Modern Programming Practices

Robert L. Glass books published by Prentice-Hall

SOFTWARE RELIABILITY GUIDEBOOK
SOFTWARE MAINTENANCE GUIDEBOOK

Modern
Programming
Practices

A Report from Industry

ROBERT L. GLASS

Prentice-Hall, Inc., Englewood Cliffs, New Jersey 07632

Library of Congress Cataloging in Publication Data

Glass, Robert L., date
  Modern programming practices.

  Includes bibliographical references and index.
  1. Electronic digital computers—Programming.
2. Computer industry—United States. I. Title.
QA76.6.G559   001.64′2   81–8715
ISBN 0-13-597294-9   AACR2

Editorial/production supervision by Lori Opre
Manufacturing buyer: Gordon Osbourne

Printed in the United States of America

10 9 8 7 6 5 4 3 2 1

ISBN   0-13-597294-9

PRENTICE-HALL INTERNATIONAL, INC., *London*
PRENTICE-HALL OF AUSTRALIA PTY. LIMITED, *Sydney*
PRENTICE-HALL OF CANADA, LTD., *Toronto*
PRENTICE-HALL OF INDIA PRIVATE LIMITED, *New Delhi*
PRENTICE-HALL OF JAPAN, INC., *Tokyo*
PRENTICE-HALL OF SOUTHEAST ASIA PTE. LTD., *Singapore*
WHITEHALL BOOKS LIMITED, *Wellington, New Zealand*

Contents

Acknowledgments

The real authors of this book are the software engineers from industry who wrote the original six Modern Programming Practices reports. In alphabetical order, they are:

Boeing Computer Services: "BCS Software Production Data," RADC-TR-77-116

Rachael K. E. Black
Richard P. Curnow
Malcolm D. Gray
Robert Katz

Computer Sciences Corp.: "Software Production Data," RADC-TR-77-177

Susan Carter
John Donahoo
Robbie Farquhar
James Hurt

Martin-Marietta Corp.: "Viking Software Data," RADC-TR-77-168

Nelson H. Prentiss, Jr.

Sperry Univac: "Modern Programming Practices Study Report," RADC-TR-77-106

W. E. Branning
W. A. Erickson
J. P. Schaenzer
D. M. Wilson

System Development Corp.: "An Investigation of Programming Practices in Selected Air Force Projects," RADC-TR-77-182

Grover H. Perry
Norman E. Willworth

TRW Defense and Space Systems Group: "Impact of MPP on System Development," RADC-TR-77-121

John R. Brown, with
J. W. Dowdee
D. E. Hacker
G. R. Keludjian
D. S. Lee
M. Lipow
G. R. Paxton
T. R. Savage

Project Engineer for Rome Air Development Center was

Roger W. Weber

DEDICATION

Software-skilled people are found in both the academic and the industrial worlds. Unfortunately, sometimes those two worlds work toward different goals and speak in different languages. This book is dedicated to all those who are building bridges between the two worlds.

ROBERT L. GLASS

Seattle, Washington

Modern
Programming
Practices

One

Introduction

1.1 BACKGROUND FOR THIS BOOK

Industry is the Gary Cooper of technology.

Remember Gary Cooper? He was the strong, silent star of a lot of American motion-picture historical epics, probably best remembered for his Academy Award-winning role in "High Noon."

"Yep," he would say in response to a complex philosophical question. "Yep," he would say in response to a highly personal probe. "Yep" was the Gary Cooper trademark response to all inquiries.

Why is industry like Gary Cooper?

Because it is the strong, silent, technological creator of the products of society. Because it builds a lot of things, but seldom takes the time to talk about the technology behind them.

Take the computing software literature as an example. Look at where the authors of papers or books come from. Places like Ivyclad University, or perhaps Think Tank, Inc.; but rarely places like General Electronics, or International Software Works.

It is not that the software people in industry do not have anything to say. It is, rather, that they rarely take or are given time to say it. They are so busy designing the latest micro-widget that they do not take time to tell the world how they did it.

Attempts to solve this problem have often failed. There is some controversy about that failure. Some people say that industry people are reluctant to submit papers based on practical experience because of a perceived bias on the part of program committees toward theory.

Others say that industry people who have *done* something simply do not bother to submit things. This problem was explored in depth in the context of a controversy over the content of one computing conference in recent issues of the Association for Computing Machinery's *SIGPLAN Notices.* * Whatever the true reason, works that reflect the lessons of experience, thought, and observation are rarely published.

This book is an attempt to present an industry view of industrial software practices. "Modern programming practices" is the theme around which the book revolves. There is a story behind that theme.

Early in the 1970s the concept of *structured programming* exploded on the software scene. Strong claims were made for the benefits of using structured programming, some of which were borne out by later experiments, but many of which were not. Nevertheless, as time passed it became obvious that the goodness of structured programming outweighed the badness of the outrageous claims sometimes made on its behalf.

In 1975–1976, the U.S. Air Force and U.S. Army jointly procured a milestone definition of structured programming for in-service use. Objectively prepared by IBM and called the "Structured Programming Series," it presented in a 15-volume set definitions, rationale, and examples for and of the structured programming milieu. This series helped the Department of Defense agencies come to grips with the newly exploding methodology.

A nagging question remained. Was structured programming really the best of the software engineering methodologies? Or were there better concepts floating around behind the cryptic "yeps" of industry?

The possibility of such better concepts was tagged *modern programming practices* (MPPs). The Air Force, as a follow-up step to its structured programming procurement, paid six American industrial software giants to share the best of their technologies—in print.

Money talks. Spurred on by the Air Force contracts, each of the companies produced a volume detailing its experience with software engineering technology. Better yet, they were *good* volumes. Each company told, with only a little corporate puffery, how they went about their software construction tasks. Each company described its involvement in one or more leading-edge applications of the software technology. Each company enumerated the modern programming

---

* Rosen, "How Practical Is POPL?" *SIGPLAN Notices,* January 1980; Abrahams, "Some Observations on POPL," *SIGPLAN Notices,* May 1979.

practices they had employed, told what was good and bad about them, and contrasted their own MPPs with structured programming.

Scattered through the six volumes ran a vein of golden information. Surrounding that vein was a raw ore of redundancy and wordiness. This book is an attempt to mine that vein. The superfluous words have been stripped off, and a common structure has been imposed. Sometimes the material has been more intensely focused, but sometimes the rambling original words provide more insight than any more formal approach could provide. The overriding philosophy has been that of retaining the flavor of the original industry writing, cutting only for pomposity and redundancy.

After all, when industry *does* get around to talking, it is worthwhile to listen to a relatively unadulterated version of what it has to say!

Try on for size these excerpts from later in this book. The honesty level is especially impressive:

From Martin-Marietta Co.:

> The Critical Design Review was held in a high school auditorium before an audience of several hundred people; included were Flight team members, directors, and outside software experts brought in by NASA to critique the Viking software development approach. To accommodate such a large audience, the Integration Engineer used very large diagrams for each subsystem, the largest of which was 10 feet high and 40 feet wide.

From Computer Sciences Corp.:

> This project encountered several problems during the development cycle. The major problem arose when a complete redesign of the subsystems was required after sensor data collection hardware could not meet the performance requirements. The original hardware, known as the Information Transfer System, was replaced by special-purpose hardware using an AN/UYK-20 computer as a control unit. This involved a major change in the concept of operation. The decision to make this change was made only after the first two levels of the monitoring subsystem were delivered to the customer.

From Boeing Computer Services:

> Project B currently consists of 20 members reporting to the Program Manager; personnel size has fluctuated from 2 through 27. This project experienced a rather severe and abrupt personnel turnover immediately after Critical Design Review. The Program Manager stated that their design documentation and configuration management practices cushioned the shock of the turnover and a greater amount of productive work was salvageable.

From Computer Sciences Corp.:

> On the AEGIS project, as a test, several programs were written by CSC programmers using the SP constraints and then rewritten using a structured format with free-form code. The results of the test indicated that structured pro-

grams required 5 to 8% more core. Since the core allocation was a key factor on the AEGIS project, a modified version of SP, functional programming, was selected for this project.

From System Development Corp.:

> The writers also had the Preliminary Product Specifications to help them, but usually preferred to depend on the source listing for information about the modules they were describing. The Preliminary specs were useful in expanding upon the intent and functional requirements of the modules, but so many changes in designs and requirements had occurred that the previous specifications could not be trusted for program details.

From System Development Corp.:

> In a pressure situation, whenever there is a choice between risking delivery of a questionable product and the onus of missing a schedule, production-oriented people almost always opt for taking the risk. This undoubtedly happened in COBRA DANE, for programmers reported that programs that were not adequately unit tested appeared in the System Master library from time to time.

1.2 HOW TO READ THIS BOOK

Most of this book is the story of industry software development, told in its own words. These words of editorial introduction are echoed as appropriate throughout the book, to establish a framework for the industry words that follow.

In each case, the industry words are clearly identified as to source, and are set in a typeface different from this. The name of the contributing company is contained in the paragraph heading. Paragraphs subsidiary to a paragraph originated in the same company as the master paragraph. If no name is presented and the material is in this typeface, the paragraph is written by the editor.

The book begins, in Chapter 2, with an industry description of the project environment in which the software was created. It moves on to the technical MPPs in Chapter 3, and the management ones in Chapter 4. Following the description of the MPPs, Chapter 5 discusses each company's approach to evaluating the MPPs, and Chapter 6 then provides industry conclusions about the value of the MPPs and their relative value with respect to structured programming.

Thorough readers should read the whole book. Impatient ones may want to skip ahead to Chapter 6 to see how everything comes out. Be aware, of course, that society frowns on the impatient reader who starts a book at the back!

As an example of how the book is organized, the paragraph that follows, written by the Air Force procuring agency—Rome Air Development Center (RADC)—is included. Note that its RADC origin is included in the heading.

1.2.1   Summary of the MPP Reports (RADC)

This report describes the software development technology and management practices employed on a large and complex system development.

The intent of the RADC program to which this document relates is to describe and assess software production and management tools and methods that significantly affect the timely delivery of reliable software.

The study contract is one of a series of six, with different firms, having the similar purpose of describing a broad range of techniques that have been found beneficial.

RADC is engaged in promoting utilization of Modern Programming Technology, also called Software Engineering, especially in large complex Command and Control software development efforts.*

1.3   THE SOFTWARE LIFE CYCLE

The software life cycle has been adequately described elsewhere.† It is one of those "goes without saying" concepts which can almost go without saying!

However, there are a few nuances to the concept, such that one person's software life cycle is not identical to someone else's. With that in mind, a quick trip through the concept is presented here. It is important that it be presented because the life cycle is the outside structure imposed on the original MPP documents to make them more readable, and thus it lies at the heart of this book.

The life cycle is presented in Figure 1.1 as a circle. Within that circle lie ordered slices of the circle, each representing a task to be performed in the software production process.

The bottom half of the circle represents software development. Someone inputs user requirements into the process on the left, and out pops a user solution some person-months later on the right.

The top half of the circle represents software maintenance. In many ways, maintenance is a replicate image of software development since it includes all the tasks of the original development process.

---

* This paragraph was written by Roger W. Weber, RADC MPP Project Engineer.
† See, for example, Glass, *Software Reliability Guidebook,* Prentice-Hall, Englewood Cliffs, N.J., 1979, Section 2.2.

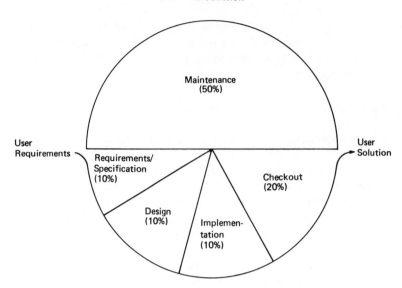

Figure 1.1   Software Life Cycle: Costs per Phase

Several studies have been conducted on actual costs of the various phases of the software life cycle. Although there are variances between them, Figure 1-1 presents a roughly accurate breakdown. Note the dominance of the maintenance phase.

REFERENCES

1. Boehm, "The High Cost of Software," *Practical Strategies for Developing Large Software Systems,* Addison-Wesley, Reading, Mass., 1975.

2. Alberts, "The Economics of Software Quality Assurance," *Proceedings of the National Computer Conference,* 1976.

3. Lientz, Swanson, and Tompkins, "Characteristics of Applications Software Maintenance," UCLA Graduate School of Management, 1976.

Requirements/specification. Requirements/specification is the first phase of software development, and it usually consumes about 10% of the total software costs. It is here that the user's problem is analyzed and restated in the form of a specification.

Design. Design is the second phase of software development. Here the "what" of requirements is translated into the "how" of a solution.

Implementation. Implementation is the third phase of software development. The design is converted into a computer-executing solution.

Checkout. Checkout is the fourth phase of software development. Here the solution has its errors removed.

Maintenance. Maintenance is the final and continuing phase of software production. While the user uses the checked-out solution, the maintainer removes residual bugs and installs the inevitable changes. To the surprise of many, maintenance has been found to consume roughly 50% of the software dollar.

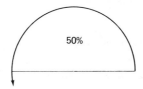

1.4   TRADITION

If it is the purpose of this book to describe and evaluate modern programming practices, there needs to be a good definition of what practices went before. Fortunately, one of the MPP companies provided an excellent summary of our industrial software traditions.

1.4.1 Traditional Programming Practices (BCS)

Traditional Programming Practices are those techniques and procedures which have been (and in some cases are still being) used in software development. These practices form the foundation for Modern Programming Practices. To understand the implications of Modern Programming Practices, we must first describe the traditional environment in which software development occurs, and the methods applied within that environment.

The traditional approach is to partition the required software problem solution into basic functional components which are assigned to groups of programmers for development (design, coding, and checkout); then to integrate the resulting components into a package of software which provides the required capability. The software development "team" is therefore composed of "programmers" and "integrators." The traditional approach results in a software life cycle similar to that displayed in Figure 1.2. This model tends to stress the parallelism of design, code, and testing activities, while delaying production of documentation until just prior to delivery. The tasks accomplished during the operation and maintenance portion of the life cycle include, in addition to the completion of supporting documentation, the operation of the capability; necessary housekeeping functions, such as data set manipulation; and repairs and enhancements to the capability as needed.

The specific practices traditionally employed within this life cycle are discussed in Sections 1.4.1.1 through 1.4.1.7. The practices are categorized and presented in terms of:

Software development and management procedures

Documentation standards

Design methodology

Programming standards

Support libraries and facilities

Testing methodology

Configuration management and change control

1.4.1.1 SOFTWARE DEVELOPMENT AND MANAGEMENT PROCEDURES

The traditional approach to software development can be characterized by (1) a concentration on computer code as the primary end product, and (2) an emphasis on the delivery date of the end product as the overriding commitment of the developer. In the paragraphs that follow, these characteristics are illustrated in traditional practices involving software development and management procedures, respectively.

A software development team is usually headed by a "lead programmer,"

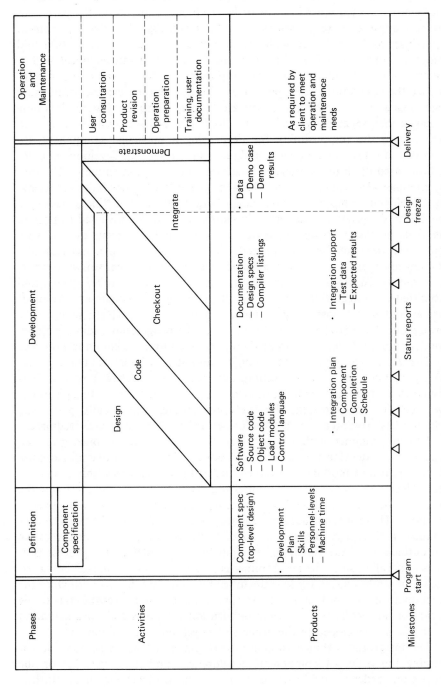

Figure 1.2 Programming Practices Life Cycle—Traditional

9

who reports directly to the manager responsible for development. A lead programmer is selected, based on his or her technical expertise in the particular software application (e.g., command and control, digital modeling, financial reporting), and familiarity with the specified hardware configuration and computer language. The lead programmer, because of this technical skill in the basic software functions required to provide the desired capability, can influence the selection of team personnel with appropriate experience in those functional areas (e.g., executive software, display/control software, data base management). Once personnel are acquired, the lead programmer assigns to each person the responsibility for developing a particular component appropriate to his or her experience and sets a target date for development completion based upon the responsible manager's delivery commitment. The lead programmer also assigns one individual or group the responsibility for receiving developed components and integrating them into a final, packaged capability. Programmers assigned development tasks are assumed to possess the skills necessary to design, code, checkout, and document the software component to which they are assigned. The integration group consists initially of a few test planners, and is augmented by special functional software expertise from the cadre of programmers as their components are completed and submitted for integration. This mode of planning and assignment presumes that an individual possessing required experience can perform many tasks throughout the software development cycle; the progression from developer to integrator to documenter (and finally to maintainer) is common practice.

The lead programmer, in assigning development or integration tasks, relies principally upon the assignee's estimate of requirements for resources, such as keypunching and machine time, needed to accomplish a task. Using his or her own technical background, the lead programmer will usually personally validate these resource estimates before arranging for the services required.

The programmer within a software development team, once given an assignment to develop a functional component, lays out an overall structure of subroutines or modules to perform defined subfunctions within a component. Then the programmer determines which of these identified pieces are the "kernels" (i.e., the routines most technically difficult or critical to the overall function). These subroutines are designed, coded, and checked first. The programmer then repeats the design, code, and checkout process for successive subroutines, until the functional component is complete. This process proceeds in parallel, since the programmer is planning work to take advantage of slack time while waiting for keypunching and computer turnaround. Once the functional component is complete, the programmer hands over the code to the integrator, and collects for formal publication the notes and documentation he or she has developed in the process of developing the component.

The integrator within a software developmental team is responsible for defining the order of component development and handover. He or she defines this order in such a way as to minimize the development of "throwaway" test drivers which may be required to tie functional components together. The integrator then devises test data cases which will exercise all of the various options of the functional capability; these test cases may consist of "synthetic" data or (pieces of) "live" data provided by the customer. As each component is handed over by the programmer, the integrator executes it with previously received components, using the test data cases to determine if the set of components perform together as expected. If any interface incompatibilities are discovered during test execution, the integrator modifies the components as required. The integrator continues this process until all functional components have been received, exercised, and corrected.

The software development team determines that the capability is complete when all components are present and function smoothly together. A common working definition of completeness is that, in exercising the capability with the complete repertoire of test cases, the software "does not unexpectedly halt, loop, or exit." An additional criterion for determining completeness is that the results obtained from the test runs match hand-calculated results derived from the input values used as test data.

The completed capability is then made available to the client. Usually, delivery involves a demonstration of the capability plus delivery of a package of instructions, control cards, etc., required to operate the software. It is not uncommon for one or more members of the software development team to be "on loan" to the user for an interim period as usage consultants. The final task for the software developers is to produce a formal Maintenance Document containing all the information they believe is needed to explain, describe, operate, and modify the capability.

Reviewing and reporting project activities concentrates on performance against schedule. Progress, in terms of completeness of the total capability, is based upon the judgments of the lead programmer and the technical personnel to whom specific tasks have been assigned. Usually, the schedule is structured in terms of specific development tasks (the production of independent software components), with as much time as possible allotted for the integration process (the consolidation of independently developed components into a working capability).

To review the status of specific tasks, the lead programmer obtains the assignee's assessment of progress to date against the total development or integration task. If the assignee feels that progress to date is such that he or she will meet the task completion date, the lead programmer assumes that performance to schedule is satisfactory and that the supporting resources planned are sufficient for task completion. If the assignee indicates that he or she anticipates difficulties in meeting the task completion date, the lead programmer requests permission of the responsible manager either to allow the assignee to spend overtime on the task, or to acquire additional resources (personnel, computer time, keypunch) necessary to meet the schedule.

In addition to these informal status reviews, a software development team traditionally conducts milestone reviews to apprise the client (both system users and management) of progress in a more formal fashion. There are two points in the development cycle when milestone reviews are usually conducted. The first is a design review, held after the principal functional components of the capability have been identified, and the development and integration schedule for these components has been planned. The second is an acceptance review, held after the capability has been integrated into a functioning system. The objective of the design review (commonly called a Preliminary Design Review, PDR) is to apprise the client of the nature of the functional components which the developers determine are necessary to perform the required capability, and to assure the client that all the functional components will be developed and integrated on a schedule which will provide capability on the date required. The objective of the acceptance review is to effect the transfer of the completed capability to the client. This transfer usually involves a demonstration and delivery of the basic materials the client will need to operate the capability.

In projects associated with Department of Defense (DoD) procurements, a second design review (called Critical Design Review, CDR) is required. The objective of this milestone review is to present to the client the details of the design of functional components identified at the Preliminary Design Review. Design details are presented so that the client understands the format of input data required and the type of output which the capability will provide. Since the traditional development life cycle permits staggered development of functional components, the Critical Design Review may be phased so that groups of functional components are reviewed as their designs are completed.

When supplying a capability to a client, the software developers traditionally develop and integrate their product on the computing hardware where the program will be used. In the case of DoD procurements, the required capability may be used on computing hardware different from that used to effect development. Delivery, in this instance, involves transporting the capability to the client's site, as well as installing and demonstrating the package.

1.4.1.2 DOCUMENTATION STANDARDS

The traditional approach to software development considers documentation as an activity distinct from and subsidiary to the primary objective —delivery of a specified capability. Documents, when produced, are oriented toward "recording the history" of completed development tasks. The criticality of complete and usable documentation for subsequent system operation and maintenance tends to go unrecognized during the development cycle. In the following paragraphs, the pertinence and content of traditional software documentation are described.

The traditional objective of software documentation is to describe fully the capability as it exists at the point it is handed over to the client. Figure 1.2 shows that documentation activities are delayed until just before delivery. This deliberate scheduling of documentation minimizes the impact of changes occurring in subroutines and components during design and testing. Final documentation tends to be in compendium form, and is developed from the informal documentation which the programmer has created in the process of designing, coding, and checking out a component. This informal material is not available until a component is submitted for integration (or shortly thereafter). Component changes occurring during integration must be reflected in the material the programmer supplies; documentation activities (writing, typing, reviewing, editing, and publishing) are therefore not attempted until the integration of a component is considered complete.

If the client requires material describing how to use the computing capability, it is commonly produced after the capability has been delivered. This User Guide is developed by the member of the software development team "loaned" to the client as an interim consultant, and is oriented toward specific consultation questions that have been raised once the client's staff has used the capability for its intended purpose.

Traditional maintenance documentation is collected into a single volume or volumes, and typically contains the following information:

1. Purpose
    a. Problem description
    b. Development objectives
2. Method
    a. Algorithms implemented
    b. Scope
    c. Limitations (accuracy of results, etc.)
    d. Recommendations (for usage, for enhancement)
3. Input preparation
    a. Card formats
    b. Deck setup
    c. File descriptions
4. Output description
    a. Annotated report page formats
    b. Display layouts, etc.
5. Installation/operating instructions (including list of diagnostics)
6. Program details
    a. Method of invocation
    b. Library subroutines and operating system services used
    c. Top-level organization (relationship of functional components,

of components to files and intermediate storage, of components
to program input and output)

d. Intracomponent organization (hierarchical list of subroutines,
showing dependencies)

e. Alphabetical set of subroutine design specifications, flowcharts,
and compiler listings

7. Standard test case

a. Annotated listing of standard input deck
b. Sample output resulting from input deck

Portions of the Maintenance Document (e.g., 3, 4, and 5 above) are
sometimes broken out into a separate volume called an Installation/Operation
Manual. This volume is produced in conjunction with the (abbreviated)
Maintenance Document.

The User Guide prepared after delivery of the capability varies in format
and content, depending largely upon the needs and sophistication of the
client. It usually does not contain all of the information required to exercise
the capability and interpret its output, unless the using audience is relatively
unsophisticated. Rather, as mentioned earlier, it addresses those specific usage
questions that have arisen as a direct result of the client's exposure to the software. Typically, the User Guide includes discussions of how to invoke certain
functional options, and how to interpret output reports, error messages, and
dumps.

1.4.1.3 DESIGN METHODOLOGY

The traditional approach to software design is iterative, and spread
throughout the development and integration activity. The Definition phase involves the activity of component specification, that is, partitioning the
specified capability's requirements and allocating them to functional components of software. This is usually performed by the lead programmer. The
details of component design are determined initially by the programmer
assigned the development task, and may be changed by the integrator as required to make the component execute properly with other pieces of the
capability.

Unless the client specifies the required formats for data input and output,
their specification is part of the programmer's design responsibility. Where
these formats involve files to be used in passing data from one functional
component to another, the lead programmer typically convenes an informal
Interface Working Group involving the programmers responsible for the components affected. This group resolves the communication protocols between
components.

To assure that the resulting components perform together, an integration team is established. Completed components are exercised as a package, using test data developed by the integrators. In order to perform their task, the integrators require the programmer to provide definitions of the component input and output interfaces when he or she releases them. These definitions can then be compared with the definitions for interfacing components already received by the integrators. If interface and communication problems are discovered during integration, it is the responsibility of the integrators to make the design and code changes necessary to correct them.

A benefit of the integrator's role as traditionally constituted is the design visibility available to the client as functional components are completed and handed over. The definitions of component input and output formats supplied at this time can be made available to the clients so that they gain advance visibility of how the complete capability will appear externally; the clients can therefore begin to plan how they will use the capability they will ultimately receive.

1.4.1.4 PROGRAMMING STANDARDS

Traditional software development projects establish programming standards in three basic areas:

1. Language
2. Commentary
3. Linkage conventions

The objectives of these standards are (1) the effective use of available hardware and software resources, and (2) the consistency, and hence quality, of the delivered capability. These standards result from recognition of the superiority of certain coding practices in minimizing compilation and execution errors, and the realization that program modification and enhancement are facts of life that demand preplanning during the coding process. In the paragraphs that follow, the types of standards traditionally defined in these three basic areas are described.

In traditional software development projects, a specific higher-order language is usually prescribed as a standard. The choice is based on language availability, type of application (business: Cobol, PL/1; scientific: Fortran, Algol, APL; real time and simulation: GPSS, SIMSCRIPT), as well as client preference (Jovial for the Air Force; CMS for the Navy).

The use of certain language forms or special, perhaps unique, features of specific language implementations may be restricted. Examples include mixed-mode computations in Fortran or "direct" instructions in Jovial. Deviations from these standards are typically permitted only when necessary to achieve required efficiencies—in execution speed or in storage usage—or to invoke specialized capabilities of the computer or its operating system which the higher-order language compiler cannot support.

Programmers are traditionally encouraged to annotate their source code with explanatory comments. The lead programmer may leave the amount and type of commentary to the discretion of the individual programmer. Specific guidelines, when published, typically encourage the incorporation of a description of function, an explanation of symbols, labels, notation, or naming conventions, and a definition of input and output variables within each component.

There are three basic kinds of interfaces associated with a computing system: (1) those used for communication between a computer program and its human users and operators, (2) those used for communication between computer programs, and (3) those used for communication within a program. Typically, a project will have formally defined standards only for the third type of interface, specifically for calls to software subroutines.

Standard linkage conventions (for subroutine call and entry sequences) are ordinarily defined by the computer vendor or the supplier of operating system/executive-level software. These conventions are established to provide a common design basis for various utility functions: debug aids, linkage editor/loader, library subroutines, etc. Because of their pervasive nature, these conventions tend to become de facto project standards; except in rare instances, there is little need for programmers to devise alternative ways of effecting intraprogram communications.

Communications between programs, on the other hand, are not ordinarily subject to vendor-established conventions. These linkages, usually by means of intermediate storage (disk or tape), must be devised to satisfy the needs of the particular communications involved; the variety of possible needs makes it impractical for the project (or vendor) to attempt standardization of all such interfaces. Instead, the affected programmers will usually convene an informal Interface Working Group to identify the required data communications and devise an appropriate protocol.

For human–machine communications, unless the client has specifically defined the input and output formats required, design of the necessary interfaces is traditionally the responsibility of the programmer whose component implements them.

Of all the types of standards traditionally imposed in software development, interface conventions are the most consistently adhered to. This is a direct consequence of the integrator's role in the team environment; the vendor-defined linkages, the programmer's documented input/output format definitions, and the agreements of the Interface Working Group constitute the rules by which the integrator assures that functional components perform together. The integrator is directed to review components received for adherence to these rules, and can refuse to accept a component that does not comply. The integrator therefore assumes a quality assurance responsibility for the software developed. In practice, the integrator seldom rejects a completed component for violation of interface conventions, both to avoid schedule risk and because the integrator can personally change the component so that it conforms. Generally, at the completion of the integration activity, all functional components (have been modified to) adhere to standard linkage conventions, interface conventions, and defined input/output standards.

1.4.1.5   SUPPORT LIBRARIES AND FACILITIES

Traditionally, program support libraries and facilities are provided within most computer centers in response to the demand for services common to all computer users. These include programming aids found in operating systems, text editors, linkage editors, assemblers, compilers, utility libraries, various language subroutine libraries, and data structure manipulation packages. System libraries, in particular, containing the standard computation and manipulation routines, are provided for general use in the traditional environment. Editors, assemblers, and compilers also provide widespread service.

The underlying rationale for all of these tools is: If the piece of software required for a job is already available, there is little excuse for building a new one. This thesis, of course, presumes that the tool is capable of performing the required function, that as a result of prior usage it has been proven capable of performing the function reliably, and that it can be acquired more quickly and at less cost than would be incurred in developing a new one.

The programmers themselves have generally instigated development of software so configured that it can subsequently be reused as a utility program operating system function, or library subroutine. In contrast, it is the project manager (or his or her subordinates) who must direct the programmers to actually use the reusable elements available to them. Projects that stress the use of higher-order languages, and projects with particularly tight schedules are typically the most dependent upon the support libraries and facilities available.

In the paragraphs that follow, traditional tools available in the form of standard subroutine libraries, operating system functions, and utility programs are described.

With the advent of standard linkage conventions, it has been possible for the software community to begin collecting libraries of subroutines to perform common computing functions, such as calculating the sine of an angle, reading a punched card, or converting a quantity from one representation to another. Continued use of such libraries by programmers has both refined the subroutines previously available and encouraged development of new contributions to the library repertoire.

Although no formal studies of this practice have been conducted in recent years, it is generally acknowledged that the availability and use of standard subroutine libraries has contributed significantly to improving software reliability while reducing costs. In fact, it is not uncommon for as much as 50% of the instructions in an application program to have originated not with the programmer who wrote it, but from the computer system library. Traditionally, software developers expect virtually any computer except the very smallest will come complete with an extensive library of standard subroutines.

A similar tradition exists for operating system software, which performs the manipulation of a variety of hardware functions, particularly those associated with data input and output. Few programmers except those employed by the hardware manufacturer possess the knowledge of equipment operation needed to design, code, and test the control program, which can transmit a data record to or from a particular portion of one track on the surface of a specified disk of a multidisk storage device. Nor, given today's requirements for data integrity and protection, would the manager of a modern computing facility want the average programmer to try.

Further, these same requirements have provided the impetus for the suppliers of "system software" (i.e., those software elements that "come with" the computer) to provide means of invoking these functions as standard elements of higher-order programming languages. Thus, for all but the most sophisticated of applications, there is no need for programmers to try their hand at the kind of coding which carries with it the greatest risk to the integrity of the system.

Beyond libraries and operating system functions, another type of tool that has become traditional is the utility program. The most commonly used utilities are those which perform various operations on a data file: compressing the data (usually to collect fragments of unused space and make them available for reuse), adding data to one file from another, deleting unneeded portions of the data in a file, reordering the data (i.e., sorting them), copying the contents of a file to another storage medium (e.g., making a backup copy of disk-stored data on magnetic tape), or simply printing the information.

There have been sporadic attempts made to develop and use utility programs of less-general capability (usually, to create data files that could be used in testing other software), but these efforts have not been so successful as to become traditional.

1.4.1.6   TESTING METHODOLOGY

Traditional objectives for software testing are (1) that the software does not unexpectedly fail (i.e., halt, loop, or exit), and (2) that the output values produced match results of hand calculations from input test data. Satisfaction of these test objectives traditionally rests upon the integrator and the client, respectively. The traditional approach to testing consists of three steps; checkout (performed by the programmer), integration (performed by the integrator), and demonstration (performed by the integrator if required by the client). These three steps in traditional testing methodology are described in the following paragraphs.

Checkout is traditionally considered an integral part of the programmer's development assignment. The programmer is presumed to have the requisite skills to test his or her subroutines and the functional component which they comprise, at least to the level where the component can be "put in context" by the process of integration. The basic test strategy applied is to use higher-level subroutines, wherever possible, to create the conditions for test. This strategy reduces the amount of resources expended in constructing test drivers, usually considered "throwaway" code. The traditional design practice of constructing "kernel" subroutines first affects the manner in which the programmer applies this strategy. Since higher-level subroutines that invoke the kernels are constructed after the kernels themselves, the programmer must either write special driver software to exercise the kernels, or (more commonly) defer testing of the kernels until enough of the component structure above them has been constructed to make checkout exercises more convenient (and more cost-effective).

A testing strategy similar to that applied in checkout is traditionally applied to the planning and execution of the integration activity. The integrator schedules component hand over in such a way as to allow previously received components (which are predecessors in the functional execution sequence) to create the conditions whereby a particular component is exercised. In performing their task, the integrators are permitted to alter functional components as required to achieve overall performance. As mentioned before, their primary objective is to assure that the components, functioning together, do not unexpectedly fail.

The second test objective mentioned earlier deserves some special discussion. While it is traditional practice to verify by hand calculation the results obtained with a particular set of input test data, it is also traditional for the software development team to accept no responsibility for the validity of the algorithms implemented in their code. The only exceptions to this are if the programmers themselves devised the algorithm, or if they had to substantially modify an algorithm provided by the client in order to implement it in computer code. In effect, this attitude on the part of the software developer implies that his or her traditional role is that of providing a logical structure of computer instructions that house the client's algorithm(s). In other words, the software developer's job is to provide (1) the code that translates the client's algorithms into computable instructions, and (2) the code that reads data, determines which algorithm to apply, and reports the results of application.

Demonstration of the completed capability for the benefit of the client is usually performed in an informal fashion. The software development team traditionally does not design, prepare, and conduct a formal demonstration of the package unless obligated to do so (usually by contract). Typically, the client provides the demonstration data, and is the party responsible for determining if the results the software produces are realistic and correct.

1.4.1.7 CONFIGURATION MANAGEMENT AND CHANGE CONTROL

Configuration management, as evidenced by formal nomenclature and identification conventions, is implemented for software when required by the client (usually to satisfy some contractual obligation). Change control is traditionally imposed by "locking up" the code at the time the capability is considered complete, and earlier when functional components are handed over for integration. Traditional software development practices for configuration management and change control are described in the following paragraphs.

Configuration management is often not practiced at all. This is a consequence of the observation that the software developer creates a product only once, and then modifies it as required to meet changing needs. This attitude is reinforced by the traditional mode of operation, in which the computing capability is developed and used at a single site.

There have been occasions when the client has imposed configuration management disciplines on the software product. This is usually accomplished through the expedient of establishing conventions for the naming and identification of items within a configuration. In this way, items can be conclusively specified as belonging to a particular configuration having a particular capability, and can be distinguished from members of other configurations having different capabilities.

Traditionally, the lead programmer of a software development delegates to each programmer the responsibility of maintaining an up-to-date copy of the source code, separate from the version that may be undergoing integration or in operational use. The practice of "locking up" source code is imposed at the discretion of the lead programmer, and may be introduced in response to or in anticipation of, problems arising during integration or subsequent operation and maintenance.

The point at which "locking up" is considered virtually mandatory is when the integrators have determined that the capability is complete. This ensures that consultants loaned to assist the client in using the capability have a baseline from which to diagnose problems.

It is common in traditional software development efforts for the "locking up" activity to occur at an earlier point as well: when each functional component is handed over from programmer to integrator. This ensures that the integrator will have the latest version of the software available to modify as required in the process of making components execute together.

One technique often employed in "locking up" software is to entrust the source code library to an individual who is not either a programmer or an integrator; ideally, the individual should not possess the skill to devise and introduce software changes. Such an individual, provided with written procedures concerning change authorization, access to controlled code, and introduction of new elements into the controlled library, can function as a vital member of the integration team and as a result enhance product integrity.

Two

The Environment— Projects and People

The projects selected for modern programming practices study had one important thing in common—they were huge. This means that the experiential results presented in this book are in marked contrast to much of what is published in the computing literature. What appears elsewhere is often based on academic research and experiments involving classroom-size personnel levels with semester- or quarter-limited schedules.

By contrast, we are talking here (see Table 2–1) about projects each of which involves

Up to 400 people
Up to 5 years' duration
Up to 500,000 lines of source code
Up to 27,000 pages of documentation
More than $7.8 million cost

We are also talking about experienced, professional programmers. Independent of company and project, the average software experience for the participating programmers was about 10 years. Most had bachelor's or more advanced college degrees. Titles tended to be things like "senior member of the technical staff." Turnover rates and

TABLE 2.1
Project, personnel data*

Company Task Duration	Personnel	Size	Cost (in millions)	Pages of documentation	People experience	Computer hardware
			Project			
Computer Sciences Corp.						
1 3 + years	100 (ave.)	310K core	$7.8		9.6–10 years	AN/UYK-7
2 2 + years	30 (ave.)	94K core	$2.4			
3 2 years	30 (ave.)	250K lines	$3.5			
Sperry Univac						
1	630 pm	90K lines		8,059		AN/UYK-7
2	2,960 pm	500K lines		27,014		
3	430 pm	26K lines		3,507		
4	115 pm	13K lines		2,259		
TRW						
5 years	400 (max.)	1 million instructions			10–15 years	CDC 6400, 7600, 7700
Martin-Marietta						
3 years	1,783 pm	278K lines		24,000		Univac 1108, CDC 6500, IBM 370
System Development Corp. Not available						
Boeing Computer Services						
1	5					Nova 830
2	27 (max.)					IBM 370
3	5					IBM 360
4	37					IBM 370
5	2					IBM 370

* pm, person-months; lines, lines of source code; core, words or bytes of object code; ave., average number of programmers; max., maximum number of programmers.

hiring practices were important considerations in the overall project environment.

Further, we are talking about striking applications of the software art. Technical breakthroughs in related disciplines were necessary elements of the total system in which the software plays a part. One company talks about a Viking space vehicle. Another describes a computer-controlled, shipboard-guided missile system. A third describes a once-controversial antiballistic missile system. These are challenging projects that have taxed the minds of their engineers beyond limits even dreamed of a few decades ago.

And finally, we are talking about major companies that are

acknowledged leaders in their fields. Sperry Univac is huge in computers and defense systems. TRW is the epitome of technology-first corporations. Martin-Marietta is a leading defense contractor. Computer Sciences Corp. (CSC) is a highly respected computing software company. System Development Corp. (SDC) is a long-admired think-tank. And Boeing Computer Services (BCS) is the computing arm of the king of the airframe producers.

In short, these are major corporations producing advanced state-of-the-art projects with highly skilled people writing enormous quantities of software.

That is not to say that the project software itself, or the corporate discussions about the software, are impeccable or Pollyanna-ish. Martin-Marietta provides a frank and confrontive discussion of their experiences. TRW uses a programmer poll to come to some conclusions that rub against the grain of other software beliefs. Boeing Computer Services describes, as we saw in Chapter 1, the traditional (pre-modern!) software development environment accurately and, perhaps, even nostalgically.

These are slices of software life, taken out of the middle of a very large loaf, original in their flavor and, in general, unembellished.

They are very real.

2.1   VIKING MISSION OPERATIONS SOFTWARE SYSTEM (MARTIN-MARIETTA)

The Viking Mission Operations Software System (MOSS) was developed over a 3-year time period. Phased deliveries of integrated software systems were needed to support test, training, launch, cruise, and planetary operations. Capability was added and improved with each new system. This overview presents a brief history of the development of these systems, stressing the problems encountered and their resolutions. Each system was delivered on schedule. The overall approach taken by Viking management was one that led to the availability of a very efficient software system during planetary operations.

2.1.1   The Operational Software System

The Viking Mission Operations Software System consisted of six interrelated software subsystems, which supported an interplanetary space vehicle whose destination was Mars. They were designed to support Mission Planning, Tracking and Flight Path Analysis, Orbiter Uplink, Orbiter Downlink, Lander Uplink, and Lander Downlink activities. The system was installed in the Viking Mission Control and Computing Center at the Jet Propulsion

Laboratory (JPL), Pasadena, California. The Center consisted of three facilities: a Mission Test Computer Facility, a Mission Control Computer Facility, and a General Purpose Computer Facility.

Viking Orbiter (VO) real-time telemetry software and near-real-time first-order image-processing software resided in a dedicated computer system.

Viking Lander (VL) real-time telemetry software, VO and VL real-time command software, and VL near-real-time first-order image-processing software were processed by a multimission real-time 360/75 computer system also used by other space projects. A second 360/75 computer was supplied to support batch operations.

The batch operation was under control of a real-time operating system and lacked many features common to general-purpose computers.

The General Purpose Facility provided two 1108 computers to the project. One was used for Mission Planning, science analysis, and data record generation; the second was used for flight path analysis and sequence-generation processing.

Second-order image-enhancement software was developed by the Image Processing Laboratory, a separate division of JPL. This software was not considered a part of the MOSS and was not subject to Viking MOSS Configuration Control.

The Deep Space Network supported the command and telemetry link between the spacecraft and JPL. High-speed and wideband data lines connected the lab with Deep Space Stations, where command stack and telemetry receipt software interfaced the MOSS with the ground radar portion of the communication link. This Deep Space software was considered an integral part of the MOSS and was subject to Viking Configuration Control.

2.1.2 Multiagency Responsibilities

The Langley Research Center was directed by NASA to manage the Viking Project. Contracts were awarded to the Denver Division of the Martin-Marietta Corporation (MMC) and several divisions of the Jet Propulsion Laboratory to develop the operational software system.

MMC was responsible for Lander batch and Mission Planning software, specifying requirements for real-time software, and the integration of the six software subsystems.

One division of JPL was responsible for Orbiter batch and Tracking and Flight Path Analysis software, specifying requirements for real-time software, and supporting the integration of the Flight Path Analysis software subsystems.

Another division of JPL was responsible for institutional software, implementing the real-time Lander and Orbiter software requirements, and maintaining the integrity of the operational software system through a process called the Mission Build.

Still another division of JPL was responsible for the development and maintenance of the software installed at the Deep Space Stations.

2.1.3 Quantitative Software Description

A total of 278,575 source cards were delivered to mission batch operations for the 22 Viking Lander software functions developed by MMC in Denver. Approximately 24,000 pages of documentation was written to support these deliveries. The cost to accomplish this task was 1783 person-months.

These figures account for all activities conducted by the Cognizant Engineers and Cognizant Programmers to develop the 22 programs from mid-1972, when the effort to write the Software Requirements Documents began, until early 1976, when the final versions of the programs used to support planetary operations were delivered. (The term "cognizant" implies both knowledge and responsibility. Cognizant engineers were responsible for software requirements, cognizant programmers for software development.)

The documentation figure includes all Functional Requirements, Software Requirements, General Design, Program Design, Users Acceptance Test Plan, and User's Guide documents developed for the 22 programs.

The estimated effort expended by development phase is as follows:

Requirements	20%
Design	10%
Code and debug	15%
Test and integration	25%
Change traffic	30%

The requirements, design, and code phases cover initial program development. The test and integration phase covers certification tests at MMC, program conversion at JPL, acceptance testing, and redeliveries caused by errors detected during initial integration plus any new requirements incorporated prior to January 1975. At that time all planetary programs had been delivered to the integration build and all launch and cruise programs were incorporated on the initial launch and cruise operational software system.

The change traffic phase represents the level of effort required to redeliver programs for reasons of new requirements, program errors, and performance improvements.

2.1.4 Organizing for the Task

A Flight Operations Working Group was formed and made responsible for the development of the Mission Operations Software System. Its membership was made up of the managers responsible for the development of the software, and it was chaired by a Project Software Manager.

The group created a Software Subworking Group to manage the details of the MOSS development. Its first assignment was to document a Flight Operations Software Development Plan. The subworking group consisted of a Project Software Systems Engineer, an Integration Contractor Software Systems Engineer, a Viking Orbiter Software Systems Engineer, and a Data Systems Project Engineer. As chairman of the subworking group, the Integration Engineer was responsible for the coordination of interagency agreements and the software development plan.

The Flight Operations Software Development Plan became the controlling document for the development of the operational software system. It defined the change control procedures to be followed within and among the software developing agencies; specified program documentation requirements on a paragraph-by-paragraph basis; defined development, test, integration, and delivery milestones that would allow monitoring development progress, identifying roles and responsibilities, and specifying configuration management control procedures. It was concurred upon by each member of the Group and approved by the Viking Project Manager.

2.1.5 Defining the Software System

Software Functional Descriptions were written to document the purpose, description, input/output requirements, and estimates of frequency of use and computer CPU, core, and mass storage resources required for each operational software system candidate program. They were used to develop an Integrated Software Functional Design, which showed the top-down design of the data flow for the six software subsystems. This task required a considerable amount of iterative effort in obtaining interagency coordination and agreement. Functions were combined, separated, created, and discarded.

2.1.6 Different Development Philosophies

The Jet Propulsion Lab had more than a decade of experience in developing software to support space exploration missions. Most of the software functions needed to support the Orbiters were therefore obtained by modifying existing programs already operational at JPL. This led to a bottom-up program development approach which required that the Viking Orbiter software subsystems adapt to the established conventions and procedures for using the individual programs. Subsequent computer loading studies, geared from a cost-effectiveness point of view, took into account where software already existed.

The challenge to MMC to develop the Lander software subsystems was significantly different. Some descent analysis, power, and thermal programs had been developed on MMC computers that could be modified to support Lander Flight Path Analysis and spacecraft performance functions. But the mission planning, ground resource, sequence generation, command generation, flight computer simulation, data decommutation and decalibration, and science analysis functions had to be built from scratch. The process was further complicated when the computer loading studies indicated that these software subsystems would have to be split between two computers. This added the requirement that a file management program be designed to control intercomputer data transfers to prevent the overloading of available tape-drive resources.

A top-down approach to Lander software system development was adopted. It included parameter passing and common data base file management control functions, common time utilities used by all programs, and required the use of unique file header records that were compatible with both computers.

Commitments by JPL to other projects limited computer resources available to the Viking Project. For this reason the MMC software was developed in Denver on nontarget computers, using a Guidelines and Constraint document that specified module size, number of tape drives, and mass storage requirements for the off-site-developed software. Programs destined for JPL were developed on either CDC 6500 series computers, or IBM 370 computers. Minimal HOL coding standards were adopted to simplify the process of converting to the target computers. Pathfinder studies were made that indicated the conversion process would not pose any serious problems.

Considerable effort was expended in an attempt to standardize interface naming conventions and header record requirements for the Orbiter and Lander software subsystems. However, because of the differences in development philosophies, a common approach agreeable to both parties could not be found. Eventually, interfaces between the two subsystems were kept at a minimum. They were individually negotiated, often with considerable compromise.

2.1.7   Milestones and Schedules

A hierarchy of schedules were developed to provide an orderly delivery of software to JPL that would not compromise available computer resources. High-level schedules provided significant milestones for upper-management visibility. Lower-level schedules were very important for monitoring programmer progress on coding and testing. They were very detailed.

2.1.8   The Development Cycle

A cognizant engineer and a cognizant programmer were assigned to each program. The cognizant engineer formalized the program requirements in a Software Requirements Document. Approval of the Requirements authorized the cognizant programmer to design the basic flow for the program and write a General Design Document. After it was approved, the cognizant programmer began coding and the cognizant engineer wrote a Users Acceptance Test Plan. The rationale was that the programmer would test the code during the debug stage and implement the design, whereas the engineer would assure that the program formally met the requirements specified for it. Some software developers do not like this approach, claiming that the programmer, rather than the engineer, knows best how to test the program. Nevertheless, the process adopted by Viking proved very effective. Its weaknesses were that many vague requirements were approved because users did not understand all that was needed, which led to confusion, replanning, reprogramming, retesting, and redelivery, and that some engineers failed to write tests that fully tested the requirements. Its strengths were that it uncovered numerous misunderstandings of requirements by programmers and disclosed cases of poor program design. Observe that the weaknesses can be controlled by management, whereas the strengths are difficult to realize if the programmer testing approach is adopted.

Concurrent with the requirements/design/code phase were the development of two extremely important and useful documents. They were the Software Data Base Document and the Lander Orbiter Software Test Plan.

The Data Base document described in exacting detail each file and parameter that would reside in mass storage accessible by Viking program software. The cognizant engineers and programmers were required to sign an agreement for all files produced or processed by their programs. This agreement indicated that they understood the file structure and data contents, and that the file was compatible with their program. The document was invaluable in locating errors and resolving interface problems; when an interface test failed the document invariably could be used to point directly at the cause.

The Test Plan specified the requirements for individually testing each interface. It included test descriptions, resources required, success criteria, and procedures. This permitted management to foresee, early in the development cycle, the facilities, personnel, and data that would be required. The plan also described single-thread tests for the major software subsystems that would demonstrate the data flow and indicate what procedures would be required to use the software as a system.

During the software coding time period, plans for how the software system would be integrated and implemented were finalized. MMC software would be required to pass a formal certification test in Denver prior to being taken to JPL. Following this the programs would be subject to change control, placed on an Integration Build, and unit-verified by Data Systems Integration. At JPL at specified points in time, copies of the Integration Build would be made that became the current version of the Mission Build. Spacecraft compatibility and Ground Data System test and training could then be conducted using the Mission Build. Finally, after test and training were completed, the Mission Build would become the Mission Operations Software System.

2.1.9 Additional Comments

During the Requirements and Design phase, progress toward generating the three Mission Operations Software Systems (MOSS) proceeded relatively smoothly. Milestones were added and changed under Flight Operations working configuration control as the process unfolded. Schedules were modified to accommodate new requirements, and plans for future testing evolved as management gained insight into the system description and integration approach. A clear-cut, workable approach to the development cycle was formalized.

Management had some concern about the constant reworking of schedules caused by changing requirements. The software was being developed in parallel with Flight hardware and software. Changes in those areas created the need for changes to the operational software under development. The result was that the time period allotted for integration functions had to be reduced, since the delivery date for the on-line MOSSs could not be changed.

The schedule for MOSS 1 proved to be overly optimistic in that it moved scheduled software delivery dates forward by several months. This was to affect the development of MOSS 2 significantly, because it prevented programmers from developing MOSS 2 software during the MOSS 1 integration time period. The impact should have been foreseen, but it was not.

File management software should be developed before any program that will be dependent upon it is developed. This was not accomplished on Viking because of a combination of events. When MOSS 1 was defined, the file management software delivery schedule was moved forward 2 months so that it would be delivered first. The Software Integration group, responsible for its development, was understaffed at the time, so that only one programmer was available to write the software. This was further complicated by the fact that the JPL computer systems were not well documented at that time. The result was that the MOSS 1 file management software was poorly designed relative to MOSS 2 software requirements, especially in the area of Orbiter/Lander interfaces. It became mandatory that a redesign effort be undertaken in parallel with MOSS 2 software deliveries, resulting in frequent failures during MOSS 2 interface testing. Had it not been for the fact that it was under development by an exceptionally competent and dedicated individual, serious schedule slippages would have occurred.

An item that was not worked properly during this time period was the negotiation of the structure, contents, and naming conventions of Lander/Orbiter interface files. The responsible people agreed to negotiate file naming conventions and header record structures, and continued exchanging information as the individual systems developed. As matters turned out, there was not sufficient Project support to force compliance with agreements made, and because of the divisional organization at JPL there was not full control of the

Orbiter software. This proved to be a mistake, since final negotiations impacted developed software in both systems.

Software requirements should have been given far more attention by middle management than they received. Items that should have been stressed more include program run time, printed output formats and quantities, and plot requirements. In addition, had this attention been extended to include critical reviews of the initial program designs, some of the design problems uncovered after program delivery may have been avoided.

A rather interesting technique was used by NASA to validate the management approach and system design. NASA gathered a committee of software experts from around the country to review and critique Viking software during this phase. The committee agreed with the overall approach, and contributed many constructive suggestions.

2.1.10   User Acceptance Testing

Conversion of MMC developed software and User Acceptance Testing proceeded nominally on the 1108 computers, but were difficult to accomplish on the 360 computers. The 1108 was a general-purpose computer with considerable mass storage capability, which made it easy to use. In addition, turn-around time on the 1108 was reasonable.

The 360 was controlled by a real-time operating system designed to be efficient for command and telemetry functions. Batch operations were restricted to 400 to 500 kilobytes of core. No roll out/roll in features were available. Programs were scatter-loaded. Direct-access storage space was limited. The user was required to request a specific disk pack computer configuration be mounted to permit Viking software to operate.

The first programmers to bring their software to the 360s for conversion and User Acceptance Testing began slipping their schedules almost immediately because of poor turnaround time. Two- to three-day delays were not uncommon. It became apparent that Viking software, which was the first major batch software system supported by the 360s, would require special treatment.

The resolution of the 360 computer turnaround problem was to block computers for Viking users. Schedules were issued which allowed Viking users to know when computers would be available during the week. Typically, 4- to 6-hour blocks of time were scheduled on second and third weekday shifts, and during daytime hours on weekends. When a computer was blocked for Viking, programmers could access it from peripheral equipment located in an adjacent user area. They could monitor the computer run and load status, and receive their output promptly.

The 360 blocked computer environment caused programmers to develop bad habits. They would come prepared to make as many job submittals as possible during block time, often making conflicting ones that would hang the computer. They would overload the computer, causing the system to crash or their programs to abend. They only glanced at their output during block time, and submitted many sloppy and unnecessary runs. They overworked themselves and became inefficient. However, generous amounts of block time were made available to them, and ample time had been scheduled for conversions and testing. As such, they were able to meet their delivery-date commitments.

Reviews were held at the completion of User Acceptance Testing. The cognizant engineers were required to demonstrate that their programs had met all success criteria specified in the User Acceptance Test Plans. The Review was a profit-incentive milestone. Management kept a close eye on conversion and testing progress to assure that the milestone would be met on or ahead of schedule.

Occasionally, waivers had to be issued for specific subfunctions that were not included, or because the test demonstrated that a program violated a computer-set constraint of size, run time, or peripheral equipment usage. Programs delivered with waivers often were required to be scheduled for corrective redelivery at a later date.

Waivers were also required for functions that had to be tested artificially because the true environment was not available. This occurred for some early deliveries because the file management functions that accessed the common data base, the common data base itself, the time utilities, or interfacing programs were not ready.

2.1.11   Unit-Verification Testing

As soon as the User Acceptance Test review was completed, the program was incorporated on the Viking Integration Build, where it was no longer accessible to the programmer for modification. During peak delivery periods, the Integration Build was updated weekly. It was necessary to unit-verify the program to assure that it had been correctly incorporated on the build.

The unit test sometimes failed because the program had not been incorporated properly on the Integration Build. This happened primarily with 360 operations because of the complexity of the build decks, or because a required module was not on the build, or because a programmer had not turned all the required build slip forms into operations. When this occurred, the program, or components thereof, had to be redelivered via the same responsive but rigid change-control procedure used for the initial delivery. The fix would then be incorporated with the next Integration Build update, and retested. Since a month was allotted between milestones, these failures rarely jeopardized schedules.

2.1.12 Lander/Orbiter Software Test Integration

The initial integration was conducted following unit-verification testing of the MOSS 1 programs on the Integration Build. It demonstrated that what had been delivered was a collection of programs that individually worked fine to perform their required functions, but could not communicate with one another to form a workable software system. This finding was to prove true for MOSS 2 programs as well.

It should be emphasized that the purpose of integration was to assure that every interface would work. Since they were being tested for the first time, it was anticipated that a large number of errors would be uncovered.

The high rate of failure detected by integration established the extreme value of the data base document. The reasons for failures could be detected very quickly. Invariably, only minor changes to code were required to correct the situation. Had the data base exercise not been done as detailed and complete as it was, it is reasonable to conclude that the integration failure impact would have been major, and the Mission Build would have been compromised. In addition, the data base document permitted management the visibility to know that when a change to a program did not affect the data base in any way, the change would not affect any other program in the system. Thus, the software system itself was structured by the data base as well as the functional design.

The reasons for failures detected by integration were numerous: there had been misunderstandings in the file header structure, precision requirements, file access methods, fixed- vs. floating-point data, file structures, number and types of records generated, data units, and operating system differences between originating and receiving computer sets. Overall, 80% of the interface tests failed the first time they were attempted, and 50% of retesting uncovered new errors.

The fact that the User Acceptance Test was made an incentive milestone was a contributing factor to this finding. Rarely was a schedule missed. But emphasis had been placed on unit testing. Rarely had interfaces been tested because that was not required. Scaffolds had been used to demonstrate that interfaces would work, but they had been built based on individual programmer's interpretations.

The significant failure rate uncovered by integration, combined with a much greater change traffic caused by new requirements than had been anticipated, was not compatible with meeting Mission Build schedules. Therefore, after failure reports were issued and program corrections made, integration was performed prior to redelivering the software. This permitted corrections to be made for newly discovered interface failures prior to placing the redelivered software under rigid change control. This modification of the development cycle proved to be workable, permitting programs to be placed on the Integration Build that formed a usable software system.

2.2 SYSTEMS TECHNOLOGY PROGRAM (STP) ENVIRONMENT (TRW)

TRW chose the Systems Technology Program (STP) as the "guinea pig" for studying MPP impact for several reasons. First, software development to date spans almost 5 years, during which many modern programming practices have been applied, most from the beginning but some during only more recent development activity. Second, a great deal of data has been collected and is regularly used to analyze and evaluate the performance of STP developers and the software they produce, and based upon these analyses, an effort has been made to define new production practices and supply developers with new tools to improve performance.

There is one overriding reason for the large number of MPP used in the STP development activity. At the outset of the project [formerly called the Site Defense (SD) program], there was considerable feeling outside TRW that the SD data processing subsystem, and especially the software, could never be built to meet the demanding performance specifications, and certainly not within the projected cost and schedule. To meet this challenge, it was necessary to produce not only the heart of the SD system (the real-time software) but also the development support software and test support software required to demonstrate that satisfactory performance had been achieved. The sheer magnitude of the software (nearly 1 million machine instructions) and the project (as many as 400 people) demanded unprecedented rigor in the development process and led to the establishment and enforced application of a variety of both existing practices and new practices unique to STP.

The following subsections provide a brief description and historical account of STP to provide the reader with a general understanding of the environment within which these modern programming practices were applied.

2.2.1 System Description

Site Defense (SD) was intended to be an antiballistic missile terminal defense system. It was designed to possess a performance credibility sufficient to deter an aggressor from a first-strike attack against the Minuteman Missile force and to ensure that an acceptable number of Minutemen would survive in the event of a first strike. Furthermore, the SD System would be capable of countering attacks of various levels and tactics, and of degrading gracefully in the event of subsystem overloads or failures, or in the event of attacks of greater severity than the design threat parameters. The SD System development has been redefined to be a Ballistic Missiles Division (BMD) Systems Technology Program (STP), to provide objective evidence of the performance of the key functions of a tactical SD System. The primary objectives of STP are:

1. Validating the data processing subsystem by demonstrating the performance of the engagement software (the tactical applications program and the tactical operating system) executed by the computer, a CDC 7700, against both real targets and simulated threats
2. Providing the framework for incorporating currently deferred data processing subsystem elements
3. Supporting data gathering during system tests at Kwajalein missile range

The STP software being developed by TRW has been organized into engagement software, test support software, and development support software categories. The software in these categories consists of 10 major computer programs.

The engagement software is the software necessary to identify and track ballistic reentry vehicles through the use of STP system resources. Its logic and algorithms consist of those needed to satisfy functional and performance requirements that support the system engagement functions: detect and designate objects, track objects, and discriminate objects.

The software that actually runs on the CDC 7700 (the STP processor) is referred to as a *process*. A process is composed of a data base, an operating system, and one or more application programs. The Tactical Application Program is composed of tasks, which are composed of several levels of routines. The operating system is a table-driven, real-time system designed specifically for the CDC 7700. The application program and the test support programs operate under its control. It provides the following basic functions: task supervision, scheduling, dispatching, real-time input and output, system timing, data management, history logging, error detection, error processing, initialization, and termination.

The primary component of the Test Support Software is the Kwajalein Test Support Program. It is required to test key functions of the engagement process and to support system test operations. Additional test support functions have been provided in the Data Processing Subsystem Simulator and a variety of test tools used in the generation of test data and evaluation of test results. Development of two other test support components (i.e., the System Environment and Threat Simulator and the System Test Driver) was initiated, but continued development was deferred.

The Development Support Software consists of the Basic Operating System, the Process Construction Program, specialized development support tools, and the Data Reduction and Report Generator. The basic operating system, the primary operating system used in software development, consists of a specially tailored version of the SCOPE 2 operating system for the CDC 7600/7700 plus the associated loaders, compilers, assemblers, and utilities. The functions of Process Construction are data base definition, data base generation, task/routine compilation, process consolidation, and process adaptation using a higher-level, Fortran-like language which facilitates construction of the real-time software. Using the process designer's input directives and definitions and a library file of coded routines and tasks, Process Construction assembles the application program, constructs the tables defining the program operation to the tactical operating system, and links the entire process together.

Specialized tools consist of a number of utility programs that aid developers in the design, execution, and evaluation of SD software. They provide information useful in static and dynamic analysis of the software and relieve developers and testers of many repetitive and tedious tasks.

Data Reduction is an off-line program used to postprocess in a non-real-time environment the data generated by the test processes. It supports analysis and reduction of real-time execution history logs and generates reports based on user requests.

2.2.2 The Computing Facility

The major elements of the computer hardware system consist of CDC 6400, 7600, and 7700 computers. The CDC 6400 computer is used primarily as an input and output station for the 7600 and 7700. The 7600 was used in the early phase of software development and was replaced by the 7700, which is essentially two 7600s with a shared large core memory. The 7600 and 7700 mainframes have been supported by an extensive complement of peripherals driven by the CDC 6400. At the peak of the configuration, the system contained two card readers, one card punch, six tape drives, eleven disk packs, six printers, one large disk file, and three operator's consoles. Off-line peripherals consisted of one IBM 360–20 and three Calcomp plotters.

All STP software development up to July 1976 was done in the batch mode with some stand-alone testing of the real-time system. No time sharing or remote job entry systems were used. After the CDC 7700 system was shipped to Kwajalein (July 1976), a remote job entry (RJE) system connected to the McDonnell-Douglas Astronautics computer facility in Huntington Beach, California, was used by TRW for software maintenance and additional development. At the peak operation (mid-1974), approximately 600 batch jobs per day were processed by the computer facility at TRW. Availability of the hardware grew from 85% (in early 1973) to an average of 97% (mid-1976). Turnaround time was greatest (4 hours) in mid-1974 for classified runs and has averaged approximately 40 minutes for all runs from mid-1974 through mid-1976. Throughout 1975, the second 7600 processor was devoted for one full shift to real-time testing. The computer facility was available for 1.5 shifts in 1973, 2.5 shifts in 1974, 2 shifts in 1975, and 2 shifts for the first 6 months of 1976.

A systems support group was established to be responsible for maintaining the CDC-supplied software. This group had the responsibility to develop STP unique improvements and additions to the CDC software.

2.2.3 The People

At its peak the project staff exceeded 400 personnel. A history of the project population through mid-1976 is shown in Figure 2.1. The figure also illustrates the personnel mix (educational background, degree level, and experience), which has remained relatively constant despite the large variation in project size.

The programmers on the STP project fell into three major categories: (1) CDC operating systems support programmers, (2) real-time systems programmers, and (3) application programmers.

2.2.4 STP Chronology

The STP Program began with the award of multiple-contract definition-phase contracts to three teams of contractors, one of which was the team of McDonnell-Douglas, TRW, GE, and CDC. At the end of this phase, each team was required to submit proposals for future STP development and the McDonnell-Douglas team won this competition. Since that initial award, the program underwent multiple redefinitions (here called "Reprogramming")

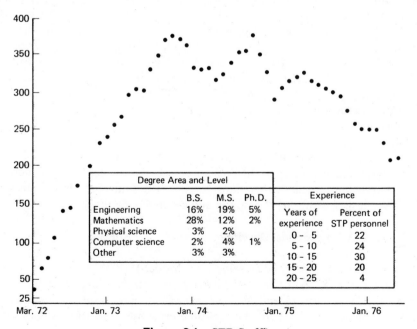

Figure 2.1 STP Staffing

mainly as the result of congressional action. The major effect of this reprogramming was to stretch schedules and redefine the content of the computer program deliverables. The approximate contractual chronology for STP was as follows:

Contract definition contract award	April 1971
Contract definition complete/STP proposal submitted	November 1971
STP contract award	March 1972
First reprogramming (66-month program)	April 1973
Second reprogramming (72-month program)	March 1974
Third reprogramming (80-month program)	February 1975
Fourth reprogramming (86-month program)	March 1976

2.3   PROJECT DESCRIPTIONS (CSC)

The three CSC projects studied had many similar characteristics, and yet they were diverse enough to have varied environments for employment of MPP. Each project involved either direct or indirect contractual relationships with the U.S. Navy. The software in all those projects was developed for real-time command and control systems for shipborne employment. The earliest and largest (in terms of manning) of the three provided the nucleus of experienced personnel for the other two. Also, much of the support and test software was common to all three. This was due to the standardization of computer hardware and software for Naval tactical systems. The Univac AN/UYK-7 computers are used for Navy shipborne tactical systems, and all software is developed using the CMS-2 compiler. The CMS-2 compiler is the responsibility of the organization that makes all modifications and enhancements to the compiler to assure that all Navy installations are operating with a current standard version.

Nevertheless, development environments, management approaches, and system requirements were all different, and the success achieved in each of these acquisition projects varied considerably. The following discussions will provide a basis for the MPP analysis and recommendations.

2.3.1   AEGIS Engineering Development Model-1 Project

The AEGIS Engineering Development Model-1 (EDM-1) project was a subcontract with RCA for the U.S. Navy to design and develop engineering models of the Command and Control subsystem, Radar subsystem, Operational Readiness Test System, the real-time executive, and the support software.

AEGIS is an integrated, computer-controlled shipboard weapon system composed of a guided missile, acquisition and guidance radar, and an auto-mated control system. EDM-1 is a proof-of-concept system now at sea on the USS *Norton Sound*. The computer selected for operational software was the Univac AN/UYK-7, and the language selected was the CMS-2 high-order language.

The CSC contract performance evaluated by this research project was from January 1970 through April 1973 for the EDM-1 version of the system. The data collected for this research covers only the EDM-1 software develop-ment; however, CSC also provided level-of-effort support to RCA in the areas of system integration and testing of EDM-1 software.

The AEGIS technical staff averaged approximately 100 over the contract period. This staff had an average of 10 years of data processing experience and 90% had related experience prior to assignment on the AEGIS project. Related experience was determined to be experience in the subsystem to which the person was assigned (i.e., real-time executive, radar, command and con-trol, etc.). The staff was comprised of 67% senior members of the technical staff or higher, and 70% of the staff possessed college degrees. The re-quirements for a senior member of the CSC technical staff are: B.S. degree, M.S. preferred; minimum 5 years of professional experience, with some supervisory or management experience. The average turnover rate for the technical staff during the contract period was 21.6% per year.

The EDM-1 was a research and development effort with customer em-phasis on quality. The hardware and software for the system were developed in parallel, which resulted in several restarts and modifications to the original design. The project personnel interviewed during this research felt that the success of the project was due to the very close working relationship among all personnel and good overall systems coordination. The CSC developed soft-ware amounted to over 310,000 words of core, at a cost of $7,850,000.

2.3.2 TRIDENT Monitoring/Data Acquisition Subsystems Project

The TRIDENT Monitoring/Data Acquisition subsystems project was a subcontract with IBM for the U.S. Navy to develop the Monitoring subsystem and the Data Acquisition subsystem software for the TRIDENT submarine sensor system. CSC had responsibility for design specification, detail design, program generation, coding and checkout, and subprogram integration. All system testing and integration was accomplished by CSC personnel at the Navy Land-Based Evaluation Facility in Rhode Island.

The TRIDENT class submarine is the largest of the Fleet Ballistic Missile Submarines and will carry a complement of 24 TRIDENT I missiles. Each submarine is designed for quiet operation, high systems reliability, and ex-tended cruise endurance.

The subsystems operate within the ship's central computer complex to provide automated sensor signal analysis, supporting quiet operation of the ship. The on-board computers to support these programs are the Univac

AN/UYK-7 and AN/UYK-20. The computer programs are written in the CMS-2Y high-order language.

The CSC contract performance period for this effort was April 1974 through August 1976. The technical staff consisted of approximately 30 persons during the coding and testing phase; of these, 60% were senior-level personnel. The average data processing experience for the staff was 9.6 years, and 73% of the staff possessed college degrees. Some of the technical staff members were transferred from similar CSC projects, and of the total staff, 47% had directly related experience using the Univac AN/UYK-7 and the CMS-2Y language prior to assignment to the TRIDENT project. The annual turnover rate was 24% during the contract period.

The subsystems developed by CSC totaled 94K words in size and the development cost was $2.4 million over the contract period.

This project encountered several problems during the development cycle. The major problem arose when a complete redesign of the subsystems was required after sensor data collection hardware could not meet the performance requirements. The original hardware, known as the Information Transfer System, was replaced by special-purpose hardware using an AN/UYK-20 computer as a control unit. This involved a major change in the concept of operation. The decision to make this change was made only after the first two levels of the monitoring subsystem were delivered to the customer.

The project also had a problem with program sizing caused in part by the added requirements that accompanied the replacement of the Information Transfer System hardware. Also, the subsystems were coded using structured programming with the CMS-2Y language, which further extended the core budget. Even after several test cases proved that structured programs required 5 to 8% more core than nonstructured programs, the decision was made by the customer to continue with structured programming. A major effort was undertaken to reduce the size of the program late in the development cycle, and monitoring of the core budget became a high-priority effort.

Hardware, compiler, and facility problems further slowed progress and resulted in milestones being rescheduled. The customer became concerned and was given additional visibility into development activities. Additional controls, resources, and techniques were applied to the project and most of the problems were resolved.

The problems resulted in the final product delivery date being rescheduled from May 1976 to August 1976.

2.3.3   DD-963 Project

The U.S.Navy is constructing a new class of destroyers to assure protection of the fleet through the 1980s. This class, known as DD-963, will be equipped with the most sophisticated weapons and control systems available today. The heart of these systems will be a real-time automated command and control system. CSC as a prime contractor to the Navy developed the operational software for this advanced system based on a prototype system developed by another contractor.

The mission of the DD-963 class destroyers is to operate offensively in the presence of air, surface, or subsurface threats as an escort for strike forces or antisubmarine warfare (ASW) aircraft carriers. In addition, it is designed to seek out and destroy enemy submarines. The system is also capable of providing friendly aircraft control during ASW patrol and surveillance, and search and air rescue.

In May 1973, the Navy requested CSC to assume responsibility for two activities associated with DD-963 development. The first activity was to monitor Litton Industries production of a prototype version of the DD-963 command and control system known as Model III. In this task CSC reviewed the computer program design specifications, subprogram design documents, program test plans, and program test procedures. Also, CSC personnel witnessed all levels of computer program testing. The objective of the second activity was to upgrade the prototype version of the command and control system. This involved developing a totally new system, designated Model IV. The following subtasks were completed for the Model IV development:

1. Revise Computer Program Performance Specifications.
2. Write the design specification for this model.
3. Modify the real-time executive as required.
4. Code, debug, test, and integrate the application programs.
5. Produce system test procedures and assist the Navy in conducting program acceptance and system integration testing.

It was the second activity associated with development of the DD-963 command control system which was evaluated under this study—system development efforts for Model IV of the DD-963 system.

The project technical staff, which averaged 30 people through the life of the project, was located on site at Dam Neck, Virginia. These personnel averaged 10 years of data processing experience and 46% had directly applicable prior experience. This included UYK-7 hardware and CMS-2 language experience. Half of the staff were senior members of the technical staff or higher, and 73% of the staff possessed college degrees. The average annual personnel turnover rate was 13.2%.

System development took place over a period of $2\frac{1}{2}$ years at a cost to the customer of approximately \$3.5 million. The software system developed under this contract consisted of 14 modules comprising 250K lines of code. These modules form the ship operational program, which is an element of the Naval Tactical Data System (NTDS) command and control system supporting the ASW mission of DD-963 class destroyers. Processing is handled by an AN/UYK-7 computer system configured with three control processor units (CPUs), two input/output channels (IOCs), and ten memory banks. A fourth

CPU runs with one IOC and two memory banks as a reserve processor. Scheduling of the modules, core allocation, timing, etc., is handled by the real-time executive program.

The primary output device is a Hughes display console, which displays a radar/symbology presentation and amplifying data. Track symbology for air, surface, and subsurface tracks will be displayed, with modifiers showing velocity and direction, assignment or engagement status, etc. Also special points, such as reference points, sonobuoys, and electronic warfare fixes, will be shown.

2.4   PROGRAM ENVIRONMENTS (SPERRY UNIVAC)

This section discusses the environment of software development at Sperry Univac of four large real-time command and control programs completed for the U.S. Navy. This section reviews each program's magnitude, operating system(s), hardware suite(s), special requirements, and deliverable items. It summarizes schedule, work assignments, and personnel attributes.

The four programs reflect the evolution of modern programming practices at Sperry Univac over a seven year period. Each program involved modification and expansion of existing available programs, and generation of new programs. Each program was separately documented in conformance with standards set by the Navy. Each used a common set of software for its baseline operating system (common program), and each operated on the Navy's standard large central computer, the AN/UYK-7. Each operating system required adaptation to the applications unique computer/peripheral configurations.

A summary of the magnitude of each program is shown in Table 2-2.

2.4.1   Program 1

Software was developed to provide a real-time Command and Control System (C&CS). C&CS included the operating system software for integrated use by two real-time application programs: a navigational program produced

TABLE 2-2
Program capabilities

Program	Number of Lines of Source Code Generated	Number of Pages of Documentation in Final Edition	Number of Person-Months
1	90,000	8,059	630
2	500,000	27,014	2,960
3	26,600	3,507	430
4	13,150	2,259	115

as a second part of this program, and an application program produced by another contractor.

The Navigation Program was a task state application program that operated under the real-time operating system. It provided the computational functions required for collecting, interpreting, and supplying navigation information (e.g., ownship position, altitude, speed, and heading) for subsequent system use.

2.4.2 Program 2

Program 2 consisted of software developed to provide a large centralized integrated Command and Control System (C&CS): the operating system, operational application programs, test programs, and simulation programs.

The operating system was based upon the advanced operating system from Program 1 at the start of the Program 2 development. This baseline program was expanded in capacity by expanding control tables, and enhanced in capability by adding new I/O interfaces and new functions. Since the central computer for Program 2 was not fully hardware-integrated, two operating system designs were developed using a single program source; one allowing dual CPU multiprocessing and the other allowing single CPU processing. Each operating system supplied its own I/O interfaces as determined by the hardware suite design. This dual operating system design shared use of certain computer memory units, I/O handlers, and an intercomputer I/O channel which provided a degree of software integration to the two operating systems.

Concurrent with operating system development, a separate working group developed the modular task software, which, when integrated with the operating system software in the central computer, provided the C&CS operational program. This provided command personnel with the capability to continuously monitor the ship's tactical mission environment and to control the weapon systems. The operational program was subjected to simulated operational testing before acceptance.

The simulation program was modular and ran under the Program 2 Operating System, but in a separate AN/UYK-7 computer. It simulated the real-world environment and the weapons system via intercomputer I/O interfaces and operator-generated scenario.

The resulting system provided simulation and recordings for acceptance of the operational program, and provided a basic C&CS training tool.

2.4.3 Program 3

Program 3 comprised a set of specialized system functions which expanded a Navy-furnished baseline program to provide the real-time operating system for a large integrated C&CS.

These specialized functions provided centralization of:

1. System loading, system initialization, system casualty recovery, and reconfiguration functions
2. Input/output of intercomputer channel data shared by multiple-application subsystems
3. Management of the system-shared data
4. Semiautomatic control of on-line C&CS hardware confidence tests and manual control of computer diagnostics and peripheral performance tests
5. Control for standard peripheral devices

2.4.4 Program 4

Program 4 was a real-time application subprogram that used the Program 3 operating system software. It was the software component for a complex process control system which featured both automatic and computer-aided manual control. This program provided display outputs, logic functions, and performance monitoring, performed calculations, and gave location assistance required for maintaining real-time operations.

2.4.5 Target Hardware Suites

The hardware used during the Program 1 software development was an AN/UYK-7 configured with two mainframes, each containing 16,384 32-bit-words of core memory.

The Program 2 central computer was the AN/UYK-7, containing varied internal configurations of four mainframes and three CPUs each containing 16,384 32-bit computer words of main memory. The network integrated these components but did not allow for total memory sharing.

Programs 3 and 4 were developed using the UNIVAC 1108 system. The generated program listings and machine-loadable tape of absolute program elements were taken to a Navy-furnished center and integrated with the baseline operating system. The resulting programs were debugged and tested under simulated real-time conditions using the furnished center equipment, four fully integrated AN/UYK-7 computers.

2.4.6 Special Requirements

Each studied software development was designed to accomplish many unique real-time requirements.

Program 1 met the following special requirements:

a. The system automatically detected, isolated, and recovered from all first-level hardware failures in the central computer, and from peripheral failure.
b. The system maintained navigation accurately across main-memory program reloads and program reconfigurations.
c. The system supported a minimum time period to recovery from a hardware component failure of a few seconds.

Program 2 met the following special requirements:

a. Reconfiguration of the on-line software for varying conditions of hardware operational readiness
b. Real-world simulation interface testing of the four interconnected computer systems so each could be operationally tested independently within the target equipment suite

Program 3 met the following special requirements:

a. Operation in multiple states, reconfiguring automatically following hardware failure, or manually under operator direction, to ensure continuous real-time support of the critical C&CS functions
b. Support for seven simultaneous test, development, and integration centers, each with different hardware and software configurations

Program 4 met the following special requirements:

a. Integration with the results of the Program 3 development before testing and delivery
b. Full-cycle processing at 8Hz using less than 15% of a CPU

2.4.7 Personnel Considerations

The total person-months of paid expended labor for each program is shown in Table 2-3.

TABLE 2-3
Person-months for each program

Program	Labor (person-months)
1	630
2	2960
3	430
4	115

2.5 SELECTION OF CRITICAL STUDIES (SDC)

SDC selected two of its most recent experiences with MPPs for inclusion in this study. The first was the COBRA DANE project, selected because initial planning for the project laid down a broad set of standard practices. These practices were representative of both new technology and accepted practices. A mix of both technical and managerial standard practices was used. At the time of selection, the COBRA DANE project was nearing completion and offered unique opportunities to estimate how well the standard practices were observed and to assess the impacts of levels of observance on productivity and quality.

The second instance selected was the COMPOOL-Sensitive System employed by the Air Force Satellite Control Facility (SCF) to define and control data structures. It was selected because this tool was specifically developed to solve an extremely difficult set of problems that faced the SCF. These problems involved such conditions as encountering a large number of interface problems in integrating the software products of a variety of independent software developers, redundancy and inefficiency in the definition and use of data structures, and severe limitations on computer capacity. The system has met its original objectives.

2.6 SOFTWARE PROJECTS SELECTED FOR ANALYSIS (BCS)

Five in-house developmental software projects were selected to provide the software production data we collected. These projects vary in size, complexity, and the extent to which both traditional and modern programming practices were exploited.

In order to provide the greatest amount of project specific information without compromising the identity of any one project, there is no relation between the names and the order of the functional description of these projects, and the project labels A, B, C, D, E used in the following descriptions of project characteristics.

2.6.1 Project Functional Descriptions

CASA (Configuration Accountability System Aerospace) is the first of a four-phase development to redesign and upgrade the computer support for the Boeing Aerospace Company (BAC) engineering and operations divisions. BAC's computer processing support, which originated in the 1950s and early 1960s, was studied in 1973. The study concluded that significant improvem ıts could be achieved by eliminating fragmentation in computers and systems, exploiting recent advances in computer technology, and redesigning software instead of converting it to newer hardware.

CASA is primarily designed to support engineering in the establishment and maintenance of design configuration information. In addition, other organizations, such as manufacturing, material, quality control, and finance, are supported by the system. The system serves as a baseline for all manufacturing and procurement activities and creates program unique parts lists that form the basis for configuration control, maintenance of engineering release records, and easier accessibility to current engineering data.

EML (Estimator Modeling Language) is a software system used to estimate system costs. It provides a user-oriented computer language developed for use by estimators in the processing of cost estimates and allows a convenient means of describing any cost estimate model. EML is used to aid cost estimators in preparing intersystem and intrasystem cost studies, cost trades, and cost proposals.

EML consists of three major components: a Precompiler, System Utility Processes, and a Run Time Program. The Precompiler accepts (in EML language form) cost estimates for items in a Work Breakdown Structure expressed in terms of cost relations. It translates these into output directives, initialization, and compiler source code. The System Utility Processes consist of compilation, which fuses special user-supplied compiler routines with the main program, table look-up and calculations; and loading or link editing, which provides the augmentation of EML user and system libraries. The resulting Run Time Program, which performs arithmetic calculations and produces tabular results, forms a baseline against which cost relations can be varied for trade study alternates. Figure 2.2 shows an abbreviated EML system flow and processing.

MIDAS (Management Information and Data Automation System) is a system designed specifically for the purpose of information processing. It is a generalized data base management system providing on-line, interactive file creation, data insertion and updating, a query language for data retrieval, report generation, and a programming language with arithmetic and comparison capabilities. Two modes of operation are supported: interactive, from user terminals, and immediate access, via callable subroutines from application programs.

The MIDAS system support functions provide a Communications Subsystem, a Data Base Access Subsystem, a System Monitor, and a Terminal Task Foundation Module.

Features of MIDAS include an integrated data base, minimal redundancy data sharing, biasing of data to multiple applications, a variety of access procedures, a data base administrator with control functions, a variety of data structures, direct user–computer interface, selectable/automatic report formatting, dynamic file management, and comprehensive selectable data and system security.

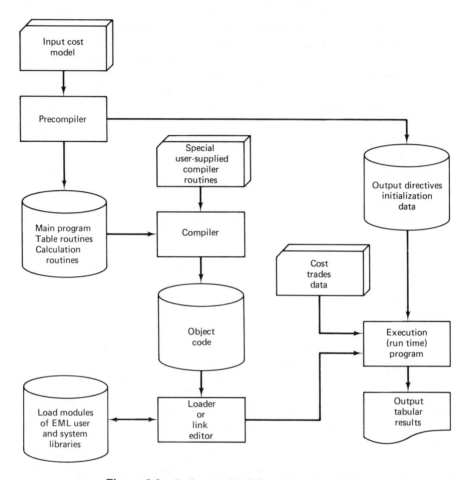

Figure 2.2   Estimator Modeling Language (EML)

SARA III (System Analysis and Resource Accounting) is a computer performance analysis program. It provides capability for reporting—from raw accounting data collected by an operating system—information describing the characteristics of the work load presented to a computing system, and the performance of the system in processing that work load.

WIRS (Wire Information and Release System) was developed to support Boeing Commercial Airplane Company's engineering and manufacturing activities, including the design and release of wire-bundle assemblies to manufacturing, the assembly and test of wire-bundle assemblies, and the control of the configuration of wire bundles through the design and manufacturing processes.

Input to WIRS consists of data on wire-bundle assemblies provided by integration engineers. Output from WIRS consists principally of wire-bundle assemblies, control of status reports, shop aid packages, and CRT displays for the engineer, planner, or fabricator.

2.6.2   Project Characteristics Descriptions

Computer characteristics. The computer hardware used on the projects that were studied was predominantly IBM 360 and 370 machines; one project used the NOVA/830 minicomputer. Two projects each used Cobol and Fortran IV

Project	Principal Hardware		Support Software	Machine Access
	Host	Target		
A	Data General NOVA/830	Data General NOVA/830 compatible	RDOS operating system, MAC macro assembler, Algol compiler, text editor, debugger, precompiler	Time sharing; stand-alone
B	IBM 370/158 (VS 1.0) 370/168 (VS 2.4)	IBM 370/168 or 370/158 (MVS)	Cobol compiler, Bal assembler, IMS, TSO, CTS (time sharing), BTS (batch terminal simulated) IEBUPDATE, KAPEX Cobol optimizer	RJE; time sharing
C	IBM 360/65 (OS/MVT)	IBM 360 compatible	OS/MVT MAINSTREAM TSO, Fortran IV (level H) with precompiler, programming support library aid	RJE; time sharing
D	IBM 370/158 (VS 1.0) 370/168 (VS 2.4)	IBM 370/158 or 370/168	Cobol compiler, BAL assembler, MARK IV utilities, MAINSTREAM TSO, IMS	RJE; time sharing
E	IBM 370/65 370/158 370/145	IBM 360, 370 compatible	Fortran IV (level H) compiler, TSO, CTS (time sharing)	Remote batch (mailed decks)

Figure 2.3   Computer Hardware, Software Types, and Accessibility Characteristics by Project

languages, and Algol was used in one project. Machine access methods included stand-alone, remote batch, remote job entry, and on-line terminal. Figure 2.3 details the computer characteristics for each project.

Personnel characteristics. Project A was composed of five members, including the Program Manager.

Project B currently consists of 20 members reporting to the Program Manager; personnel size has fluctuated from 2 through 27. This project experienced a rather severe and abrupt personnel turnover immediately after Critical Design Review. The Program Manager stated that their design documentation and configuration management practices cushioned the shock of the turnover and a greater amount of productive work was salvageable.

Training of personnel for Project B included courses in Cobol, IMS, and top-down design and structured programming. Less formal training was also provided in the areas of Job Control Language procedures, Data Management Systems, and project specific procedures.

Project C was made up of five members (on the average), including the Program Manager. The Program Manager was replaced midway through the project, and the identified customer was changed at about the same time. The four design team members had been trained in top-down techniques prior to assignment to the project.

Project D consists of 37 full-time project members. All project personnel received training in top-down design and structured programming, and in data base management concepts. They were all experienced in Cobol, and 75% of them had prior experience in a large-scale (IBM) environment. The project has thus far experienced a 10% personnel turnover rate, consisting principally of planned and phased entry and departure of outside contractor personnel.

Three

Technical Practices

In the mid-1970s, it was popular to be suspicious of the software technologist.

"Software is always behind schedule, overbudget, and unreliable," some said.

"Industry takes too long to do what are essentially simple software jobs," said others.

It was in the midst of this growing suspicion that the MPP studies were conducted. The companies and the Air Force were looking for dramatic solutions to the schedule/budget/reliability problems, and felt that they could be found, given the "simplicity" of the problems involved in software construction.

The passage of time, and the enlargement of awareness of the complexities that are modern-day software, has blunted the thrust of those suspicions. However, some of the flavor of the era still emerges in the MPP reports. It was as if no one had yet absorbed the importance of the opening of Fred Brook's classic, *The Mythical Man-Month:**

> One occasionally reads newspaper accounts of how two programmers in a remodeled garage have built an important program that surpasses the best efforts of large teams. And every programmer is prepared to believe such tales,

* Brooks, *Mythical Man-Month Essays on Software Engineering,* © 1975, Addison-Wesley Publishing Company, Inc., Chapter 1, pp. 4–6. Reprinted with permission.

for he knows that he could build ANY program much faster than the 1000 statements/year reported for industrial teams.

Why then have not all industrial programming teams been replaced by dedicated garage duos? One must look at WHAT is being produced.

In the upper left of Figure 3.1 is a PROGRAM. It is complete in itself, ready to be run by the author on the system on which it was developed. THAT is the thing commonly produced in garages, and that is the object the individual programmer uses in estimating productivity.

There are two ways a program can be converted into a more useful, but more costly, object. These two ways are represented by the boundaries in the diagram.

Moving down across the horizontal boundary, a program becomes a PROGRAMMING PRODUCT. This is a program that can be run, tested, repaired, and extended by anybody. It is usable in many operating environments, for many sets of data. . . . The program must be thoroughly tested, so that it can be depended upon. . . . Finally, promotion of a program to a programming product requires its thorough documentation, so that anyone may use it, fix it, and extend it. . . .

Moving across the vertical boundary, a program becomes a component in a PROGRAMMING SYSTEM. This is a collection of interacting programs, coordinated in function and disciplined in format, so that the assemblage constitutes an entire facility for large tasks. To become a programming system component, a program must be written so that every input and output conforms in syntax and semantics with precisely defined interfaces. The program must also be designed so that it uses only a prescribed budget of re-

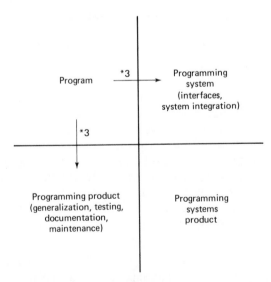

Figure 3.1   Evolution of the Programming Systems Product (after *The Mythical Man-Month,* Addison-Wesley, Reading, Mass., 1975)

sources—memory space, input–output devices, computer time. Finally, the
program must be tested with other system components, in all expected combinations. . . . A programming system component costs at least three times as
much as a stand-alone program of the same function. The cost may be greater
if the system has many components.
In the lower right-hand corner of Figure 3.1 stands the PROGRAMMING
SYSTEMS PRODUCT. This differs from the simple program in all of the
above ways. It costs nine times as much. But it is the truly useful object, the
intended product of most system programming efforts.

The importance of the programming system product in the MPP
reports should already be apparent from the preceding sections of
this book. It will become even more apparent in what follows. Fortunately, the suspicions of the era did not taint most of the findings of
the MPP technologists. The material that follows describes an evolutionary, achievable set of improvements to the software engineer's
toolbox. The result of their use, it is important to note, is not the
hoped-for dramatic solution to the schedule/budget/reliability problems of software. The result, instead, is an effective process for constructing the programming systems product that Brooks described.

For the purposes of organization, the material that follows is
grouped by phases of the software life cycle described earlier.
Technical practices related to requirements for software development are dealt with first.

3.1   REQUIREMENTS

The several companies utilized a variety of requirements techniques.
Some techniques, such as using simulation to assist in the definition
of requirements and using "threading" to assist in the traceability of
requirements, were commonly used by several companies. Others
were mentioned by only one or two.

3.1.1   Requirements Generation

The definition of requirements is critical to the success of a software project. It is also a hard problem, in the sense that requirements
do not leap at the system analyst from their problem domain, but
rather evolve from a process of human interaction.

The number of techniques mentioned by the MPP companies to
deal with this problem was limited. Basically, requirements generation is still largely a sociotechnical process.

3.1.1.1 REQUIREMENTS GENERATION
(MARTIN-MARIETTA)

The Viking Lander Guidance and Control system was extensively analyzed via simulation and other supporting techniques before hardware and software specifications were written. This led to the generation of detailed specifications for hardware and software which later produced results that were compatible across integrated software/hardware closed-loop tests and actual flights, with minimal revisions. An auxiliary technique of this process was the Fortran specification of the Flight software routines to be consistent with the overall system analysis and simulation models.

This approach has been used generally on aerospace guidance and control contracts, but more often than not the simulations evolve too late to influence the hardware design or significantly change the software. In this case, having a complete six-degree-of-freedom simulation early in the program, models for all components (inertial sensors, radars, actuators, aerodynamics, etc.) could be evaluated closed-loop with preliminary flight software control laws and algorithms for overall system accuracy, stability, and response.

In the development phase of Viking, a simulation was used to analyze different radar designs, variations of parachute and aeroshell mechanics, propulsion dynamics, and flight software algorithms. The models were all written in Fortran. These formulations, after considerable experience, were directly translated into models for an analog–digital hybrid real-time simulation which was used for closed-loop testing of the descent-phase flight software and guidance and control hardware. Having the Fortran flight software models in the hybrid simulation allowed a three-way comparison of the Fortran program, the hybrid real-time simulation, and the hybrid real-time simulation mixed with Flight software/hardware combinations. Because of this testing, timing and phasing problems were identified and corrected very early in Viking development.

The six-degree-of-freedom simulation provided a modularized structure which handled dynamic integration of differential equations, intermodule communication through a common array, random noise generation, standard data input, standard print output, vehicle dynamic staging control, and plots. Therefore, within this structure it was a simple process to develop the Viking peculiar models, using Guidance and Control engineers who only had rudimentary Fortran experience. This program later evolved into the Flight Operations Lander Trajectory Simulation program used for preseparation analysis of candidate landing trajectories.

The Flight Software Requirements Document (descent phase) was written directly from the Fortran algorithm models. This had to be transposed by hand to a typed version using Greek letter symbols, etc., because the customer objected to the style of Fortran-type equations.

Fortran has several other shortcomings as a specification tool for flight computations. It is not a sufficiently high order language for specifying conditional computations, identifying accuracy constraints, and performing vector and matrix operations. Thus, these operations tend to force undesired detail on conditional statements and matrix-element calculations, and allow accuracy specifications to be ignored or only implied.

Complete, precise, consistent, and concise requirements are highly desirable but difficult to obtain. Typically, the programmer must carefully analyze a partial problem statement, ask questions, fill in missing detail, and resolve inconsistencies. Some of these problems were solved through use of the Fortran simulation and could have been expanded to integrate all descent-phase functions with minor additional effort.

The program documentation should use a consistent nomenclature which can be related directly to the simulation model. Fortran provides this (upon agreement between the system analysts and flight programmers) with some limitations that can be worked around. Furthermore, it is highly desirable to use nomenclature common to standard keypunches and typewriters as opposed to special Greek letters and math symbols. As such it would have been preferable to structure the requirements directly from the Fortran listings using comment fields to specify accuracy and range of variables because many typographical and reproduction errors resulted from the Greek letter translation.

Other Lander system requirements for sequencing during the descent phase which did not affect guidance and control were not included in the simulations. Therefore, these requirements were confusing to the flight programmers since they were not integrated into the specifications. For consistency, the simulations should have included a Fortran sequencing module which would have been a direct analog of the Flight program version.

It is very important to have a system analysis group which is capable of integrating, simulating, and specifying all requirements in a consistent language. The language should have one-to-one correlation with the simulations and the actual software/hardware. Although this is commonly done in Guidance and Control, it could and should be extended to any spacecraft flight software operations. On Viking, many hardware/software and software/software incompatibilities resulted from the lack of end-to-end simulation modeling of portions of the system, and the lack of an analytical systems group working those mission phases.

The labor cost involved in developing the simulation to analyze and generate requirements was approximately 40 person-months. The additional effort required to develop a 12,169-source-card Lander Trajectory Simulation program for Flight Operations was 73 person-months, which, with overtime, amounted to about 80 person-months.

The total effort required to develop the hardware and software requirements was approximately 25 person-years, of which 12 to 15 involved the development and use of the simulation.

3.1.2 Requirements Analysis and Validation

We have already seen that requirements generation is a nontrivial task. Not only is it subject to the vagaries of the social process, but it may also require complex simulation assistance.

It is not surprising, then, that the requirements, once generated, must be subjected to considerable analysis and validation activities.

3.1.2.1 REQUIREMENTS ANALYSIS AND VALIDATION (TRW)

Software requirements engineering is the discipline for developing a complete, consistent, unambiguous specification which can serve as a requirements baseline for common agreement among all parties concerned, describing "what" the software product will do. Requirements analysis and validation is the practice through which a given software requirements specification can be analyzed to validate its content prior to design and coding. It is a general consensus that it is extremely cost-effective to analyze thoroughly the given requirements and detect errors early in the software development cycle. The lack of a good requirements specification makes a top-down design impossible and testing meaningless, obscures management monitoring capability, and prevents good communication between user and developer.

The first step in the software development process is the definition of data processing, and subsequently software, functional, and performance requirements which represent the primary input to the subsequent process design activity. Requirements from the system specification which the Data Processing subsystem must perform are allocated to hardware and software. They are iterated with the system-level requirements to assure completeness and traceability.

Once all the Data Processing subsystem-related requirements have been identified, the generation of the requirements specification is the next order of business. Special attention must be given during this activity to what makes a good requirement and specification. For real-time systems, the Data Processing subsystem functional requirements are best expressed in terms of

Input
Processing requirements
Output

That is, for each external stimulus, the subsystem must perform certain processing functions in order to produce the desired output. Requirements expressed in such a manner aid in assignment of performance requirements, establish a one-to-one correspondence between requirements and interface specifications, facilitate the verification of requirements and preliminary design, and facilitate testing.

Equally important are the properties a specification should have. The attributes that are most important are completeness, consistency, traceability, and testability. By careful definition of Data Processing subsystem requirements adhering to the general attributes described above, the resultant requirements specification will enhance the software design solution.

Interface definition parallels the Data Processing Subsystem requirements generation. Since the processing requirements are organized by stimuli, it is absolutely essential that for each external interface a complete message catalog be established. Furthermore, compatibility between interface and functional requirements must be assured: that is, the one-to-one correspondence discussed above.

Once the Data Processing Subsystem functional requirements have been identified and documented in a traceable fashion, they must be analyzed and verified for their adherence to the critical attributes. The requirements analysis group utilizes a formalized method of describing requirements in terms of paths. The requirements are functionally grouped and then decomposed in flowchart forms which illustrate the interaction between them. These flowcharts, called Requirements Networks or R-NETS, consist of:

1. A set of nodes representing processing steps called alphas
2. A set of nodes identifying processing conditions, called "OR-nodes"
3. A set of nodes identifying "don't care" sequences of alphas, which could be performed in any sequence or even in parallel ("AND-nodes")
4. A set of interface nodes where external messages are received or transmitted
5. A set of initial and terminal nodes
6. A set of arcs joining the nodes to form a network
7. A set of events and conditions for R-NET enablements
8. A set of validation points used to uniquely identify transitions

Each alpha is associated with two subsets of data identifiers, which represent data input to and output from the processing step. These, together with the definition of the interface data and the identification of the choice variables, form the basis for consistency checking of the paths. On the other hand, if an R-NET processes data from an interface, the net shows all possible processing paths emanating from the interface. Thus, the processing of each message for each possible condition is identified. This provides a significant aid in verifying completeness of requirements.

Performance requirements are assigned to validation points, providing a connection between these and processing requirements. Each validation point is associated with a set of data identifiers. If performance requirements are expressed in terms of these identifiers, then the requirements will be testable.

A collection of R-NETS define a set of Data Processing functional requirements that can be checked for completeness, consistency, and testability.

A functional simulator is utilized to analyze and validate the requirements further. Simulators model the functional characteristics of the candidate Data Processing Subsystem and the way its resources are utilized. Significant stimuli, hardware characteristics, and critical processing paths from the R-NET are modeled.

Via functional simulation, the requirements analysis team can demonstrate that the given Data Processing subsystem requirements are implementable on the selected hardware configuration. In the event that incompatibility exists, system/subsystem trade-off studies are conducted until a viable baseline is established. An important by-product of the use of the functional simulation is that it provides another method by which the viability and compatibility of the Data Processing Subsystem requirements are demonstrated.

Once a viable hardware configuration has been established, the requirements are allocated to hardware and software. It is important that a complete traceability be maintained from the system to the hardware and software specifications. Interface specifications are also established at this point of the preliminary design phase. From the message catalog defined earlier, interface specifications are generated which define functional requirements and quality assurance provisions for each Data Processing Subsystem interface. They specify communications in terms of external messages, format, rate, and the data transfer protocol applicable to the interface.

3.1.3   Baselining Requirements

Achieving an appropriate set of requirements may be a lengthy process, subject to considerable iteration and validation. Once obtained, a set of requirements must be made firm. The software designer must know that, within reason, the requirements will not change as the design proceeds.

3.1.3.1   BASELINING REQUIREMENTS (TRW)

The baselining of requirements occurs in a review process after the preparation of a software requirements specification and prior to the first software design review. It is intended to achieve a mutual understanding and written agreement as to proper interpretation of mandatory provisions of the requirements specifications which are the basis for software end-item acceptance prior to delivery.

Prior to baselining the software and interface requirements, it is necessary to demonstrate that:

1. The Data Processing Subsystem (DPS) is compatible with the overall system definition.
2. All applicable system-level requirements have been allocated, in a traceable manner, to the DPS and subsequently to hardware and software.
3. Software requirements are complete, consistent, and testable.
4. Consistent interface control has been established.
5. The DPS requirements can be implemented on the selected hardware configuration.

In preparing for and conducting the review activities that precede baselining of the specification, the requirements are analyzed and evaluated for technical and contractual acceptability and any identified problems are documented. All issues and problems are discussed and resolved and all agreements and action items resulting from the review are documented prior to baselining of the requirements specification.

3.1.4 Requirements Tracing

Having established a set of requirements, the software developer has only opened the door to a significant set of tasks: design, implementation, checkout, and delivery of the software system.

As these tasks proceed, it is important to retain awareness of the requirements that spawned the subsequent activities. Most of the companies used some form of requirements tracing capability. The mechanism for tracing is usually somewhat formal, but not (as yet) automated.

3.1.4.1 REQUIREMENTS TRACING (TRW)

Requirements Tracing is the use of documentation techniques and functional processing thread diagrams to establish and maintain forward and reverse traceability from requirements through design to code and from requirements to validation tests.

3.1.4.2 REQUIREMENTS TRACING (CSC)

The THREADS methodology is a requirements tracing tool. A thread represents a sequence of events that contributes to the satisfaction of a specific system function. This sequence is an internal process and may be defined at any functional level. A single thread demonstrates a discrete series of operational activities from stimulus to response.

In threading the system design, the following steps must be carried out for each operational process:

1. Isolate inputs available (stimuli).
2. Identify outputs to be produced (responses).
3. Determine processing required to produce each output from the inputs (processes).
4. Define the sequential processing path from each stimulus to its response (thread).

A complete set of threads defines all processing required to satisfy all system functional requirements. Thus, threading a system design is a process employing a discipline that is external to the system to verify design consistency relative to requirements. Threads is a uniquely functional approach to design verification that may be used effectively in other roles, such as test plan development and, in conjunction with the Threads Management System (TMS), management control.

The three CSC projects reflect three distinct management philosophies with respect to the use of threads. In the case of AEGIS, one subsystem was threaded and those threads were used to verify design specifications and to monitor software development progress. The TRIDENT software system was not threaded. For DD-963, the entire software system was initially threaded during the design phase, and in conjunction with the Threads Management System, threads were aggressively used throughout the period of system development. It is worth noting that both AEGIS and DD-963 were successful projects in that they were completed on time and within budget. TRIDENT, on the other hand, encountered serious development problems and as a result was not successful.

Threads are most effective when they are introduced early in the system acquisition process. Threads employment should be defined within the project management plan as an integral part of the total management effort. System-level threads may be used in the iterative process of evaluating alternative architecture concepts preparatory to selecting the optimum architecture for system development. These system-level threads must be defined based on the system requirements specification. As system development continues, lower-level threads support activities such as system and subsystem design verification, interface definition, test plan development, and system integration.

For the DD-963 project, analysis and design phase activities included revision of Computer Program Performance Specifications and writing the Computer Program Design Specifications. During these phases, CSC personnel threaded the system. The threading process was carried on in conjunction with writing the Design Specification. This provided an extremely effective vehicle for linking the design document to the performance specifications. Developing threads during the analysis and design phases assured more effective use of available manpower in addition to improving the quality of the design. Also, these threads, developed early in the acquisition cycle, continued to enhance the system development process throughout later phases.

The AEGIS Command and Decision subsystem was not threaded until after detailed design was established. Threads were defined after the fact to verify the design specifications. This was the first use of the threads methodology and thus involved a period of learning for those developing the threads. Nevertheless, they were effective in design verification and continued to be used in support of later development phase activities.

During the code and checkout phase for both the AEGIS and DD-963 projects, threads were used by project managers to monitor and report system development status. Thread development status is a reliable indicator reflecting progress toward achieving project milestones. Completion of specific threads within each build was easily recorded, and periodically these data would be reported in summary form for project monitors and managers to review. This provided all concerned personnel with current, easily understood project status information. Recording the thread data requires the expenditure of some labor, but not a significant amount. For instance, on the DD-963 project approximately 50% of one person's time on a weekly basis was devoted to maintaining a threads data base.

Test and integration phase activities for the DD-963 project included developing and executing test plans built around the system, subsystem, and module threads. Threads provided the basis for the stimulus/response-type material included within the test scripts. This was a natural outgrowth of the development process to this point. Test team members could be assured of thoroughly exercising all software functions because of the one-to-one correspondence with system design elements. Later, the integration of system components was facilitated for both DD-963 and AEGIS personnel because of the close correlation among all system components achieved through threads definition. Threads provided the framework for positive control of the test and integration phase.

There are few research data to support positive conclusions concerning threads effectiveness in the installation, and operating and support phases. Research was limited to preinstallation development for all the projects. It seems reasonable to assume, however, that the operating and support phase would benefit from threads documentation. With the system functions clearly defined, it should be easier to make the modifications and functional adjustments normally associated with this phase.

The AEGIS and DD-963 staffs made effective use of the system or subsystem threads. Threads were employed with equal success on both projects as a design verification tool. Later threads became an invaluable aid in maintaining management and customer visibility of software production status. Threads status reports were considered by the staffs to be one of the most current and definitive indicators of production progress. For AEGIS the reports were primarily used for internal management control and monitoring. The DD-963 staff employed the reports internally and also used them regularly to keep the customer informed. Once the build demonstrations and phased integration began on the DD-963 project, the threads played a dual role. They continued to be used to report progress. In addition, the test group used threads to develop and modify test scenarios. In general, the DD-963 staff seemed to employ threads a bit more aggressively than the AEGIS staff did. Thus, threads had greater impact on the DD-963 project.

Recommendation. The decision to use threads should be made early in the acquisition life cycle. Threads are most effective when introduced early in the analysis phase to support the design verification effort. Once the commitment is made to use threads and they are defined, their utility increases over the life of the project. In addition to providing traceability directly from requirements to all levels of design, threads support effective management of software development and maintenance. This includes management visibility into development progress, test scenario definition and execution, and system and subsystem integration. Threads must be considered an important element of a coordinated software management plan.

3.2   DESIGN

Design is a deeply intellectual activity, subject to individual differences and intuitive leaps. In spite of that, the several companies agreed on several common design approaches. Whether the term used was "top-down design," "integrated functional design," "process design," or "complete preliminary design," all of the companies used a systematic approach to carving up the design task into manageable chunks, where each chunk kept its driving requirements clearly in view. Design reviews to analyze and appraise the design were commonly held. And designs were translated into implementation plans by a technique called "builds."

It is interesting to note that little space was spent discussing design representations. Apparently, none of the companies saw the flowchart/program design language/hierarchic input–process–output chart controversy as being important to the total software system task.

3.2.1 Design Approaches

Nearly every company said *something* about their methodology for approaching the problem of taking a large set of requirements for a large software system and incorporating them into a design. Often, what they said was quite similar.

3.2.1.1 TOP-DOWN DESIGN (CSC)

The AEGIS designers decided on a top-down approach to the software system design for several reasons, the most important being the system size and complexity. The AEGIS system was at that time one of the largest ever developed by CSC and the top-down design was to provide a systematic approach to segment the system into manageable development units. The decomposition and refinement of functions down to the program level during a top-down design requires the identification of the interfaces necessary to communicate between the levels of the system. Once these interfaces between levels of the system are identified, the system becomes less complex as components become smaller. In contrast, the bottom-up approach becomes more complex as the next higher level of a system is built and lower levels dictate what system interfaces are required. Thus, top-down design was chosen for AEGIS.

The total system development concept for the AEGIS program was to develop the EDM-1 version for maximum functional flexibility and system maintainability to enable future enhancements to be made with a minimum effort and cost. The top-down design provided CSC with a system architecture that was compatible with development of functional subsystem components.

For the DD-963 command and control system there were a number of diverse operational capabilities which had to be linked through a single executive to a master display/control subsystem. This was a complex design problem with the level of intermodule message traffic as a paramount consideration. The functional capabilities had to be designed so that they maintained their unique characteristics, and yet communicated efficiently with each other and the display/control subsystem.

For the DD-963, top-down design was also compatible with the use of threads for design verification. The threading process involves decomposition of the system design, proceeding from high- to low-level processes. Thus, threads definition logically followed the design methodology applied to the DD-963 system. Top-down design and threads were compatible with the modular system architecture necessary for this real-time system to provide the flexibility required to meet the dynamic operational requirements placed on a command and control system. A modular system is the best design.

The top-down design methodology would benefit any system that can be specified to operate with multiple functional levels. For example, if an executive function will exist which exerts operational control of a system's subfunctions, then top-down design would be beneficial. On the other hand, where a system is composed of autonomous functions with limited interfunction communication, top-down design would not be called for. In fact, it might be counterproductive to attempt a top-down system design.

3.2.1.2   PROCESS DESIGN (TRW)

Process design is the assignment of functional requirements into distinct software functional units; and the performance at the overall software system level of such tasks as the estimation of timing, accuracy, and storage requirements; the evaluation of processing limitations; and the analysis of system behavior and computational loading characteristics. The objective is to ascertain that the entire process fits together and can perform the required functions within the given time limits and accuracy requirements, that all interfaces are properly specified, and that the data base is correctly defined. Subpractices within process design include the allocation of software requirements to software units, the specification of all data exchanges, a functional simulation to analyze timing and loading behavior, a preliminary sizing of all data processing resources, an identification of critical issues and process limitations, and a specification of the execution sequence for all logic threads.

Process design is the activity that establishes a candidate preliminary design baseline. The three major inputs to this design activity are the baselined and validated Data Processing Subsystem functional and interface requirements and the candidate Data Processing hardware characteristics.

The first step in top-down process design activity is the "mapping" of functional and interface requirements to the operating system and application program. These requirements are then further allocated downward into software architectural elements. The purpose of this mapping is to define the required operating system support services and to subdivide the application program into a number of independently schedulable modules which perform specific major processing functions.

Together with the definition of the software architectural elements, the definition of the process structure that will best meet given performance requirements is required. This activity defines how the operating system and application program will perform as a result of external/internal stimuli. Software analysis determines intermodule communications, scheduling/dispatching criteria, priority servicing, load handling, error processing, and recovery. The impact of external intermodule communications upon the data base structure is folded into the data base design activity.

Once the modules of a program have been defined, functional and interface requirements are further allocated downward to the lowest, meaningful entities of the software structure, that is, to routines.

Two important guidelines are followed in this series of downward allocation of requirements. First, complete traceability of requirements must be maintained to the routine level. A traceability matrix must be generated which identifies the allocation of each software and interface requirements paragraph to software modules and routines. Second, performance budgets of storage, accuracy, and timing must be allocated down to the module and routine level. These budgets are derived from software performance specification, hardware constraints, and software analysis. Allocation to software architectural elements can assure that software performance requirements are controllable within the given hardware limitations.

An important activity that supports the generation of realistic routine budget estimates is the key algorithm design. This design activity is conducted to solve critical areas before detailed design and production coding begins. Candidate critical areas are identified with as much detail as possible during process design. Prototype software is developed to find appropriate techniques for solutions.

The data base design is also accomplished as part of the top-down process design activity. The top-level, functional data base is defined. For a process designer, this chart provides a top-level base from which data flow and design modularity for the entire Data Processing Subsystem can be assessed. The global data base is defined by the process designers in terms of data files. The preliminary data base design activity establishes the data base constants and variables, formats, units, etc. Sizes of data files are estimated and fed back to the budget allocation process for modules and routines.

In summary, the process design allocates Data Processing Subsystem requirements and interface requirements in a traceable manner to hardware and various programs that comprise the entire software. Furthermore, the software architecture is defined and requirements and performance budgets allocated to the module/routine level. The process interaction and control have been established and data base structure designed. Consequently, a candidate development baseline has been established.

3.2.1.3 INTEGRATED FUNCTIONAL DESIGN (MARTIN-MARIETTA)

Software Functional Descriptions were written for each candidate Mission Operations software function. Concurrence by Flight Team members established the requirement for a program. The Descriptions were combined to form an Integrated Software Functional Design of the entire software system. The Design was subjected to preliminary and critical design reviews by the Flight Team Directors and the Mission Director. Upon acceptance by the Mission Director, the Design was placed under change control to establish the baseline design for the Mission Operations Software System.

Each Flight Team group was in a position to define the functions they would need to support and control the Viking spacecraft during Mission Operations. A requirement that these functions be documented offered management a tool by which they could combine functions used by more than one group, determine which should be performed through procedures and which through software, and establish the program need date as a function of mission phase. By integrating and combining the individual functions, the data flow for the entire software system could be established.

The Flight Operations Software Plan specified the need for software functional descriptions and an integrated software functional design of the Mission Operations Software System. The lander, orbiter, and institutional software systems engineers were required to gather software functional descriptions for each candidate element of their software systems. They delivered them to the Integrating Contractor Software System Engineer, who was responsible for publishing them.

This proved to be a lengthy iterative process, wherein numerous meetings were held among the software systems engineers and the various Flight team groups to understand the need for and interplay between the various functions. An initial Design was generated and subjected to considerable review by each of the Flight team groups, primarily to determine interface requirements and uncover system deficiencies.

Eventually, six software systems were defined to support mission planning, lander and orbiter uplinks and downlinks, and tracking and flight-path analysis. Diagrams for each of these systems were used to conduct a preliminary design review of the system, which was held before the mission directors and representatives of the various Flight team groups.

Following the Preliminary Design Review, the iteration process continued and brief text descriptions were developed for each of the software systems.

The Critical Design Review was held in a high school auditorium before an audience of several hundred people; included were Flight team members, directors, and outside software experts brought in by NASA to critique the Viking software development approach. To accommodate such a large audience, the Integration Engineer used very large diagrams for each subsystem, the largest of which was 10 feet high and 40 feet wide.

Following the CDR, the Mission Director approved the design. It was then incorporated as an appendix to the Flight Operations System Design document and placed under Viking Integration Change Control. The software system was now structured such that any change to the design would affect system data flow and affect more than one program.

The software design and development process began with the identification of software elements. This was accomplished by the appropriate Flight Operation subgroup by preparation of a Functional Description for each required function. The Description was written in accordance with the following format and requirements.

1. *Program title*

2. *Functional description:* Give a brief description of the general functions to be performed by the program. Although the functions are of main interest, some information on capabilities and mathematical method is also desirable.

3. *Utilization:* Describe the intended use for Viking operations in general terms with reference to mission phase, frequency of use, use in program run streams, etc. For new programs, a step-by-step functional description of the program operation is recommended to facilitate the integration process.

4. *Input/output:* Describe all data and program interfaces, both internal and external to the particular operations software element. This section shall be broken up into subsections entitled ''Input'' and ''Output.''

5. *General:* State whether the program is essentially a new program, an existing program, or one that will be derived from an existing program. If the latter, name the baseline program, computer developed on, and the magnitude of modification. If possible, give some indication of expected program size and running time. Specify any anticipated or known program constraints.

6. *Bibliography:* Give references to pertinent documents which would provide more information about the planned program or which describe the existing program.

The Design was developed in a series of increasingly complex stages. A target program, such as the Lander Sequence Generation Program, was shown as a box. The input section of the Design for this target program was then used to determine what information was required to be made available to the program. A logical subset of the remaining Functional Descriptions was examined to see if it could or did generate output for the target program. When a source for input to the target program was found, the source program was added to the diagram and an arrow was drawn to indicate the data flow. This sometimes required modifying the output section of the Functional Description of the source program. If no input source for the target program could be found, the input was shown to be manual. The output section in the Functional Description of the target program was treated in a similar fashion, showing each output item either going to another program, to a printer, a plotter, or to archives. In this fashion, a simplistic overview of the entire software system was generated.

The basic system flow diagram was next iterated upon by the various Flight team groups to determine if manual inputs would require new software functions to be defined, to ascertain which prints and plots would generate information required to produce manual input to other programs, and to assess whether some functions should be moved from one program to another.

Following this iteration, more detailed diagrams were drawn that indicated the means by which interfaces would be accomplished. Symbols were used to show mass storage files, tape files, card files, and manual interfaces. The latter illustrated that printed output from one program would become punched-card input to another program. File management functions were now determined and added to the diagrams.

Computer loading studies were conducted to balance the computational loads on the available computer systems. The Designs then were expanded to show the computer systems involved. A rough estimate of throughput time for data to be passed through the system could now be made.

The final step in the generation of the final Design was to write a short narrative describing the software programs used by each subsystem, how they would be operationally used, and how information would flow through the system.

The Design Document was extremely valuable to the success of developing a software system that was both reliable and minimized the amount of software necessary to be developed to support all mission objectives. It permitted the project to assess system capabilities during the design stage. It provided a structure for the overall system that was visible and easily controllable by management. It lay the foundation for the system integration requirements and the development of the Software Data Base Document.

The document was maintained through integration of the software system, after which the Software Data Base Document was used to control changes to the system structure and integrity.

The cost to develop the Functional Descriptions and the Design Document was approximately 5 person-years. Changes to and maintenance of the descriptions cost an estimated 2 additional person-years. A total of 130 Functional Descriptions were written. The total number of functions shown in the Design adds up to 156, which illustrates that 26 adaptations were made to allow functions to support more than one subsystem. Thus, had the Design Document approach not been taken, it is reasonable to conclude that some redundant software functions would have been developed at additional cost in labor and computer resources.

3.2.1.4   DESIGN (SPERRY UNIVAC)

This phase defined the design requirements of the Application Program. The design is based on the approved functional requirements of the performance specification. The resulting design specification described these requirements and provided for formal control of the program design.

The performance specification testing requirements were also expanded in this phase and documented in the test plan and informal test guidelines. The test plan defined the procedures for qualification testing. The test guidelines aided in program debugging and checkout and in design of the simulation and testing functions.

Inputs to the Design Process

The program design was based on the requirements of certain documents:

Specification: identified the integrated processing facility and the required hardware and software component specifications.

Design Data Document: identified common design functions and resource allocation.

Software Management Plan: defined the approach to the planning, management, control, generation, testing, integration, and acceptance of the computer programs.

System Interface Design Specification: identified the system interface.

Configuration Management and Quality Assurance Plan: defined the design standards, design review requirements, performance testing requirements, and internal configuration control requirements.

Design Process

The design phase is discussed in three areas: program structure, implementation approach, and testing requirements. Each area has its own distinct outputs and characteristics.

Program structure. Since the program structure provided the framework for completing the task, it was defined early in the Design Specification.

The program structural design was based on the multiple-entry module concept of the Common Program. This program also provided general services to the user modules. In particular, it provided the major portion of the I/O services as performed by Program 3 and the Common Program message handler. Besides providing these Common Program interfaces, the design provided compatibility with the other system programs, including interfaces; and compatibility in shared computer resources, including core, Central Processing Unit (CPU) time, common data definition, and common functions.

Design trade-offs in design analysis were based on the following critical standards listed in order of importance:

1. Optimized system performance
2. Optimized software performance
3. Practical degraded performance
4. Practical development and testing characteristics

5. Suitability for functional changes and additions

6. Suitability for dedicated operation

The functions defined in the performance specification were allocated to specific modules. This was done by a review and tradeoff study of the characteristics of each function, including the timing requirements, priority requirements, interrelationships, and applicable modes. The modules were formed from functions with similar requirements, with consideration for multiprocessing. The functions performed in each module were described, including the logic for the call. Also, the regional data stores were defined based on the module common data requirements.

Studies were made of the data flow and control path flow in each program structural design considered. An error analysis was made, including studies of data loss, data modification in conversions, and timing interactions. The special requirements of the system for recovery from system-detected errors and from data loss due to component malfunctions were also studied. Finally, the propagation of errors through the system, whether from data loss, erroneous input, or loss of significance in the calculations, were studied. In all cases, suitable error-recovery procedures were devised to minimize the effects of these errors.

During the design, the Computer Program Operators Manual was developed from expanded definitions of program control characteristics. The final details of the manual depended on completion of the coding and debug and program checkout.

During the design study, certain features were found which improved the design. Change proposals were generated to update inadequacies or to add improvements in the Performance Specification. Other features were not within the scope of the current project, but useful in a future update; these were collected for turnover with the program. Ideas on the design of subroutines were also saved and provided to aid the development efforts.

Implementation Approach. Implementation guidelines and standards were provided to support the design. The development of specific computer program generation guidelines were critical for standardization and support of follow-on maintenance. A programmers' handbook was developed which contains all applicable development guidelines. Based on the contractor's experience and compatibility with the other system developers, these guidelines helped standardize the following programming practices and techniques:

1. CMS-2 language usage rules

2. Common Program usage rules

3. Program debugging and logical path testing

4. Program correction control and records

5. Program development historical records
6. Top-down structured programming usage, including progress reporting procedures
7. Program development protection and backup procedures

Other management procedures were developed to provide control, visibility, and communication. These were included in the programmers handbook, and include the following:

1. Progress reporting and development control procedures
2. Procedures for reporting and processing trouble reports
3. Procedures for project information storage and access
4. Procedures for collecting new design features
5. Maintenance of project notebooks providing collected requirements and guidelines

The implementation of the design was monitored by the design personnel through informal review meetings. This procedure allowed the free exchange of ideas to promote the design understanding required by coding personnel.

Test Requirements. This portion of the development was a separate and parallel activity to the design of the application program. It designed the exact tests and facilities needed to support the qualification testing. The result of this design effort was the development of the Computer Program Test Plan. This document provided the testing requirements for qualification and required formal approval after an In-Process Review. As an aid to other testing, including debugging, checkout, and facility and test software development, informal test guidelines were prepared.

Design Outputs

The primary output of the design phase was the Design Specification. This document provided the basic structure of the developed program, and guidance on the development of this program.

The design phase also developed other documents which, except for the informal test guidelines, were approved and maintained through the In-Process Reviews. These documents were:

Computer Program Test Plan
Computer Program Operator's Manual
Test Guidelines

3.2.2 Design Reviews

For large software projects, the design review is an extremely common sociotechnical process. Often, in fact, there are two design reviews—the Preliminary Design Review (PDR), held to make sure that the early design efforts are going in the right direction, and the Critical Design Review (CDR), held to make sure that the design is rational just before it is translated into code.

Design reviews were a technique mentioned frequently by the participating companies. As will be seen in some of the discussions that follow, the design review is preferably an intricate part of the entire design process, interwoven with design approaches and design representation.

3.2.2.1 PROJECT REVIEWS (CSC)

Project reviews may not always be considered to be MPP; however, during this research all project managers interviewed felt that the use of in-process reviews kept the customer involved in the project throughout the development cycle and enhanced development progress. The normal sequence of events for most projects begins with the customer approving the system design at the Critical Design Review (CDR) and then departing until some time later when he or she returns to accept the software. This results in little or no input by the customer as the product evolves through the development phases. This sometimes causes system integration problems due to hardware or software changes or trade-offs being made without proper developer–customer coordination. CSC encourages customer involvement during all phases of the software development. This fosters awareness by all system development participants in problem areas, thus promoting their expedient resolution, and keeps everyone informed of the current status of progress on all project tasks. The AEGIS project staff had a monthly status meeting in which problem areas were identified, action items were assigned to the appropriate personnel, and progress was reported since the last meeting.

3.2.2.2 DESIGN REVIEWS (SPERRY UNIVAC)

Upon Sperry Univac's delivery of the preliminary Computer Program Design Specification, the Navy held a formal Critical Design Review (CDR) based upon detailed questions and comments from the customer's design analysis group and other Navy-contracted development agencies affected by interfaces in the program. The documented minutes of this CDR and the results of testing the Level 1 and 2 program were accounted for in the approved final Design Specification.

3.2.2.3 COMPLETE PRELIMINARY DESIGN (TRW)

A complete preliminary design consists of the definition, documentation, and baselining of a design prior to detailed design and coding, and includes as a minimum, the top-level software structure, data base definition, interface characteristics, scheduling criteria, and analysis of critical algorithms. The preliminary design specification contains all the conceptual design information needed to support the detailed definition of the individual software system components and, upon completion of the Preliminary Design Review, becomes the work statement and design baseline for development of the detailed design specification used in coding. The preliminary design specification has a previously agreed upon standard format, identifies the mapping from requirements to software design, identifies the organizations responsible for the software to be developed, defines the software structure, specifies required processing resources, specifies the data base organization, and makes uses of the results furnished by the process design to specify the estimated resource budgets.

During the design process a candidate preliminary design baseline is established. A significant step in modern programming practice is the demonstration that the preliminary design baseline is viable. The software preliminary design baseline is considered complete when the following conditions are met:

1. All applicable system-level requirements have been allocated to the software structure.
2. Interface control has been defined and implemented via interface specifications.
3. Allocation of stated software and interface requirements into basic software structural elements has been completed.
4. Storage, execution timing, and accuracy budgets have been established for each software module/routine.
5. The data base has been defined in sufficient detail to demonstrate software operability.
6. A satisfactory design approach for the entire software process and its elements has been demonstrated.
7. Software performance requirements can be met under required operational loading conditions.

Primary methods of demonstrating the foregoing points, that is, the completeness of preliminary design, are the use of functional simulation, thread analysis, and preliminary design review.

The functional simulator models the characteristics of the Data Processing hardware, external stimuli, operating system, and each module of the applica-

73

tion program. Each module is modeled by its service requests (data and operational) to the operating system, its logical structure, and the execution time for each segment in the logic structure and data base interaction (both external and internal). Performance budgets established during process design are utilized in the simulator. This detailed level of modeling allows an evaluation and insight into the software preliminary design and its complex interaction. The simulator is used by the process designers to examine the sensitivities of computer capacity, timing responsiveness, loading conditions, and port-to-port timing. Process design issues such as proper allocation of requirements to software modules, data base interaction efficiency, and recording capacity can be studied. Expected operational conditions are simulated to verify that the software can meet its performance requirements.

Thread analysis is another method of demonstrating the completeness of the preliminary design. This analysis identifies each unique input to the DP Subsystem and, for each, a thread is generated identifying the applicable software module involved in processing this input. The unique software requirements which are involved in such processing, the data base interaction (at the file level) associated with the given input processing, and the output produced are identified on these threads. Port-to-port timing requirements are also identified and are verified by the use of the functional simulator.

Thread analysis is employed by the process designers to provide additional assurance that:

1. Each unique input is properly processed and the required output is produced.
2. The requirements are complete.
3. All requirements have properly been allocated to software modules.
4. Intermodule interactions and data base definition are complete.

At the completion of the preliminary design phase, a Preliminary Design Review is conducted. This review provides the media by which the soundness and completeness of the preliminary design can be demonstrated. Simulator results, thread analysis, and other material are presented to this effect. A successful Preliminary Design Review becomes the foundation from which software detailed design and code production can emanate.

3.2.2.4   DESIGN VERIFICATION (BCS)

As the design details of a software functional component are determined, and at the point when the design is considered complete, an explicit verification of the design can be performed; the mechanism for this is usually a peer review called a structured walkthrough. Such a review has as its basic objective verifying that requirements for a particular component have been adequately satisfied, and that the design itself is consistent. Beyond this basic objective, verification of design consistency may assume a more formal posture, in that reachability and modularity analyses of the design may be performed. This analysis can be performed manually as part of the structured walk-through, or it may be performed with the aid of a computerized logic analyzer.

It must be acknowledged that traditional practices have often allowed the software developer to proceed through coding, integration, and even demonstration without realizing that some requirement was not implemented. The basic objective of this new practice is to prevent such oversights. Deliberate review of design against requirements may also point out less costly implementations or reveal possible reductions of scope to meet cost targets; this helps ensure that the tasks planned for after Critical Design Review are those necessary and sufficient to implement the capability the customer requires.

Design verification is primarily a way of performing a portion of the traditional testing activity much earlier in the development process (i.e., before code is composed). In a project, design verification is often implemented by assigning the component designers and the test designers the responsibility of reviewing each other's work.

An additional benefit of design verification is that it may reveal that the requirements, as originally stated, were mis-prioritized. In attempts to trim the cost to a fixed price, the developer (with the customer's concurrence) may have deleted a requirement which was crucial to successful operation, or design verification may reveal that a requirement was simply missed during Definition. Armed with this information at the Critical Design Review, the developer and customer can agree to (1) revise the requirement priorities to get a working capability and still stay within the fixed price, or (2) accept the out-of-scope requirement at additional cost. This kind of visibility permits the customer to take needed remedial action in a timely fashion (e.g., revise plans for using the redefined capability, or secure additional funding).

A final observation must be made about design verification. Requiring review of one individual's design by another implies that a formal method to represent the design, the rules of which are understood by both the designer and the reviewer, should be established as a project standard. The traditional design representation is the flowchart; newer representation techniques such as HIPO (Hierarchical Input–Process–Output) diagrams can also be used for this purpose. The important point is not which specific design representation technique is used, but rather that one be used consistently on the project and serve as an effective communication aid in the verification of the design.

3.2.3 Builds

The build is a concept seldom seen in the software literature. In essence, a build is the implementation of a thread. If a thread is a set of related requirements, attached by pointers to those software elements related to those requirements, then a build is the constructed program portions which are defined by that thread or more than one related thread.

Builds are a logical way to attack the problem of large software development. They are a way of converting a massive effort into a set of manageable small ones.

3.2.3.1   BUILDS (CSC)

The build concept was primarily used on the AEGIS project as a means of incremental system development. A build is a group of functionally related threads which can be developed and demonstrated as a partial system capability. By grouping the threads into controllable entities, the total software production can be scheduled and controlled at a manageable level. This technique allows management to schedule the development based on hardware availability, critical areas of software, and other constraints; and to utilize development resources to the maximum degree. This technique provides visibility if replanning is necessary due to unavoidable problems, such as late delivery of a hardware component. The build completion dates were used as intermediate milestones by lower levels of management to measure progress.

The technique also promoted progressive testing and integration, which is discussed in Section 3.4.2.2.

Threads Management System

After the threads were defined and documented, other uses of this information were conceived and computer programs were developed to obtain the full benefits of the data. This collection of programs was called the Threads Management System (TMS) because many of the reports generated by the system were used for management control.

The data base for the TMS contained identifying information about each system thread, such as:

Thread name
Thread number
Performance specification paragraph reference number
Design specification paragraph reference number
Modules required to process the thread
Thread input source
Thread output format
Thread status, such as designed, coded, tested, and integrated
Milestone reporting dates

The AEGIS management used the TMS report to monitor production progress of modules by threads within a module. The status is reported in a binary format; a module is either 100% coded or 0% coded. This type of status reporting eliminates estimates by the programmers and reports the true status of a software package. The system also reports missed schedules on an exception basis, as well as current and projected activity status. Other reports include any changes to the data base, such as rescheduling of milestones and providing change impact analysis for proposed system changes.

This system has been enhanced since its development on the AEGIS project to provide extensive management reports. The system served AEGIS as a control tool and provided visibility to CSC management and the customer.

3.2.4 Design Control

Often in a large system it is desirable to have an outsider look at the ongoing process to interject some disinterested objectivity into what is happening. We have already mentioned design reviews as a part of this process; audits, which are more of a continuing activity than scheduled reviews, are another part.

Reviews and audits sometimes are performed by a separate organization called quality assurance. This is becoming more and more common, for example, in DOD-related activities.

Design control is an umbrella name for this family of concepts.

3.2.4.1 DESIGN CONTROL (SPERRY UNIVAC)

The Software Quality Assurance (SQA) group worked independently of the project software development group during software analysis and design. This SQA work specified controls necessary to ensure program design and design documentation to satisfy the program mission. SQA conducted a critical review of the developed interface design specification and the program specifications to remedy discrepancies.

The objectives of SQA design control were:

1. To assure quality program specifications for interfaces, performance, and design
2. To assure quality and timeliness of program documentation
3. To assure functional adequacy of contractually deliverable computer programs
4. To ensure that the documentation and design adhere to the established standards and conventions
5. To provide for identification of, and report the resolution of, all specification and design discrepancies

Design Control Procedures

The following procedures provided design control:

1. SQA specified the criteria for program quality by providing material for the Quality Assurance Provisions section of the performance specifications and design specifications.
2. SQA provided assurance that the developed interface design and performance specification met the requirements. A report documenting this review was presented at the Preliminary Design Review.
3. SQA participated in design reviews, internal biweekly reviews, monthly customer reviews, and Navy-sponsored design reviews.
4. SQA audited the program design specifications to ensure adherence to the interface specifications, performance specifications, design standards, and documentation standards. The report from this audit was presented to the customer for inclusion in the design review.
5. SQA prepared the Computer Program Test Plan based upon the customer requirements and the program performance specifications. Upon review and approval by the customer and the Navy, this plan was implemented.

3.3 IMPLEMENTATION

Commonality of approaches is much more prevalent in the implementation phase than in the prior life-cycle phases. Most of the companies included in their report some mention of:

1. Structure, modularity, and style
2. Top-down implementation
3. Methodologies and tools
4. Standards
5. Performance concerns

Although fewer of the companies mentioned them, these two additional approaches are known to be commonly used in industry:

6. High-order language
7. Information communication

3.3.1 Structure, Modularity, and Style

It is no surprise that software structure is a common concern in the structured programming era. It is equally no surprise that modularity, long known to be a vital consideration in software construction, is also a common concern.

It may be more of a surprise that style, until recently seldom discussed in the literature and a somewhat elusive concept, is also a common concern.

These three concepts are grouped together here because they all relate to how the software is organized internally. These are vital concerns at the nitty-grittiest level of software.

3.3.1.1 PROGRAMMING TECHNIQUES (CSC)

There were three distinct programming techniques used during development of software for these projects. Collectively they represented formal attempts to structure the programming process. Structuring the process is important because it provides a standardized product (program code) and introduces a procedural approach to what has a tendency to be a disorganized activity (programming). The name of the technique or the particular rules that support it are less important than the fact that a structured technique is used and enforced. This is the key to success in using any programming technique.

Structured programming is a method of writing programs with the logic flow always proceeding from a single entry through a single exit without arbitrary branching. To support this method, a system must be segmented into small programs that can be written with a limited number of logic structures to develop clear, readable, and maintainable programs.

Functional programming involves the development of software based on functional routines that are integrated to create system and subsystem capabilities. This programming technique employs well-defined coding conventions to produce routines in standardized formats for use within the system.

Structured modular programming is a modification of structured programming which is less restrictive in the area of structured constructs. For structured modular programming the technical staff is permitted to use "GO TO" statements and may deviate from the single entry/single exit requirement of structured programming. However, the intent of structured programming is followed with respect to data names, code indenting, and program length.

These programming techniques are applied during the program design and coding phases, with the benefits realized not only in the coding phase, but in the test and maintenance phases as well. For structured programming the detail design will involve more intense activity than for other programming techniques, because of the level of detail required for structured programming. However, this detail will decrease the effort required to produce program code. All three of these techniques improved productivity in the test phase because of the smaller (usually one program per computer print out page), less complex programs. Also the improved readability of the standardized coding structures will have a positive effect on program maintenance in the operation and support phase.

The comparison of these techniques over the three projects reviewed is difficult because only one project used pure Structured Programming (SP) and the other two used a modified form of SP. The TRIDENT project, which used the pure form of SP, had some problems during the development of the software. One of the problems was core usage under SP constraints. It was realized toward the end of the coding phase that the core budget would be overrun. This resulted in some reprogramming to optimize core usage while maintaining SP code. During interviews with the TRIDENT staff, the analysts stated that they felt the program design required a longer period of time than that for free-form programs because of the need to define the program structure at a more detailed level. But the coding phase was reduced to almost half the normal time, due to the design being developed at almost the code level. The supervisors on these projects thought the constraints of SP did not affect the productivity of the senior-level personnel to any degree; however, a noticeable adjustment was required by the junior-level personnel to develop program logic in a structured manner. It was also felt that the quality of the programs produced by the junior staff members using SP was higher than would ordinarily be expected.

The total effect of structured programming on the TRIDENT programs cannot be determined at this time since one of the measures of effectiveness is maintainability and the product has not reached that phase in its life cycle.

On the AEGIS project, as a test, several programs were written by CSC programmers using the SP constraints and then rewritten using a structured format with free-form code. The results of the test indicated that structured programs required 5 to 8% more core. Since the core allocation was a key factor on the AEGIS project, a modified version of SP, functional programming, was selected for this project.

A similar technique was used on the DD-963 project where structured modular programming was employed. The modified versions of SP used on the AEGIS and DD-963 projects were successful in producing high-quality programs within the core limitations. The programs written on these projects did not adhere to SP constraints; however, both projects were developed under rigid coding conventions and used a structured format to ensure standardization of programs.

3.3.1.2 ELEMENTS OF PROGRAMMING STYLE (SDC)

The elements of programming style include rules for:

Commentary
Paragraphing
Naming
Modularity

The objectives of these rules are to increase the legibility and understandability of the program, to contribute to the control of program quality, and to enhance the ease of maintenance and modification of the program.

Commentary, both explanatory prologues to modules and internal annotations of instructions, is intended to explain the intent of the module and to clarify processing steps. By identifying the author of the module, listing its data and subroutine environment, and estimating sizing and timing parameters, programming control operations are enhanced.

Paragraphing, which may be extended to punctuation and formatting rules as well as blocking and indentation, is aimed at increasing the legibility of the program. Paragraphing helps reveal the internal structure of the program and organize its contents as well as make the program easy to read.

Naming conventions for program and data elements are aimed at increasing the semantic content of the program through mnemonic associations and construction rules. Legibility may also be increased by arranging names in lists and calls in sequential order, by adopting standard abbreviations for common words, and by stating simple rules for the hyphenation and continuation of expressions.

Modularity has several functions beyond breaking a large program into more easily understood partitions. Rules for modularization include (1) the minimization of interaction among modules, (2) making module subordination apparent, (3) singularity of function for a module, (4) reducing entry and exit points, and (5) decoupling modular interdependence. The objectives are to increase the ease of understanding through greater structuredness of the program, to simplify functional performance and decrease complexity of interaction, and to enhance maintainability by providing replaceability of modules and isolation of the impacts of change.

Commentary

The standard practices for program annotation are given in Table 3-1. Although not part of the initial standard, a specific requirement to annotate iterations and conditionals was added later. All programs were to be an-

TABLE 3-1
COBRA DANE commentary practices

A. Identification (Prologue)

Program name

One-line functional description and/or indication if this is a dummy or partial program for build test purposes.

Name and phone number of responsible programmer.

Name of latest update ident. This ident will include the two-letter program ID and a two-letter MOD, starting with AA and working sequentially toward ZZ.

B. Status Information (Prologue)

Schedule date for code completion.

Current state of code completion (e.g., none, partial, etc.) and date of status.

Scheduled date for completion of unit testing.

Unit testing status and date of status.

Program under change control (yes/no).

Scheduled date for completion of integration.

Integration status and date of status.

Date of last program update.

C. Descriptive Information (Prologue and Internal)

Common cards describing program purpose and usage.

Subroutine calling parameter descriptions.

*CALL statements obtaining global COMMON blocks.

Local data definitions and descriptions.

DIMENSION and EQUIVALENCE statements.

D. Return shall be made to the main program

EXAMPLE

```
*DECK INLOOP
      SUBROUTINE INLOOP (IN)
C     PROG = J. CODER   PHONE = 617-862-0050
C     INLOOP IS AN INFINITE LOOP FOR EXAMPLE PURPOSES
C     INCL
C     CODING COMPLETION -   - APR 75
C     CODE STATUS          - PARTIAL
C     UNIT TEST COMPLETION - MAY 75
C     UNIT TEST STATUS     - UNTESTED
C     INT TEST COMPLETION  - DEC 75
C     UNIT TEST STATUS     - UNTESTED
C     LAST PGM UPDATE      - 16 JAN 76
C
C     INLOOP = INFINITE LOOP PROGRAM IS CALLED WHEN EVERYTHING IS
C     GOING TOO WELL. IT WILL HANG IN AN INFINITE LOOP UNTIL RTC
C     TIMES THE CALLING PROGRAM OUT
C
C     INPUT PARAMETERS
```

```
C     IN - THIS ITEM IS TOTALLY UNNECESSARY
C

* * * * * * * * *•••••
*CALL CAL
*CALL ROBI
* * * * * * * * *•••••

C
C     LOCAL DATE
      TYPE INTEGER ITEMPA; ITEMPB
            ITEMPA AND ITEMPB ARE TEMPORARY STORAGE
C
C     IF THERE WERE ANY DIMENSION OR EQUIVALENCE
C     STATEMENTS, THEY'D GO HERE
C
C     HOUSEKEEP TEMPORARY STORAGE
      ITEMPA = O
      ITEMPB = O
C     LOOP
C
      100 IF (IUA) 200,200,300
      200 GO TO 100
      300 GO TO 100
      RETURN
      END
```

notated. Changes to controlled programs were to be accompanied by comments giving the reasons for the change and citing the problem report resolved by the change.

Indentation and Paragraphing

Programs are to be segmented into small, single function modules. Subordination and ownership will be clearly indicated.

Coding will be clearly indented to show subordination and grouping of the instructions. Executable statements are to be restricted to one instruction per card. More than one data declaration per line of code is permissible. Wherever possible, lengthy statements such as complicated conditional branches should be broken down into a sequence of shorter code. Blank comment cards should be used to block the listing and enhance readability.

Naming Conventions

The conventions of CDC Fortran Extended are to be followed. Module and data names are to be mnemonic tags up to eight characters in length. Special prefixes and suffixes may be appended but the remainder of each name must be descriptive of its function.

Reserved prefixes for tasks, programs, and subprograms were:

BD—Block Data Programs
CD—Main task entry point programs

Reserved prefixes for variables for Fortran standards were:

B through H—Real
O through Z—Real
I through N—Integer, octal, or logical
G—Real variable in Global Labeled Common
IG—Integer, octal, or logical variable in Global Labeled Common

Using the prefixes avoided declaring the item type in Fortran. Type could be declared or redefined.

Reserved suffixes for variables were:

xF—Base address of an allocated file
LF—Forward link pointer for a threaded list
LB—Backward link pointer for a threaded list

Tags within a program are to be numbered sequentially.

Table item tags are to be composed of a two- or three-character table name followed by a mnemonic item tag. One of the reserved variable prefixes may be appended to define the item type.

Module Construction

Programs shall be segmented into relatively short, single-function modules. Recommended segment length is one to four pages of executable code (i.e., excluding commentary and data declarations). Segmentation should not be arbitrary but based on such logical grounds as singularity or commonality of functions, operational interaction, and temporal occurrence.

Modules shall have single entry and exit points insofar as possible. Ownership of submodules shall be clearly indicated. Upon completion of submodule processing, submodules shall return to the main routine, not exit to another module. Submodules may pass information and control among themselves, but may not do so outside their master module. Interfaces (entry and exit conditions and parameters) shall be clearly indicated and defined.

Observation of Style Conventions

Observation of the standard practices proposed for programming style was very good, perhaps best for the mission support programs, somewhat less for the executive programs and post-mission processing, and least for the simulation programs. The standards were enforced by the Chief Programmers, reviewed and updated by the System Librarian, and polished during integration and test. Although not perfect, observance was well above average for known projects.

In forming this opinion source listings for approximately 60% of the COBRA DANE program modules were inspected, consisting of some or all modules associated with 50 of the 90 CPCs (Computer Program Components.) Additionally, the survey considered the System Librarian's assessments, Production Specification writer's evaluations, and Integration and Test Team comments.

Upon delivery of source programs for entry into the controlled Program Library, the System Librarian reviewed the programs for proper annotation, structure, and tagging. If the standards were not observed, the Librarian attempted to obtain conformance, largely by rewriting prologues and indicating substandard blocking and naming.

Observation of commentary conventions. The System Librarian estimated that 70% of the modules were annotated when first submitted to the Program Library for entry into the System Master library.* At the time of the review of the source listings and the preparation of final Product Specifications, the proportion was nearer 90%. At the end of integration and test, it is estimated that 95% of the modules were commented.

The specification writers who had the best opportunity to evaluate the commentary stated that it ranged from "absolutely nil" to "fantastically good." Overall, the specification writers felt that COBRA DANE Commentary was well above average compared to other projects they had worked on.

Although not an area covered by the proposed standard practices, one deficiency noted in the source listings, especially by the specification writers, was the lack of maintenance of annotations for program changes. Every change made to a controlled program had to be covered by commentary cards justifying the change and citing the Software Problem Report the change resolved. However, the changed processing was not often commented and old annotations were not always purged.

Observation of indentation and paragraphing. Proposed standard practices for blocking, indentation of code to show subordination, and use of spacing and outlining to show program structure were almost invariably followed. Except for data declarations, programs were always written one statement per line and conditionals were broken down. The specification writers did not report a single instance where the rules were violated.

Observation of naming conventions. Although there were slight variations in interpretation of the naming rules by different Chief Programmer Teams, the

---

* Library files contained old compilation listings that could have verified this estimate, but the difficult task of researching extensive old listings was not attempted.

rules for creating program and data tags were quite consistent. Violations of the rules did occur in the later stages of the project when a large number of changes were being made, especially in table items. The pressure to implement changes and corrections was high and, perhaps, the persons making the changes were no longer acquainted with the original design of the tables.

Observation of module construction conventions. Segmentation rules were quite well followed in COBRA DANE. Except for some programs in the executive area, where desire for efficiency may overrule modularization overhead, module size averaged three or four pages of executable code with very few exceptions.

Observation of standards for hierarchical structure and ownership was harder to verify. Fortran does not lend itself to showing structure and there were no environment analysis tools, such as a system set-use listing, that would reveal the structure of the system. The programmers all claimed that ownership rules were followed. Hierarchical structures were specified in designs and accounts were kept of which modules were part of which CPCs.

Rules for single-entrance, single-exit, and simple control structures were very closely followed with only minor exceptions. There were some violations of the flow rules (calls outside a program's area of control) that resulted from removal of redundant code to save core as the system became core-critical. Such convolutions were very rare, however.

Impacts of Programming Style

Following the rules for programming style made the programs quite easy to read and understand and made modification and maintenance easier. Deviations from the rules created difficulty in understanding and in program maintenance.

Impact of commentary. The specification writers found the commentary of greatest importance in preparing the Final Product Specifications. Unannotated modules or less-well-annotated modules were harder to flow and to follow and the intent of the module was hard to derive.

The writers also had the Preliminary Product Specifications to help them, but usually preferred to depend on the source listing for information about the modules they were describing. The Preliminary specs were useful in expanding upon the intent and functional requirements of the modules, but so many changes in designs and requirements had occurred that the previous specifications could not be trusted for program details.

The specification writers reported that annotation of data items was more important than of processing steps in contributing to their understanding of the modules. As programmers they had no difficulty interpreting the logic of a mathematical or logical expression, but could not interpret the intent or meaning, "what it really does," without knowing what the data items meant. One of their most useful documentation aids was a well-annotated listing of the global data items. A listing of all tags by class would have also been of some further assistance.

The commenting of flags gave the specification writers difficulty that had not been anticipated in the proposed standards. Several COBRA DANE programs, largely those interfacing with radar controllers and other equipment, would pass or receive long registers of flags or control bits. The entire register was handled and described as a single data element in the Global Labeled Common, but a great deal of processing involved building or parsing the registers. To truly understand the programs, annotation for every flag is required.

A similar situation is found in program-calling parameters. Where the rule for defining these had not been observed, the specification writers had difficulty in evaluating both module process and interactions between modules. In Fortran, where the item type declaration is implicit in the item name, a little extra effort is required to list and annotate parameters. Calling parameters also are not normally the sort of items that are globally defined. Hence, if the parameters are not annotated, it is very difficult to tell what meaning is associated with the call. That is, it is difficult to evaluate what the called subroutine has been asked to do.

Subroutine calls themselves also profit from annotation. The subroutine names usually have some mnemonic value and normally there is a list or catalog of available common routines that may be consulted if the function of the subroutine is obscure. However, it is much more convenient if the description is immediately available in the source code.

Since it is somewhat tangential to the main task, maintenance of commentary for correctors and changes is also easily overlooked. The specification writers said that encountering a section of unannotated code was a clear signal of a trouble spot in a program since no commentary meant that the program had been amended. If obsolete commentary had not been purged, it could be quite misleading. Most correctors and changes are introduced either during integration and testing or during the operations and maintenance phase, when the pressure to get the program back into service is very high. In a crisis situation, one tends to concentrate on solving the problem and not upon the niceties of maintaining commentary. Hence, this is a matter requiring some quality assurance attention and perhaps a cleanup pass at the source code after the crisis is over.

Although the System Test Support Team members were much more familiar with the software than were the specification writers (many of the former were Chief or senior programmers from the developmental effort), they still found the commentary of real use in understanding and maintaining the programs. In fact, the programmers reported that if commentary were missing or inadequate, they would insert it for their own use in understanding the module's function and in diagnosing its flow. Reportedly, as many as 30 to 100 comment cards could accompany two or three correctors. Obviously, the commentary was prized as an aid to maintenance.

The impact of extensively commenting their programs upon the productivity of the programmers is not negligible, but does not consume a major portion of their time.

Commentary is useful in program debugging and testing as well as in later maintenance. If a programmer is handling several modules, as is usually the case, he or she may easily forget prior thinking or confuse one module's contents with another. For some of the programs in COBRA DANE, the programmers were so familiar with the applications that writing the modules was almost second nature, but the value of commentary for maintenance work was universally recognized.

Impact of indentation and paragraphing. Blocking and formatting the code made it easier to read. The specification writers reported that they never had any difficulties perceiving the structure or internal subordination of the code. Blank spaces, punctuation, and outlining with asterisks emphasized the logical blocks and broke up the code into easily grasped segments. Breaking down conditionals and restricting code to one statement per line revealed internal structure and made following the logic easy.

Programmers reported that indentation and paragraphing took little effort. After a while it became almost automatic and required little thought.

Impact of naming conventions. Following the naming conventions contributed to the understandability of the items. It helped locate programs and data and gave some idea of data type and usage. However, unless very long, tags have limited mnemonic value and are most useful if accompanied by commentary.

When the tags did not conform to the naming conventions, as occasionally happened when the burden of changes and production pressure grew, difficulties resulted in a lack of understanding. This was especially so in tracing table items to their source when the table identification was omitted from the tags.* When the conventions were followed, the global data definitions did not have to be referenced so often since better inferences could be drawn concerning the source and meaning of the items.

Following conventions does require a little more care in programming, but does not consume a great deal of time. In the case of common data that are used by several programs, the care readily pays for itself in increased understanding.

---

* If an alphabetical listing of names had been available, this difficulty would have been alleviated. The Fortran compiler alphabetical listings were not exceptionally helpful and are not normally available as part of a source listing.

Impact of module construction. Modularization helped to make the programs readable. The System Test Support Team reported that the modularization aided maintenance a great deal. In diagnosing problems it helps localize and pinpoint errors by restricting the area of search. It breaks the program into small pieces that are easy to understand especially by a person unfamiliar with a program as is likely to be the case in the operational maintenance situation. If modularization is done correctly, interfaces are well defined and it is clear what one module passes to another. In making changes or corrections, if neither inputs to, nor outputs from, a module are changed, the change is easily checked and understood, and should not impact the rest of the system. Modularization localizes the impacts of corrections. A whole module may be replaced by another without undue labor. The modules reported to give the most trouble during final integration were one or two rather large, monolithic programs. The programs were reported to be well written, but the greater complexity and volume were harder to handle and understand. A greater amount of information had to be kept in mind when tracing through the code, for instance. Debugging dumps were always large, requiring more searching to diagnose errors and trace logic.

As reported, efforts to reduce code did lead to structural violations—largely calls to subroutines in other modules and some modules combined to conserve code. The collapsed code was more complex logically and more difficult to understand. The calls outside the parent area of control increased the difficulty of following the flow. In sum, the redesign to accommodate core limitations disrupted what had been a very clean, tight design.

Difficulty in following the flow was also caused by the Fortran IF statements not falling through into the main sequence. If the programmer was not aware of this idiosyncracy of Fortran, the flow jumped back and forth in a sometimes confusing fashion.

Complexity in flows resulted in a few cases from the use of multiple entrances and exits in programs. This is partly due to the obscurity of secondary entrances (one wastes time looking for a module rather than an entrance or trying to find the module the entrance is in), but partly it is due to complications in the information flow. The writers recommended that modules that were umbrellas for several entrances either be broken apart or that the module have a single interface to which parametric values determine the case to follow, rather than multiple entries.

The specification writers frequently indicated that they needed more structural information on the system to do a good specification job. Although top-level structure was available, internal structure could be obscure and Fortran does not represent ownership well. The writers would have liked a system set-used matrix like that normally available from a COMPOOL system. Modularization for COBRA DANE was quite extensive and, although a module was immediately easy to read and understand, it was hard to grasp the larger picture if one did not know the relationship of that one miniscule module to its parent and sibling modules.

Summary

In general, it may be concluded that the rules for programming style were effective in making the programs easier to understand and to maintain. Specification writers' complaints centered on those instances where commentary was missing and where structural information was inadequate. Although the Integration and Test Team members did not stress commentary, they supplied it for their own use when it was missing. The programs that gave trouble during integration were those that were monolithic, not because they were badly written but because their length and complexity made them difficult to understand and difficult to handle. Multiple entry points did contribute to confusion. Data annotations were judged to be more important than process annotations. COBRA DANE software was technically and structurally complex, much complicated by the interruptability and reentrancy requirements. Its modularity makes its maintenance feasible.

3.3.2 Top-Down Implementation

One of the more confusing elements of the structured programming milieu is the concept of top-down implementation. Often erroneously used interchangeably with top-down design, it is rather the implementation and checkout of modules in an increasingly large integrated whole, with each newly implemented set of modules attached to the existing product as a new and more detailed layer of code. The result is an implementation that eliminates the traditional software integration phase, because integration is continuous.

A surprising number of the companies have at least nominally embraced this concept.

3.3.2.1 *TOP-DOWN PROGRAM DEVELOPMENT (SPERRY UNIVAC)*

Top-down program development comprised a reasonably simple set of concepts which had natural appeal due to the many benefits afforded to the management and development of a software project. Top-down program development included program design, production (coding and checkout), and formal testing. Practical utilization of these ideas in a serious, large-scale program development called for the preparation of methods, procedures, and tools; some adaptation to the particular software architecture; and consideration of management and contractual requirements. This section describes an actual application of top-down program development. With variations on the techniques used, the management, design, production, and testing proven on these programs is applicable to a wide range of software developments.

The principal advantages of top-down program development compared to other development methods were:

1. The ability to establish multiple fixed and visible milestones within the production and testing of a computer program
2. Early production and verification of the control logic which enabled a program to execute as a component of a data processing system
3. The ability to begin system integration prior to the completion of program development

Program production and testing proceeded element by element from the top tier downward. After the proper operation of each element was verified, that element was integrated into the subprogram, which, when completed, became a part of the deliverable program. During the software system development, the program elements which had not yet been produced and integrated into the system were represented by "stubs." A stub was a dummy program element which took the place of a program element not yet coded or checked out. Stubs were placed on the source library just as real program elements were. In the object program the stubs satisfied the element calling (control passing) functions depicted in the tiered hierarchy. A stub also modeled the consumption of computer resources through the occupation of main memory and processor time use. A stub contained as many of the actual element characteristics, or simulations of characteristics, as a programmer or system designer deemed necessary for the particular program development.

The stubs defined the element name and provided as header commentary (a required convention) a description of the inputs, processing function, and outputs so the listing could be read as a complete representative of the program design. Throughout program production the combination of completed elements and stubs provided a complete representation (target machine model) of the operating program modules.

One of the many benefits to be gained through top-down software development was the early realization of the proper operation of the program's control functions (e.g., it would start up, cycle, and interface properly). This avoided the production difficulties created by disproportionate attention given to the application (purpose-oriented) functions prior to the satisfactory working of the control (EDP-system-oriented) functions.

After individual program elements had been coded and checkout tested, they were integrated into a software system. The produced elements, with the required stubs, were then tested as a whole program without affecting the production of lower-tiered elements. Detailed design of lower-tiered elements may have occurred during or after this portion of program testing. The practice of design-a-bit, produce-a-bit was not considered satisfactory because the produced software was required to pass through comprehensive and rigorous design reviews prior to its production. Also, the program was designed as an integral whole to better attain efficient use of computer main memory and processing time. This method of modeling the final program design by accurately stubbing the uncoded elements of a program facilitated early appraisal of the developing program.

Specific top-down development techniques were established to meet the special constraints and requirements of the systems' software environment. These techniques consisted of:

1. Dividing the program into large program modules in accordance with the design requirements of the real-time operating system software

2. Beginning each module's hierarchical structure with the real-time executive

3. Allowing for a natural element breakdown of each module using the coding structures of the required high-level language, CMS-2

4. Designing each program module as a structural hierarchy of elements called design objects

5. Adhering to a set of rules for determining the hierarchy of design objects

6. Providing control and visibility of the code production by the status of each design object

7. Producing and delivering the program in four levels of completeness, such that each level represented a full-scale executable model of the final program

8. Developing the qualification testing for each produced level of completeness and qualifying each level of the operational program as a baseline for the next level

The programs were produced in four levels. The general objectives of the first level were to produce each module's entrance procedures, its data design objects, and the procedures performing initialization functions (real-time initialization or startup). All design objects not produced in real and complete code as a part of the first level were stubbed. All Executive Service Requests calls were coded regardless of whether they occurred in the completed or stubbed design objects. Thus, with the completion of the first-tier entrance procedures, and the coding of the Executive Service Requests Calls, all executive interface code was in place at the completion of the first level.

The general objectives of the second level were to complete design objects below the first-tier entrance procedures which performed additional task control functions, and those design objects which provided or obtained data external to the module (input/output and intermodule communications). For many program modules the objective of the third level was to fully implement some of its major functions. This meant that hierarchies were completed vertically in selected localities. At the completion of the fourth level of production, all coding and checkout testing was done and the program was ready for final qualification testing. During each level of development, coding and checkout testing were monitored and the condition of each design object was recorded on the status reports. Therefore, not only was the use of the design object a means of documenting the top-down design of each program module, it served as a means to manage the top-down code production and provided the customer good visibility of production status.

As part of the design phase, the following data were prepared by the responsible programmer for each design object:

1. Estimated size in memory words
2. Estimated average execution time
3. Required executive service requests
4. Required external calls (e.g., mathematical subroutines)

The compilation of estimated size, for example, gave a total estimate for the size of each module, since each estimate was based on fairly detailed requirements. A production status report (see Figure 3.2) was prepared and maintained weekly for each module, showing the status of each design object:

Stubbed

Coded

Desk debugged

Unit debugged

Integrated into module

Checkout testing complete

The program production progress was monitored at least once a week by observing the status of the design objects required for the next-level completion. Deviations from schedules or expected size were visible early enough in the production phase for management to take effective corrective steps. For example, corrective actions may have been assigning senior personnel to assist the programmer assigned to a module before that module development could fall behind schedule. Corrective action taken for deviations in expected size, for example, was the update of the size in the Production Status Report, such that the visibility of the total best estimated memory requirement was given. At the completion of each production level, the program was made available to quality assurance personnel for inspection and qualification testing.

One of the major advantages of top-down software development was the incremental integration and testing of program levels prior to the completion of program production.

When each module of the program was completed to Level 1, it was integrated into a system and executed with the executive operating system software, a simulation program, and data extraction software. Proper execution of each module entrance was tested, causing execution of both the completed and the stubbed design objects. Those functions that were complete at this level were evaluated in full and the control logic and connectivity of the integrated program was evaluated. When the qualification testing of this in-

Production Status Report

Program ___SP___ Sub-program ___DC___ Level ___2___

Date ___30 Sep. 74.___ Sheet ___1___ of ___3___

ID	Description	Size in words (E=Estm. A=Actual)	Stub	Code	Desk debug	Unit debug	Module in-tegration	Checkout complete			Remarks
1A	Priority Entrance	42 A						X			
1B	Message Entrance	34 A						X			
1C	Periodic Entrance	35 A						X			
1D	Demand Entrance	21 A						X			
1E	SDCIOC Interrog Chains	118 A						X			
1F	EATIOC Chain	25 E	X								Reqmts TBD
1G	Term. Active Ioc Chains	6 A						X			
1H	Preamble	20 A						X			
1I	BRAT	20 A						X			
1J	Data Tables	604 A						X			
2A	Data Time Tag	25		X	X						
2B	Data Validation	50 E	X	X	X						
2C	Format Navigation Data	10 E	X	X	X						
2D	Process Periscope Data	40 E	X	X	X						
2E	Update Common Data Base	15 E	X	X							
2F	Notify Ship Control of update	10 E	X	X							
2G	Check EATT Results	60 E	X								Reqmts TBD
2H	Preset Message	79 D						X			
2I	Operator Requests	25 E	X								
2J	Data Notify Registration	25 E	X	X							
2K	SDC Data Update	25 E	X	X							
2L	Display Requests DDRT	15 E	X	X							
2M	DDRT Parity Error	15 E	X								Not scheduled for level 2
2N	FM Log Step										

Figure 3.2 Production Status Report Forms

94

tegrated set of Level 1 modules was completed, the resulting Level 1 program was established as a baseline and delivered. Concurrent with the qualification testing of the Level 1 baseline program, development began on the next baseline, the Level 2 program.

Generation of the test support software and documentation was also completed in a top-down manner. Because testing of each level was based on the previously validated test, the tests beyond Level 1 were built upon the tests performed at the preceding level.

The final level of testing was a complete functional test of the program's performance similar to that which would have been performed if the program had been produced in the traditional manner.

3.3.2.2 INCREMENTAL DEVELOPMENT (TRW)

Incremental development is the coding and testing of functionally meaningful increments of the overall software system wherein each increment (1) provides a self-sufficient, executable, and testable portion of the complete software capability, and (2) adds to and builds upon the preceding increment. Incremental development is an overall software production approach involving the implementation of progressively more complete increments (or "loops") of system capability. Each increment is self-sufficient and provides an independently testable increment of the evolving program containing real deliverable code as well as dummy code for those functions that are to be developed in subsequent increments. The final increment includes all the deliverable code. Builds within each increment carry the incremental development approach to more detail and further reduce the chance of downstream problems. Incremental development reduces risk by developing critical software first, evaluating system performance gradually and allowing an early start to test and integration activities. (It is possible to identify threads involving critical functions that can be developed and tested as independent increments. With care, these increments can be chosen to provide a complete increment of system capability within which high visibility testing of critical functions can be achieved with relative ease.)

Each completed increment thus represents not only (1) a meaningful version of the evolving system containing more capability than the previous increment, but also (2) a test bed (including the process structure and test information) with which interface/integration testing of subsequently completed modules can be done.

3.3.3 Methodologies and Tools

There are emerging efforts to produce a commonly available set of tools to support software development. There is considerable published material on methodology evaluation. Still, although there is consistency in the *use* of methodologies and tools among the MPP companies, there is little consistency on *what* those methodologies and tools are.

3.3.3.1 *DEVELOPMENT METHODS AND TOOLS (SPERRY UNIVAC)*

Development methods are technical and managerial procedures employed during the stages of developing each computer program. Development tools are any items (i.e., a computer program, programmed hardware/software system, or documented procedure) that benefit software development.

Technical and managerial procedures are usually dictated by the contract procuring agent and also by Sperry Univac contract policies. Sperry Univac internal management practices are defined in the Standard Practice Manual for Engineering and Production Operations. The task and responsibilities of all key project personnel are established for each project in accordance with this standard.

The majority of compilation and system program generation was completed using an off-line CMS-2Y system. For many reasons this government-furnished tape-based program support system was inefficient. Many of the peripherals were old, slow, and worn-out, and the handling of tapes was tedious and prone to operator error. Therefore, maintenance of the program was moved on to the Univac 1108 system when possible.

After generation of a system tape containing the executive operating system and a newly compiled program module, the programmer loaded, executed, and debugged the code with hands-on equipment access in the St. Paul equipment suite. Before this on-line debugging began, each programmer assured that the program was logically complete and relatively error-free by careful inspection process.

When on-line, the programmer had use of the operating system Debug Module. The Debug Module allowed the programmer to control execution of the tasks within an identified program module, to extract data at selected breakpoints, to measure program execution point to point, and to inspect and change computer memory contents. Upon satisfaction of the debug criteria, the program module was integrated onto the system tape prepared for testing under simulation.

The test system program provided some additional debugging tools. It automatically controlled execution of the program functions in a simulated environment, made automatic data extractions at established and selectable breakpoints, and recorded the extracted data on magnetic tape. The resulting tape was analyzed using a data reduction program to obtain appropriate data listings.

The following subparagraphs describe some of the support tools.

AN/UYK-7 Simulator

This support program, running on the Univac 1108 computer, provided the capabilities of AN/UYK-7 program generation and preliminary program checkout on the Univac 1108. The following functions are provided:

The AN/UYK-7 instruction repertoire simulator

The CMS-2 compiler/loader simulator

The CMS-2 monitor simulator

The common program simulator

Program checkout aids

This simulator allowed mathematical and functional program checkout on the host computer. Once preliminary checkout was completed on the host computer, final checkout was completed on the AN/UYK-7 computer.

Automated Common Program Certification Test Support Software

A package of test support software was developed for the Common Program. It consisted of the following:

1. An automated test controller
2. Scenario input from punched cards, disk, paper tape, or magnetic tape
3. A data recording module to extract information during real-time operation and record it on magnetic tape
4. A data reduction program to print the contents of the extraction tape in a format requested by the user

Processing Evaluation Tool (PET)

This support program, which runs on the AN/UYK-7 computer, is used to extract timing information during real-time operational conditions. PET is a task state program utilizing the common program executive operating system. PET operates in either one or two processors. PET creates a magnetic tape recording for each program entry and exit.

Two types of reports are generated:

1. Percentage of processor time per module for each entry
2. Record of the maximum amount of time spent in one entrance, and the total number of times that entrance occurred within the requested time period

When reducing the data contained on the extraction tape, the operator may specify the time period he or she desires reduced. Only data from recordings made during this period will be considered for this report.

Comparator

This support program, which runs on the host computer, provides the user with the capability to compare two files and produce a printed log of the differences. For example, it allows the user to determine all patches added to a baseline system.

3.3.3.2 SOFTWARE DEVELOPMENT TOOLS (TRW)

Tools are support programs built to assist requirements analysis, software design, code generation, debug and checkout, formal software testing, and documentation in a partially or fully automated fashion. Prominent examples of software development and test tools are:

Data base building tools build and maintain data definition libraries and data value libraries, check data definitions, and supply complete data specifications to all using software modules.

System construction tools permit (1) use of a high-level, special-purpose language in describing the desired system organization, and (2) subsequent use of a tool to automatically merge system elements into a unified whole. Also, they can provide an illustration of system structure, module hierarchy, and cross-references.

Code-checking tools automatically check every line of code in the system to (1) identify and report instances in which project programming standards have not been followed, (2) identify potential singularities such as division by zero, (3) verify units consistency for each usage of each parameter, and (4) identify parameters that are used before set, set but not used, etc. (For example, PCP counts the executable source statements in a module to check for compliance with the routine-size modularity programming standard, STRUCT analyzes the detailed logic structure of a module to check for compliance with the structured coding standard, and Code Auditor automatically checks every line of code for compliance with most of the other detailed STP programming standards.)

Test tools aid generation, accumulation, and evaluation of testing information and, specifically, (1) support identification of problems early in the development cycle, (2) identify required test data that relate requirements to software capabilities and ensure thorough testing, (3) select test cases to be used in retesting changed software, (4) check actual test results against previously obtained or expected results, and (5) drive and/or monitor software test execution and measure testing thoroughness. [For example, the Code Auditor and Units Consistency Analyzer (UNIC) examine code for standards compliance and parameter usage consistency; the Product Assurance Confidence Evaluator (PACE) analyzes code, identifies overall logical structure, inserts "test hooks" into the code, and subsequently monitors test execution and reports on the extent to which the software structural components are exercised; the Data Reduction and Report Generator (DRRG) provides essential support in analysis of voluminous, detailed data logged by the real-time process for subsequent post-processing and test results evaluation.]

3.3.4 Standards

The door to the subject of standards was opened in Section 3.3.1. Standards are simply procedurized style constraints, and nearly all the MPP companies use them. In the discussion that follows, it becomes apparent that defining standards is considerably easier than enforcing them!

3.3.4.1 *VIKING SOFTWARE STANDARDS (MARTIN-MARIETTA)*

Documentation and flowchart standards were specified for all Viking software very early in the life of the project. No further standards were imposed on software other than those adopted by the software groups themselves. Mission Operations issued a Viking Software Guide that listed standards, procedures, guidelines, and constraints to be followed. Responsibility for adhering to the guide rested in most cases with the individual programmers.

Management considered that controlled, uniform documentation was the key element needed to establish visibility and understanding of the development process. American National Standard flowchart symbols were adopted to provide project-wide consistency. The multiagency development of the operational software system required nomenclature, naming, labeling, and coding standards be adopted to coordinate the effort. In addition, the project was required to adhere to computer usage guidelines and constraints that had been established at JPL.

Standards adopted at a management visibility level can be effective and are enforceable. Standards set below that level are of little value. On Viking, programmers tended to ignore guidelines and nonenforceable standards. Documentation standards make reviews easier to accomplish and lead to greater thoroughness. Labeling and naming standards are a convenient tool to avoid confusion. Coding standards are of dubious value and can have negative effects when computer run time and program size are required to be significantly constrained. This remark should not be interpreted relative to Structured Programming standards, which were not employed on Viking.

Early in the project, MMC formed a Viking Software Integration Group for the purpose of monitoring the development of Mission Operations software. The first task was to define and document a uniform set of standards. The group issued "Standards for Viking Software Development," which set documentation, flowchart, identification, and handling standards for all MMC-developed software.

The Viking Software Guide contained standards for Viking software symbology notation, use of nonminimal language, Viking Lander terminology, Viking Orbiter terminology, and Viking acronyms. The symbology notation standardized the first two characters of every program name, subroutine, and data table name that would be delivered to the Mission Control and Computing Facility (i.e., IBM 360/75 computer system) for incorporation on the Mission Build. The nonminimal-language standard required programs that operated on two or more different computer systems use comment cards to show the exact coding differences required by each system.

Guidelines included descriptions of minimal languages, language comparison charts, and programming style. Procedures addressed program conversion, documentation production, test activities, and program delivery.

File naming standards were incorporated in the Software Data Base Document. Every permanent file used by a Viking program was assigned a unique five-alpha-character designator. MMC expanded this to a 12-character string that included spacecraft, mission, date, and version designators. No file naming standard was ever adopted for Viking Orbiter programs.

The Mission Control and Computing Center documented guidelines and constraint standards required to be followed by all projects using their facilities. These standards imposed limits on core allocation, contiguous core allocation, CPU time, amount of print/plot output, number of tape drives, large-capacity storage, direct-access storage, and sizes of program card decks.

There were differences of opinion over the value of global project standards. The Mission Planning and Flight Path Analysis groups liked the idea, carried it out, and felt it was a worthwhile exercise. The remaining groups considered it an unnecessary additional step and developed their standards directly. The principal difference between the two approaches was that one provided for an intermediate requirements review and the other did not.

The use of external file naming convention standards made it very easy to checkpoint and recall data recorded by a particular instrument on a particular Martian Sol (day). The standard also permitted an efficient automated file management system to be developed.

MMC management did not place proper emphasis on the symbology notation standard and the lander programmers did not understand it. This could have had a very serious cost and schedule impact on lander software had it not been for JPL's willingness to help resolve the problem. The standard required that all subroutine names begin with the characters LM and all data table names begin with the characters LZ. The reason for the standard was to prevent MMC-developed software from conflicting in name with any other software on the Mission Build. By not following the standard, MMC was faced with the task of changing literally thousands of call statements to subroutines. However, JPL came to their rescue by creating a private Viking subroutine library which made it possible to waive the standard. This example stresses the importance for a developing agency to know and understand any enforceable standards set by a user agency.

The use of flowchart standards simplifies the design review process. Consistency is more important than the particular selection of symbols. The Viking Lander Flight software group developed their own standards in this area, rather than adopting the ANSI standards used by the rest of the project.

The setting of a standard for the use of nonminimal language effectively reduced the minimal language standard to a guideline. Although it was not enforceable (no standard set below management's visibility level is enforceable), it was followed because it eased the conversion task of the programmer.

The documentation standards cost 4 to 5 person-months to develop. The Viking Software Guide cost an additional 4 to 5 person-months. The ANSI flowchart standards were available at no additional project cost.

The automated on-line data file management system and the inter-computer transfer function were developed at less cost because file naming conventions were standardized. The estimated savings in these areas is 1 person-year. Even then each individual file would have required some form of standardization.

3.3.4.2 ENFORCED PROGRAMMING STANDARDS (TRW)

Strict rules to direct the efforts of developers in the production of code and documentation were developed and enforced. Enforcement was accomplished by the establishment of an active review/inspection procedure to ensure compliance.

The term "Programming Standards" generally refers to both (1) approved procedures to be used in the production of code and associated documentation, and (2) minimum acceptable standards against which the completed products are measured. All such standards are, to the extent possible, specified early in the project and documented in a Software Standards and Procedure Manual. One of the primary objectives of the standards is to guarantee a high degree of uniformity across all software system components. This uniformity is especially advantageous when someone other than the original developer is required to understand the function of a software component.

Establishment of standard programming practices, however, is only the beginning. If the standards are to have the desired effect, they must be followed; if they are to be consistently followed, they usually must be enforced. Enforcement of strict adherence to project standards is accomplished through a combination of informal and formal reviews of code and documentation. Performance of code reviews for compliance with standards is aided substantially by source code scanners, including the Process Construction Program, Code Auditor, and STRUCT.

Programming standards at TRW include the following:

1. *Text format:* The requirement to document descriptive information on software modules in accordance with a prescribed format.

2. *Text level of detail:* The requirement to provide descriptive information on software modules to illustrate their purpose, function, and interfaces with other modules.

3. *Flow chart format:* The requirement to develop diagrams depicting the functional hierarchy and execution flow of all software modules using the flowcharting symbols prescribed in "The International Organization for Standardization Draft Recommendation on Flowchart Symbols and Their Usage in Information Processing (ANSI X-3.5.1970)."

4. *Flowchart level of detail:* The requirement for (a) program and task level flowcharts to depict overall composition and hierarchical structure down to the lowest routine level, with a single block for each routine, containing the routine name and a brief functional description, and (b) routine-level flowcharts to illustrate in detail the basic function of the routine, including identification of all external files used, operating system service requests, decision logic and branches, calculations, calls to subroutines, and entry and exit points.

5. *Statement label format:* All statement labels to be right-justified in columns 2–5 and all labels to appear in ascending order throughout the extent of the module.

6. *Executable statement format:* All executable Fortran statements to start in column 7 except where indentation is required to illustrate code segments and nested structures.

7. *Routine size (modularity):* Each routine to contain a maximum of 100 executable source statements from the time it is initially coded until turnover for independent testing with the limit subsequently raised to 150 to permit incremental addition of new capability without major software breakage.

8. *Calling sequence arguments:* Arguments in calling statements to subprograms not to contain arithmetic or logical expressions, and routines in the real-time software to have no calling sequence arguments.

9. *Mixed-mode arithmetic:* Mixed-mode arithmetic expressions (ex-

cluding integer exponentiation) not allowed on the right side of an equal sign.

10. *DO-loop usage:* DO-Loops not to exceed six levels of nesting, and DO-Loop index parameters to be expressed only as integer constants or variables.

11. *Computed GO-TO usage:* All computed GO TO statements to be immediately preceded by a validity (range) test of the variable switch parameter. Tests revealing invalid parameter values to initiate error processing. Statement labels used as branch addresses to appear after the GO TO statement in the sequence in which they appear in the GO TO statement parameter list.

12. *Labeled COMMON vs. blank COMMON usage:* Only labeled COMMON blocks to be used.

13. *Imbedded physical constants usage:* Literal physical constants (e.g., 3.14159 for the value of pi) not to be embedded in the code.

14. *Preface commentary block requirement:* Each module to contain a standardized block of comment statements immediately following the module declaration statement. The block to contain (a) module name and version identifier, (b) functional description, (c) inputs, (d) outputs, (e) key local variables, (f) usage restrictions, (g) identification of modules called by this one, and (h) description of abnormal return conditions and actions.

15. *In-line commentary requirement:* Each module to contain sufficient in-line commentary in the source code to identify the purpose of every statement that conditionally alters a data value or alters the sequential execution of program statements.

16. *Structured coding requirement:* Each module to be structured in accordance with a prescribed, restricted list of segment structures, including (a) sequence of two operations, (b) conditional branch and rejoin, (c) loop construct with condition tested prior to execution of loop body, (d) loop construct with condition tested after execution of loop body, and (e) loop construct allowing for premature escape from unnecessary loop repetition. Permits nesting of segment structures to any level and error-condition transfers from any segment structure to a common point in the module.

17. *Execution of every program branch requirement:* The requirement to cause the execution of every program branch statement and to force the transfer of control to each of the possible branch addresses during unit testing of each module.

18. *Naming conventions:* The requirement to formulate the program and data names in accordance with established patterns prescribing the use of alphanumeric characters identifying item type and function.

3.3.5 Performance Concerns

The rapidly lowering costs of computer hardware have led to the generally accepted belief that software size and speed are no longer a concern. That is not the case in the environment of the MPP companies. Particularly for real-time software, these kinds of performance concerns loom large in the overall software development process.

These concerns were already exposed in the section on methodologies and tools, where tools were described for quantifying performance. Here they are discussed in more depth.

3.3.5.1 ON-BOARD COMPUTER TIMING AND MEMORY-SIZE MONITORING (MARTIN-MARIETTA)

Classically, memory size and worst-path timing are critical in aerospace applications. A 50% margin for each was allocated at preliminary design time. Accepting the fact of inevitable change, a margin allocation curve was also established at preliminary design time in order to control margins throughout the project development phase. The plan originally called for a margin of a few hundred words at launch time to accommodate last-minute changes during operations.

The high relative cost per change with low margins has been well established. Changes made with limited spare room or time often lead to redesign of existing code with attendant ripple effects. Some published results indicate that relative costs begin to rise where margins are less than 50%. With many of the Viking Lander devices and subsystems at the state-of-the-art, 50% margins at preliminary design time were deemed essential. Perhaps more important was the realization that margin monitoring was also essential. Where continuing system change can be anticipated, software changes rapidly consume margins unless they themselves become a part of the change controls.

Management is well advised to pay close attention to timing and memory size when a relatively small computer is to be used to perform a significant real-time task. This requires a considerable effort to obtain accurate estimates of the impact of proposed changes. The 50% growth margin used by Viking was not great enough to avoid the necessity of optimizing algorithms and designs already coded.

During the development of the Viking Lander on-board program, constant control was exercised over the growth of the program within the time and space domains of the computer hardware. This was done because there were several precedents of program development problems due to unchecked growth. To achieve good control, several tools were developed and used throughout the life of the project.

The first problem with respect to obtaining good control was to establish realistic values for the memory and time margins. The approach used was to define a hypothetical computer and then to program the descent guidance and control equations for it. The descent phase was picked for two reasons. First, a significant amount of analysis had yielded a set of descent control equations which could be coded. Second, the descent phase represented the major area of concern about timing. Based on this exercise, the number of instructions to be executed was obtained together with their frequency of execution.

The sources of good size values were (1) the code size defined by the descent software, and (2) the code size estimated by coding the flowcharts established for the remainder of the on-board program. Together, these produced the initial program memory-size requirement. To this memory size was added a 50% growth margin. That value was defined to be the limit for program size growth. The two values defined a linear growth curve, starting with the program size at the date the analysis was made and terminating with a full computer at program delivery. This growth curve defined, at any given time when an audit was made, whether the program growth was being contained.

The hypothetical computer characteristics were included within the computer procurement drawing as a statement of desired instruction set and timing. This also allowed for the generation of memory and timing impact summaries for each of the prospective computer vendors. Then once the vendor's machine characteristics were known, the impact to timing was well defined. In addition, there are instruction set vs. memory requirement relationships defined by information theory. Using them, a memory impact was defined for each of the possible computers. This exercise informed the project management that the selected computer would have little impact timewise but that the memory would have to be 2000 words larger if the initial 50% margin was to be maintained.

Following selection of the on-board computer, a software change control mechanism was installed. This provided a definition of what changes were outstanding and their associated time and size impact. Management could then weigh changes against any possible growth violations. To make this accurate, all changes were forced through this control system.

During the course of the on-board program development there were several major stresses on the control mechanism. Each of these involved the definition of a significant violation of the size or time margin curves. The first was the incorporation of a generalized on-board executive. The design change was necessitated by the total program requirements, but presented an unknown risk to the time margins. To gain insight into the timing of the then-current sequencing algorithm and the proposed processing, a discrete simulation model was constructed. The model was used to define the worst-case time consumption by the executive. With this known, it became apparent that there was minimal risk to incorporate the generalized executive.

The second major stress occurred when the development of coded modules for nearly all of the on-board program was completed. The resultant code size violated substantially the size growth curve. As a result a set of code reduction changes were proposed. Incorporation of the changes brought the program size back within the established growth curve. However, they necessitated substantial changes to the already coded and partially tested program.

The third major stress was due to the violation of time margins by the descent control code. This was isolated through the use of an emulator for the on-board computer. The descent code, run in an emulated mode, was shown to take too long during certain descent phases. As a result, the descent control equations were changed to reduce the number of calculations required. In addition, some algorithms used during descent were optimized with respect to time. This problem had been brought to management's attention quite early, due basically to the enforcement of regular time and size audits. Because of this, there was ample time to analyze and correct the problem.

The components of a good timing and memory-size monitor system are accurate software audit reports, timely report generation, and total software change control. One cannot emphasize enough the importance of any of these components. Without any one of them, the process of monitoring is susceptible to failure. In describing each, one can take the Viking on-board program development and show why each is required.

Because the on-board program was constantly changing, the size and time requirements were audited by management monthly with approximate values maintained between audits. This provided, given an accurate audit process, an actual input. The input was then used to update the graph for memory growth. Using this graph, management readily established trends of rapid growth. When they were recognized, the change traffic was interrupted and a status meeting held to define which changes to reject, together with requirement changes or design changes to incorporate.

As a result of timing and sizing monitoring, the onboard program was developed and delivered successfully. The concept of regular and highly visible audits seemed to allow for ample time to recover from major stresses. In addition, management was provided sufficient information to control a highly volatile software development task. A time when the system seemed to fail was when the entire software group was devoted to the development process to the detriment of the audit process. As a result, the audit would encompass a very long time period and nominally would define a significant change to the size and time margins. In addition, continual auditing seemed to force a more disciplined development.

The growth constraint curve was a linear line connecting a 13K memory size to an 18K memory size. Twice, large accumulations of new code caused the current memory size estimate to violate the constraint curve. The first occurred when as-built code rapidly grew from 15.5K to 18.5K. The second occurred when as-built code grew from 16.5K to 19K. On each occasion management was forwarned that an unacceptable growth was taking place, thus permitting them time to assess the need for and ramifications of candidate redesign efforts. On both occasions management required the implementation of agreed-upon design changes that brought the as-built code below the memory-size constraint curve.

3.3.5.2 RESOURCE UTILIZATION (SDC)

Control over the utilization of very limited computer resources in the face of a system that has grown very dynamically in size, sophistication, and throughput load has been very effective. This control has been accomplished through a strict program of storage on an as-needed basis, purging of redundant and obsolete data, and an active program of control and reduction of program environments to ensure efficient storage utilization and data handling.

Storage is conserved by the commonality of data structures, utilizing extensive overlay capabilities, providing hierarchical compools to reduce executive overhead, using an efficient segmentation algorithm and automatically policing current core allocations.

Using the COMPOOL on-line to determine and adjust storage allocations at load time improves the flexibility of operations by making all programs and data relocatable, providing dynamic linking and loading, and allowing symbolic correctors to be inserted with any core load. A capability exists that will avoid the dynamic allocation overhead if a core load is invariant from run to run.

The procedures employed to review and control additions and modifications to the COMPOOL and the analytic aids provided contribute to the purging of obsolete and redundant data from the system. This keeps storage requirements down. Programs are also reviewed for standard functions and software suppliers are encouraged to use standard routines wherever possible.

Analytic procedures are extended to in-depth analysis of program environments to detect inefficiencies in data storage and handling. Commonality of data items is searched for and suppliers are encouraged to use common data elements. The COMPOOL change procedures flag inefficiencies, including inefficient use of routines and segmentation procedures. Separating control data from application-specific data encourages the use of overlays and tables of constants.

3.3.6 High-Order Language

The benefits of high-order language (HOL) are well understood in the MPP companies. For real-time software construction, however, such languages are still only used about half of the time. That percentage is steadily increasing, inhibited only by (1) tradition, and (2) the performance penalties that HOLs impose. Where the project is large, HOL is generally acknowledged to be the only way to code; for smaller ones, assembler may still be used. Performance penalties are much less tolerable in a constrained environment.

3.3.6.1   HIGH-ORDER-LANGUAGE UTILIZATION (MARTIN-MARIETTA)

During the initial phase of the development of Viking Mission Operational software, the requirement that Fortran be used for code was made mandatory. Waivers were granted that permitted the use of assembly language for specific functions that could not be implemented by a Fortran compiler.

The decision to use Fortran was based on several reasons. Orbiter software could be generated by modifying existing software already coded in Fortran. Lander software was required to be developed on nontarget computers. Each computer system had assembly languages which had different instruction sets, but all computers had Fortran compilers. Many of the software functions were analytical in nature, making Fortran appear to be an ideal HOL. The level of programmer expertise required to program in Fortran is not too great, reducing the potential impact caused by personnel turnover. Finally, high-order languages ease the task of locating errors in logic when anomolous conditions are detected.

The concept of using HOL for all functions that can be accomplished by it and using an appropriate assembly language for the remaining functions will produce a software system with a good basic design. In the event that the system must operate within limited computer resources, timelines, and budget, as was the case with Viking, some functions will be inefficient. These should be replaced with assembly language to get improvements as required for specific applications.

The basic functions required to be developed for the Viking operational software system were examined during the very early stage of Viking. None of them seemed to be complicated, and it appeared at the time that they could all be implemented reasonably well using Fortran. The use of that high-order language was looked upon favorably by management because the computer selections were unknown at the time. In addition, they felt it would simplify the conversion process as well as make the software logic readable to a far wider range of individuals, thereby making management less dependent on the individual talents and personalities of programmers.

The first indication that some assembly language software would be required came during the requirements definition phase for the Lander Command Simulation program. An Interpretive Computer Simulation (ICS) program was available in Fortran and could be modified for Viking. However, its size and run time violated Viking computer resource constraints and mission timeline requirements. Considerable effort was made to resolve this problem, but no solution could be found. As a result, an innovative scheme that required low-order-language development became the only viable alternative to the Viking managers. A project-wide waiver system was adopted to permit functions to be developed in assembly language in the event that Fortran could not be used to meet Viking needs.

After the original implementation of the software, assembly language subfunctions were required to be developed for the reasons outlined below.

The file management program that transferred interfacing data files between the Univac 1108 computer and the IBM 360/75 computer required an interactive capability with the two operating systems in order to become sufficiently adaptive to changing requirements so that its code would not be impacted.

The IBM Fortran compiler did not provide some functions that were available on the Univac compiler. This resulted in poor core utilization and unacceptably large CPU requirements. Assembly language subfunctions, similar to those available in the Univac compiler, were developed for the IBM programs to resolve this problem.

A number of programs increased in size, because of new requirements, to the point where they violated the 65K-word maximum core restraint imposed on the Univac 1108. A number of subfunctions used in common by these programs were rewritten in assembly language to conserve core, which solved the problem.

Fortran DATA statements, used by the Lander Sequence of Events program, were replaced with assembly language functions that took advantage of 1108 operating systems capabilities to provide output capabilities more readable to the users.

Conversion of floating-point numbers transferred between the 1108 and 360/75 computer systems was accomplished using assembly language to satisfy the guidelines and constraints of core utilization.

On-line data management functions required interactions with the IBM 360 operating system that could only be accomplished using assembly language code.

Finally, assembly language functions were developed for both the 1108 and 360 computer systems to improve computer run times and reduce computer resource loads. These were in the areas of dynamic core allocations, compressing the use of disk space, freeing unused core during program execution, and supporting bit manipulation.

The final software system consisted of approximately 90% Fortran and 10% assembly language.

The quality of the software itself was more a function of programmer experience rather than whether Fortran or assembly language was used; some programmers were limited to using Fortran.

A large amount of this conversion task was accomplished by the 360 and 1108 computer consultants, who, as members of the Software Integration Group, were funded to support just such activities. They would have been available whether or not assembly language modifications had been required. For these reasons, the cost to replace Fortran with assembly language probably did not exceed 2 person-years, and may have been much less.

The cost that the project would have borne had it not permitted any assembly language to be developed is also subjective, but easy to assess. Assuming that mission timelines could have been met with the exclusive use of Fortran, one additional 360 and one additional 1108 would have been required to support Flight Team training and planetary operations.

3.3.6.2   PROGRAM LANGUAGE ELEMENTS (SPERRY UNIVAC)

The two programs were coded in the Navy standard Compiler Monitor System (CMS-2) language. CMS-2 was comprised of a compiler, assembler, librarian, monitor, program loader, debugging tools, and utility functions. The high-level compiler language was preferred, but a few of the program functions were coded in the low-level assembler language. Implicit in top-down design was the partitioning of programs into sets that have a specific form of connectivity.

One natural approach to achieving top-down partitioning was to take advantage of subroutining using the facilities provided by the programming language. In the CMS-2 language the PROCEDURE and the FUNCTION had closed subroutine properties.

Data elements were also included in the top-down hierarchy. The CMS-2 language elements containing data were system data designs (SYS-DD) and local data designs (LOC-DD). Each of the four language elements (PROCEDURE, FUNCTION, SYS-DD, and LOC-DD), or a closely knit group of them, were then qualified to be represented by an element block on a top-down hierarchy.

3.3.6.3   STRUCTURED PRECOMPILER (BCS)

Structured code precompilers translate structured logic forms into formulations acceptable to "standard" compilers, and check for closure and nesting consistency of the code structures. The BCS structured precompiler performs this function for programs coded in the Fortran language. Besides its capability to process common structures (IF-THEN-ELSE, DO-WHILE, etc.), this particular aid accepts an enriched set of structured formulations and provides options for statement identification and block identification to increase code readability.

The BCS structured precompiler provides only limited support to code verification. Specifically, it is capable of checking for closure of logic blocks and verifying certain other details, such as nesting consistency.

3.3.7 Information Communication

On large software projects, the apparently simple problem of information flow among participating programmers becomes grotesque.

The MPP projects were indeed large; in one case, as we have seen, 400 programmers were involved. Clearly, mechanisms for information communication become vital.

Standards, already mentioned, are one form of communication. Two other forms—development folders and program libraries—are discussed in what follows. It is important that any project programmer have access by some means to all project-relevant information for which there is a "need to know." Development folders and program libraries are alternative ways of achieving that goal. They also help achieve the goal of management visibility and control.

3.3.7.1 UNIT DEVELOPMENT FOLDERS (TRW)

A unit development folder is a collection of information that (1) serves as a repository for all pertinent development and test information (requirements, design data, code, flow diagrams, test plans, test results, etc.) for each identified software unit, and (2) requires completion of a cover sheet specifying a detailed development plan (i.e., programmer estimates of completion dates for intermediate milestones) and providing a means for indicating actual completion dates and review events to depict the status of each software unit.

A Unit Development Folder (UDF) is prepared and maintained for each software unit to provide an accessible collection of all data pertaining to that unit, as these data are produced, and to collect unit-level schedules and status information. The folders are established within 1 week after the completion of a Preliminary Design Review and are maintained until the final as-built software documentation is delivered.

Each UDF contains a cover sheet identifying the contents and schedule of each section of the folder. It is signed off by the originator upon completion of each section. The sections of the UDF are described below:

Section 0 (Cover Sheet and Schedule) contains a cover sheet delineating scheduled due dates, actual completion dates, assigned originators and reviewer sign-offs and dates, plus a change log recording the UDF revision history.

Section 1 (Requirements) identifies the baseline requirements specification, enumerates the requirements that are allocated for implementation in the software unit, and shows the mapping (by paragraph number) to the requirements specification.

Section 2 (Design Description) contains the current, working version of the design, including, at the appropriate times, the preliminary design and successively more detailed design data and flowcharts suitable as a "code to" specification.

Section 3 (Functional Capabilities List) contains a list of the testable functions performed by the unit obtained from an independent review of the detailed design by someone other than the unit designer.

Section 4 (Unit Code) contains current source code listings for the unit and a change log of post-baseline updates to the unit code.

Section 5 (Unit Test Plan) describes the overall testing approach and each test case, identifies test tools or drivers used for unit testing, and illustrates the Test Case Matrix relating test cases to capabilities tested.

Section 6 (Unit Test Plan Review) documents the findings from an independent review of the plan to provide assurance that unit test cases will adequately test branch conditions, logic paths, input and outputs, and error-handling procedures.

Section 7 (Test Case Results) contains a compilation of test case results and analyses necessary to demonstrate that the unit has successfully passed the tests prescribed by the Unit Test Plan.

Section 8 (Problem Reports) contains status logs and copies of all Design Problem Reports, Design Analysis Reports, and Discrepancy Reports which document design and code changes pertaining to the unit.

Section 9 (Notes) contains relevant memoranda, informal reports, and other notes which provide supplementary detail expanding on other UDF contents.

Each UDF is reviewed by the assigned reviewer, other than the originator, following completion of each UDF section. At completion of unit testing, the manager responsible for the unit reviews the entire UDF for technical adequacy and completeness and signs and dates the cover sheet to indicate approval. In addition, periodic audits of UDFs are conducted to ensure compliance with project standards.

3.3.7.2 *UNIT DEVELOPMENT FOLDERS (BCS)*

The Unit Development Folder (UDF) is an extension of the traditional programmer's workbook. The concept of a UDF as a combination repository and visibility mechanism was originated by TRW Systems, Inc. As implemented at BCS, the UDF concept is a standard for documenting plans and progress, as well as for recording key information developed as a product of specific tasks.

As in traditional practice, the programmer responsible for design of a functional component begins by laying out the structure of subroutines needed to complete the component. These subroutines are named, and the programmer then prepares a Unit Development Folder for each, with a cover sheet (or equivalent) which sets a schedule for the completion of design, coding, checkout, and technical documentation. As each of these detailed tasks is completed, the results are placed in the UDF and the date (actually) completed and review signatures (if required) are entered on the UDF cover sheet.

A similar approach is used for test planning. An overview of the (component, integration, or acceptance) test activity is prepared which identifies the various test steps involved and names them. A UDF and cover sheet for each test, scheduling the test design, preparation of test procedures and data, and test execution is prepared. As test designs, procedures, data, and results are produced, they are placed in the UDF and appropriate entries are logged on the cover sheet.

The Unit Development Folder then becomes the mechanism whereby a programmer or integrator can easily review his or her task schedule, report completion of tasks, and record acceptance of results. It establishes naming and referencing conventions for the products of tasks which make these products more accessible to other project personnel. Communication between the individual assigned a particular series of tasks and the person's superior can be made more efficient (and less costly), since tangible products are available for objective and pertinent review.

The cover sheets of UDFs provide information which the Program Manager can readily extract for project visibility and control. This permits the PM to make an accurate assessment of progress against plan (both schedule and expenditures). The PM can more quickly detect impending performance problems and can effect an earlier (and usually less costly) recovery.

This practice may be somewhat more costly to implement than the traditional programmer's workbook, primarily because of the emphasis on the cover sheet, which implies more deliberate and detailed review of products for status, adherence to quality criteria, completeness, etc. However, we feel that this cost is more than offset by having this controlling information readily available in a standard form for the people who require it to monitor cost, schedule, and quality; the assignees, their superiors, and the Program Manager.

3.3.7.3 PROGRAM LIBRARY OPERATIONS (SDC)

The rules that were established for program library operations included the definition of responsibilities and procedures for the System Librarian and for interacting with the Program Library. They also included procedures for program change control and the handling of system builds.

Program library operations ensure better program quality by inspection of source code for adherence to the established conventions for programming style and by ensuring that unit testing is complete before inclusion of the program or any changes to programs in the controlled or "system master" portion of the library. Management visibility is enhanced by the inclusion of the total set of programs in the library via completed modules or program stubs, maintenance of status information, and issuance of regular reports of status and activity.

Except for the record-keeping and report activities, program library operations directly support programming and are tasks that must be done with or without a librarian. Library maintenance procedures (include quality assurance and change control) organize and regulate operations upon the software product and ensure the quality and currency of the working and tested portions of the library. These activities require personnel and computer time to support them, but the cost is regained in fewer problems in integrating and testing the software, and in improved software quality.

3.3.7.4   PROGRAMMING SUPPORT LIBRARY AIDS (BCS)

A programming support library aid is used to record code (and computer-readable design formulations), data, and other card-type statements used in software design, construction, and testing. This type of aid assists in modifying recorded elements and performing related file maintenance services. In addition, this type of aid can provide the visibility needed by management for control purposes.

The BCS programming support library aid is capable of recording most of the common types of products of the programming process—source code, object code, data cases, job control language procedures, and even design-expression and macro-language statements.

This aid provides capability to modify (delete, add, update) recorded elements, and to perform several other file maintenance services commonly needed in the process of producing software.

This aid provides rudimentary support for controlling and tracking the item results of programming. In particular, it is capable of listing the identifications and dates of entry of the elements stored, but provides no other assistance in matching this list to a program plan or schedule.

If a programming support library aid is not employed on a project, the project can take advantage of (traditionally available) text editing, data dictionary, and copy library capabilities. These tools do not offer the comprehensive control and support of a programming support library aid, but can assist in recording and modifying code elements. When these tools are used in conjunction with manually maintained ledgers (identifying the names, contents, locations, versions, and relationships of code elements), visibility for management control can be provided. Where even these traditional tools are not available, the project must rely on manual techniques to develop, capture, and modify code elements, as well as to provide control visibility.

3.4 CHECKOUT

Enormous concern was expressed by all the participating companies over the checkout process. A recurring theme occurs in each MPP report, under a variety of headings—testing, verification, validation—that the software product must be done right. The approaches to checkout vary, but center on these themes:

> Reviews and walkthroughs
> Top-down, bottom-up, and sideways testing (!)
> Methodologies and tools
> Facilities and system test
> Test documentation

3.4.1 Code Reviews and Walkthroughs

Code reviews and walkthroughs are a static method of removing errors from software—that is, the software need not be executed to facilitate the error removal process.

They are also a tedious and time-consuming approach to error removal.

And they are a very productive way of removing errors. Most software errors are subject to review/walkthrough detection; no other software reliability methodology can make this claim!

Out of this mixed cost/benefit picture comes a mixed utilization picture. Although *design* reviews are almost universally used by the MPP companies, *code* reviews are used sparingly. Those uses are discussed below.

3.4.1.1 STRUCTURED WALKTHROUGHS (CSC)

A structured walkthrough is the review of a program design or program code by an evaluation committee. This review is conducted prior to coding as a design review and prior to unit testing as a program logic review. The primary programmer presents his or her design or code to the committee members, who step through the logic of the program to detect errors prior to coding or testing. This technique is sometimes referred to as peer-group programming.

The phase where walkthroughs are applied is the coding phase. However, a walkthrough of the program design prior to actual coding can be very effective in detecting misinterpretations of data base structure, communication links, and the general approach to the solution of a problem. From this viewpoint, the phases affected by this technique could be described as the design phase through the test and integration phase. This technique is similar to a mini critical design review (CDR) except that it is normally an internal process and less formal than a CDR.

This technique was used on both the TRIDENT and DD-963 projects, in a similar manner. The evaluation committee averaged five people, and normally consisted of the analysts whose programs had interactions with the program under review and the primary programmer's immediate supervisor. The design or code was reproduced and distributed to the committee members for review prior to the evaluation date. The reviews were internal to the project and informal to a degree, to encourage constructive criticism from the participants. The dates set for the walkthroughs were part of the milestones for completion of program design and coding as scheduled by the programming manager.

The effect of the walkthroughs on the projects reviewed was expressed by the personnel on the respective staffs as being cost-effective in both person-hours and machine time. The number of personnel involved in a walkthrough ranged from three to seven and the time required was about 4 hours per program. The direct benefit from these evaluations was in the test time being reduced by 50 to 80% because errors were detected prior to the test phase. The indirect benefits are (1) verification of program interfaces to alleviate integration problems, (2) expanding knowledge of system components over the staff members, (3) accelerating the software production by reduction of test time and integration time, and (4) detecting errors early in the development cycle, thus reducing the cost of correction.

3.4.1.2   FORMAL INSPECTION OF DOCUMENTATION
AND CODE (TRW)

Formal inspection is a method for assessing the quality of software documentation and code. It includes formal inspection techniques such as peer-group critiques and walkthroughs, quality-assurance reviews and audits, and design reviews.

Formal inspection of documentation and code facilitates the early detection of design errors. A design walkthrough, for example, is accomplished by having the software unit design reviewed by one or more individuals other than the originator. The scope, technique, and degree of formality of the walkthrough is established by the project manager prior to preliminary design review. The review includes, as a minimum, checks for responsiveness of design to requirements, design completeness and consistency, flow of data through input/output interfaces, error-recovery procedures, modularity, simplicity, and testability. The technique used for walkthroughs consists of either a presentation of the design and the code by the originator in the presence of the reviewers, or a review of the documentation followed by a discussion of review comments involving all participants. Problems detected during the walkthrough are identified in a written summary and made available to the managers responsible for the software.

3.4.1.3 CODE VERIFICATION (BCS)

In addition to verification of design, verification (by review) of code is employed to assist the construction (coding and checkout) activity. As each subroutine is coded, a peer review or inspection of the code is performed to assure that it is ready for checkout. This peer review assists the programmer in finding errors he or she might otherwise miss, and reduces the number of computer runs the programmer requires to checkout a subroutine.

Once the programmer has completed checkout of the functional component, another review may be performed to ensure that the code is ready for integration testing. The programmer submits evidence of successful completion of the checkout, and describes the logical and functional testing that he or she has employed. This review evaluates the adequacy of these component tests and provides a way of conclusively closing out the construction task.

Two of the projects instituted deliberate code verification procedures in the form of peer code reviews; however, only one of these attempted to continue the practice throughout the construction activity, and it met with only partial success. Both projects having experience with this practice felt that it was extremely expensive, and that it was difficult to motivate project personnel to apply this technique consistently. Furthermore, the projects observed that as the pressure of deadlines increased, this review technique was virtually impossible to employ.

3.4.2 Top-Down, Bottom-Up, and Sideways Testing

The section heading above is deliberately facetious. It reflects the fact that there is little unanimity about the merits of top-down and bottom-up testing among the MPP companies.

This is, of course, a continuation of a discussion started earlier under the heading "Top-Down Implementation." In this top-down approach, there is considerable co-mingling of the implementation and checkout phases. Therefore, there should really not be a separate discussion of top-down testing as opposed to top-down implementation.

However, the MPP company discussions of top-down testing exposed the fact that the implementation in some cases was considerably less top-down than we had been led to believe!

3.4.2.1 TESTING APPROACHES (SPERRY UNIVAC)

This section describes the testing practices employed for the programs under study. Testing methods are classified as conventional testing or top-down concept testing.

The description of conventional testing, as used for the first two programs, specifies in detail all approaches and considerations for the testing of a program as a "completed" isolated building block.

In the conventional model of the traditional program development approach there are four phases of work: analysis, design, production, and testing. These phases are time-serial with respect to each other. The usual testing method is bottom-up. That is, the independent functions are tested first, followed by the dependent ones. Certification proceeds in a building-block manner with those functions certified first being used to certify the remaining functions.

However, program testing on the MPP projects did not start in practice from a fixed point in time. Program testing may have been initiated several times only to find that the checkout, or even design objectives, had not been completed. Testing effectiveness was normally diminished at first by unexpected interactions between the large number of program elements, including the test tools which were not yet executed as an integrated software system. By the time good testing progress was being made, most of the development schedule had sometimes been consumed. As a result, program testing personnel were being asked to complete their work in insufficient time. Under the pressure of insufficient time, any technical problem may result in some question of the test integrity. For example, testing discoveries of program inadequacies may have been recorded with insufficient data to define them clearly. Therefore, testing could be questioned concerning test validity, the source of the problem, personnel competence, etc. These pressures would cause additional management problems for control of the project and for visibility to the customer. When testing was performed as a one-shot effort following completion of production, this burden seemed to be inescapable.

The sequence of testing for all programs was as follows:

1. Each programmer verified that his or her program satisfied an informal software checkout test.

2. The program was then turned over to the test group, who verified via a preliminary certification procedure and simulation that the software satisfied contractual requirements as specified by the Program Performance and Program Design Specifications.

3. The Navigation Program was delivered to the customer for formal certification testing. Sperry Univac provided support for this testing. The program was accepted by the Navy, who then turned it back to Sperry Univac for system integration.

4. The baseline Common Program Operating System was furnished by the Navy and modified as needed by Sperry Univac to provide the Operational Program. After intensive informal testing, Sperry Univac performed the formal certification tests for the customer.

5. Software Systems Integration was performed first at St. Paul using

simulation of all hardware, and then at the Navy's Land-Based Emulation Facility using live and simulated equipment. The latter tests featured full load endurance tests for periods ranging from 96 to 120 hours.

6. Sperry Univac furnished support for actual shipboard trials of the delivered software.

The purpose of program testing, regardless of the method (top-down or conventional) used, was to locate and correct errors in the design and coding of the software system, and to complete a contracted milestone for software acceptance. Testing was successful on each of the four programs studied. Conclusions reached follow:

1. Principal advantages of top-down design and development were:
   a. The ability to establish multiple fixed and visible milestones within the production and testing of a computer program.
   b. Early production and verification of the control logic, which enabled a program to execute as a component of a data processing system.
   c. The ability to begin system integration prior to the completion of program development.
   d. A tendency to localize related functions rather than scattering them through large portions of a program. This usually allowed function testing at a module level.
   e. The ability to test completed program modules as a whole using stubs independent of the production of lower-level elements.
   f. The knowledge when testing an element that all higher-level modules have been tested.
   g. The top-down testing concept could be used even if conventional design is employed.
   h. The ability to generate a test capability for level 1 and to expand and use it for more complex levels.
2. Test control software driven by scenarios was used on all four programs to control automated testing. At the beginning of Program 1 development, scenarios were embedded in testing programs written uniquely for each program module and functionally tested. When it was realized that test system control with a scenario was actually a software tool, Sperry Univac created the current automated test control software and input scenarios, providing for:
   a. Test automation
   b. Repeatability
   c. Test system viability
3. "Scripted" scenario test control, with the test inputs consisting of

timed operator key presses and other condition/response extractions, formed a dynamic, easily modifiable, repeatable test tool. However, the operator had to exercise care and the control program had to contain safeguards against the entry of erroneous commands. Entry of scenario test systems from a deck of punched cards offered stricter control while still being modifiable.

4. A scenario-generation high-level language provided simplification of the scenarios.

5. Testing was both "open-loop" (output subject to analysis only) and "closed-loop" (output both available for analysis and available for dynamic feedback to effect the next test).

6. Simulation programs simulated not only intermodule and standard computer peripheral interfaces, but also employed "wraparound simulation" to simulate the entire real environment enveloping the system.

7. A steady evolution was noted in the quality and capability of the test procedures. Additional tests were added, actions taken, and observations of results were made clearer and more explicit; notes were added, expanded, and clarified to supply background information for each test.

8. Test support software (e.g., test control programs, data recording modules, data reduction modules, etc.) was designed for viability and became tools to facilitate their use on other projects and required only minor modifications or additions.

9. The test software was designed for testing in multiple configurations, using multiprocessors, multiple computers, and a wide variety of peripheral equipment. This gave the capability to reconfigure a system for faster checkout of system problems. The simulation and test software could be executed either in the same computer as the software under test or in an external computer cabled to the tested unit. This allowed the testing of the configurations prior to live integration into the operational environment.

10. The practice of "stubbing" undeveloped, but expected, functional "design objects" in top-down development allowed early testing of the system's responses to the expected timing and memory requirements.

11. The utilization of program checkout plans, checkout procedures, and checkout logs allowed up to 20 programmers to share 4-hour open-shop-time blocks effectively and to perform highly efficient program debugging. The advantages to be gained from using this requirement outweigh the difficulties attendant to changing personal attitudes and the costs involved with generating the forms and using them.

3.4.2.2 PROGRESSIVE TESTING AND INTEGRATION (CSC)

Progressive testing and integration is the process of verifying and integrating segments of a system in a time-phased schedule as the system is being developed. The purpose is to detect any errors as early as possible, provide the customer with early visibility, and avoid the conventional process of testing and integrating the total system in one process at the end of the development phase.

This technique is applied during the code and debug phase with the benefits being realized through the system integration phase. The immediate benefit is the visibility of progress that is demonstrable to management and the customer. The prime benefit of progressive testing and integration is early error detection and correction. Figure 3.3 depicts the errors detected and documented by trouble reports during a 3-year span covering program design, program development, system integration, and maintenance for a large system development project. The peaks on the graph during the first year represent the errors detected during the testing and integration on the builds for that year. There were 755 errors detected during the program design and program development phases. Without phased testing and integration these errors probably would not have been detected until system integration when the cost to correct is much higher. With phased testing and integration, the overall development schedule is shorter, since the progressive testing and integration is accomplished in parallel with the coding of the next build.

There were two verification processes used on the DD-963 project. To verify that the program design met its requirements, a top-down verification process was used. Then the program code was verified using bottom-up verification procedures.

Top-down verification was implemented through a multistep process using threads and builds. That process proceeded as follows:

1. Prior to each build demonstration, each primary programmer reviewed the programmed threads for which he or she was responsible to verify their correctness.
2. A build demonstration scenario was developed which assured execution of every thread within that particular build.
3. The build demonstration was conducted to confirm specific functional capabilities associated with that build.
4. Monitor runs (trial executions) were conducted for selected programs or modules to confirm questionable thread execution which occurred during the build demonstration.
5. Postbuilding testing was employed to ensure that the final postbuild system configuration was functionally acceptable. It consisted of the following:

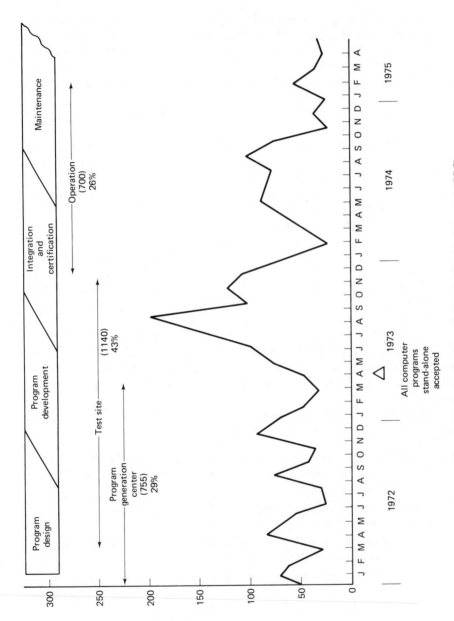

Figure 3.3 System Development Trouble Reports (CSC)

a. Exhaustive testing to execute functions over the entire range of values for input data
b. Negative testing to evaluate system responses to erroneous input data
c. Degradation testing to assess system operation under subsystem fault conditions

Bottom-up verification was achieved primarily through the use of support programs as program code was developed. The elements of this process were:

1. Compare automated flowchart generator statements with the program or segment code to assure a correspondence.
2. Create program or segment flowcharts using the automated flowchart generator.
3. Verify that the program or segment flowcharts are consistent with the development specification.

These verification procedures were first implemented during the code and checkout phase when threads were verified against the performance specifications in preparation for build demonstrations. They continued to be used through the test and integration phase as bottom-up verification was conducted to confirm that the program code paralleled the design specifications. The net result of these activities was reflected in the following:

Early definition of subsystem and module interfaces
Comprehensive design and code analysis
Error detection enhanced throughout entire period of development
Viability of system and subsystem threads confirmed

3.4.3 Methodologies and Tools

Many test tools are discussed in the software reliability literature.
Many fewer test tools are actually used by companies such as those participating in the MPP study.
The weight of the responsibility for industrial environment checkout, then, still lies in using adequate methodologies.
In the real-time world described in what follows, the use of simulators is central to the debug process. The first section describes an environment simulator which is catalyzed by a "scenario" to behave much like the physical environment in which the software will eventually run. The second section describes a way of checking out on a computer to which you do not yet have access!

3.4.3.1 METHODS AND TOOLS (SPERRY UNIVAC)

Initially, the following testing procedure was used for the application and simulation programs:

1. Punched cards containing the desired testing commands were read into a test scenario generator.
2. The generated scenarios were written to paper tape.
3. The paper tape was read onto the system disk via the keyboard printer station to provide the system test run.
4. The test results were printed on the keyboard/printer.
5. The test results were analyzed visually and were transferred to a test report log.
6. Any inaccuracies shown by testing were recorded together with test result data to a site problem log. This log was kept at the site to record any problems until they could be resolved.

In performing system integration, the capability was available to interchange real and simulated data input by recabling. The results showed that the simulated input equaled the live data. Testing of the simulation program was performed using large quantities of sample data provided by the customer.

3.4.3.2 EMULATED ON-BOARD COMPUTER (MARTIN-MARIETTA)

A ground-based, microprogrammable computer was used to emulate the Flight Computer throughout all phases of GCSC software development. This software-first approach to the Lander computer system development facilitated computer timing and sizing specification, permitted early development of critical computer programs, and provided considerable visibility into test and evaluation activities.

During the early phases of software and hardware definition it became evident that several problem areas could be satisfied by an emulation approach. Accurate sizing and timing estimates could be obtained by coding a hypothetical computer representing the class of available spaceborne digital computers. Computer memory capacity and speed have significant impact on power, weight, and volume; all were critical performance characteristics. In addition, we were committed to an Analog-Hybrid six-degree-of-freedom simulation of separation from the orbiter through soft landing on the surface of Mars. Integrated testing with real sensors and actuators was deemed important in this process. Emulated representation of the on-board computer would provide bit-for-bit fidelity. Unlike an "interpretive computer simulation" (software) approach, emulation offered the prospect of real-time test and evaluation. Finally, most of the classic problems inherent with punched tape and limited visibility associated with on-board computer usage would be avoided.

Emulation is now a proven concept in computer system development. The approach offers the same type of advantages with any embedded computer system where the target computer is undeveloped or unavailable. The power of the technique is illustrated by the fact that the first flight computer was substituted for the Emulator and was running the descent program in a full simulated environment within just 1 week of computer delivery.

Conventional approaches to software development have utilized the "interpretive computer simulation," wherein the flight computer is simulated by interpreting its instruction set and action through programs written on a host computer. A typical response time, although quite variable, might be as much as 500 times slower than the actual machine. It is also difficult to anticipate, and thereby program, situations that can occur in a real-time environment. Consequently, to develop software in a real-time environment which could include actual devices, we decided against this approach and pursued the emulation course.

Although the characteristics of the flight computer were not specified, sufficient general information was available early in the Viking project to convince us that microprogrammable computers then in existence could provide a real-time emulation of the future flight computer.

It was recognized at the onset that an emulation would not, and could not, provide a one-to-one time relationship with the actual machine on an instruction-by-instruction basis. Indeed, for this to occur theoretically, the basic cycle time of the microprogrammable computer would have to be a submultiple of that of the actual machine. The stress, in a real-time sampled data system, is upon accomplishing identical processing over a sample period.

The microprogrammable computer chosen was a Standard Computer Corporation IC-7000. It consists of two processors both of which are microprogrammable. One is the Central Processing Unit (CPU) and the second is labeled the Input/Output Processor (IOP). Each incorporates a control memory whose contents define the machine (i.e., the instruction set, interrupt structure, etc.) for that processor.

The initial use of the complex consisted of an emulation for a hypothetical flight computer. Inasmuch as the actual machine had not been specified, it was felt that software development could proceed with a typical computer representing the class of candidates available. This emulation aided sizing and timing specifications, and helped in early development of the human–machine and various system interfaces.

The characteristics of the microprogrammable complex dictated that flight computer emulation be done on the CPU and that the IOP should be used to implement I/O-related aspects and to communicate with all external devices, including the human–machine interface and control. Consequently, a basic

IOP language was defined and implemented in conjunction with development of the hypothetical flight computer emulator.

The IOP language implementation proved to be an ongoing, continual endeavor throughout the life of the project. A new instruction would be implemented as a need was generated. IOP microprogramming included implementation of an interrupt system. The IOP, in addition to providing the interface linkage for the CPU to implement flight computer I/O, also functioned as overall system problem control. Its language was used to perform tasks such as data recording, starting and stopping of runs, establishing an initialization state, etc.

Flight computer emulation began when selection of the flight computer was made. The emulation was mechanized with respect to the logic design and not with respect to the information found in what is commonly termed the "programming manual." Design changes to the computer were tracked and implemented in the emulation.

As the overall system needs and requirements developed, additional requirements were forced onto the CPU microprogram over and above the basic microprogram related to real-time flight computer emulation. The end-result real-time emulation bore little resemblance to the initial design because of these factors, and changes in computer design.

Three emulations have been mentioned: (1) the hypothetical computer; (2) real-time real computer; and (3) IOP. Another version of the emulation was also developed and warrants discussion. This was called the "Trace" emulation. Its purpose was to provide a listing to the user to aid in program development. User control was provided to allow printout to occur only as desired. The printout provided machine state information following execution of each instruction and included the instruction, its location, various register contents, and time. TRACE, in actuality, consisted of a CPU microprogram and an IOP program. Whereas much of the instruction emulation was identical to that of real time, the interface to the IOP was drastically different.

Two versions of TRACE were eventually developed. The preliminary version used IOP programming to keep track of time-related aspects (e.g., instruction execution time, sample time, delay times, etc.). As a result, the operation time was quite slow (about 300:1). A later version incorporated these features in the microprogram and resulted in a speedup (around 30:1 and in some unique instances could even run faster than real time). The latter microprogram was, of course, considerably more complex than the former.

As the characteristics of the real computer became defined, some rather drastic incompatible features became apparent with respect to the microprogrammable machine's capability. This was particularly true with respect to I/O. The design was driven by power requirements, and interfaces were required with several unique external devices. The result was several I/O registers of varying length and unique time-out periods. Also, the real computer had partial power down or "go to sleep" capability. It was readily apparent once these characteristics became known that the basic micro-programmable computer could not handle the implementation requirements. Consequently, a hardware design modification was made to the computer to aid in the microprogram implementation.

Four distinct microprograms were developed and are described separately.

1. *Hypothetical computer emulation:* The initial computer emulated was that of a "computer" typical of the class of computers available. The general characteristics were:

   a. 24-bit word
   b. 2's-complement arithmetic
   c. 24 instructions

   A simplified I/O and interrupt structure were included.

2. *IOP language emulation:* The instruction set incorporated into the IOP evolved over the life of the project and supported over 200K words of support software. The general features are:

   a. 36-bit word
   b. 2's-complement arithmetic
   c. 163 instructions
   d. Interrupt system

   Virtually the entire control core (2048 18-bit words) was utilized in the process. The IOP micro language bears little resemblance to that of the CPU.

   The IOP language supports all standard I/O peripheral device interfaces in addition to the unique devices associated with the Viking system.

3. Real computer real-time emulation: The general characteristics of the real computer are:

   a. 24-bit word
   b. 47 instructions, some of which have several subsets
   c. 2's-complement arithmetic
   d. 8-level priority-interrupt system
   e. 10 I/O registers
   f. 18K memory
   g. 2K protected memory area
   h. 3 soft index registers
   i. Multilevel indirect addressing
   j. Some error-detection logic
   k. Sleep-mode capability
   l. Programmable timer

   The real-time emulation is bit-for-bit functionally equivalent with the real computer. Emulation design was performed from the standpoint of its logical design. The priority-interrupt system was emulated, for example, on a one-for-one equivalent of the flip-flop structure involved.

Several areas of incompatibility were evident between the real and the microprogrammable computer as the real computer design progressed. In many instances, use of the microprogrammable machine capability was compromised or bypassed to meet functional equivalence. Some examples are as follows:

a. *Index registers:* Three soft index registers were utilized in the real computer, whereas the microcomputer has several hardware index registers, allowing indexing to be done as part of the instruction fetch with no additional time penalty. Use of this feature as is would result in a nonexactness of memory contents between the two machines (the three memory cells assigned to indexing). An exact equivalence could be achieved, of course, via appropriate microprogramming. However, by so doing, all instructions that are indexable must be tested, when executed, to determine if the feature is called for. The result is a critical time loss in addition to consumption of control core.

A compromise solution proved satisfactory in this case. Hardware indexing was utilized, but the three memory cells were maintained via microprogram. That is, any instruction that modified these cells also modified the hard index registers.

b. *Multilevel indirect:* This feature of the real computer was not designed into the basic hardware capability of the micro machine. Although it could be accomplished via microprogramming, the same penalties exist as for index registers: excessive execution time and core consumption. This feature was discarded as a programmer option, thereby eliminating the problem.

c. *Divide:* The real computer divide instruction contained some rather peculiar features (e.g., the l.s.b. of the quotient was always "1") which disallowed use of the divide hardware in the micro machine and forced microprogramming of the divide algorithm. Consequently, emulation divide time was significantly greater than that of the real computer. This condition was, however, of little consequence since flight programmers avoided the use of this instruction because of its pecularities. In fact, its main claim to fame was as a low-power-time killer—an instruction that consumes little power (only one operand memory reference) and takes a relatively long time to execute!

d. *I/O:* Major difficulties in emulation of the flight computer via the micro program technique were associated with I/O. Problems therein are amplified when real time is involved. Consider the differences between the two machines. I/O in the micro computer is handled through the Input/Output Processor, which is linked to the CPU via common memory and through interrupts. That is, either processor may interrupt the other at the micro level. Interrupt interpretation and data transfers are mechanized through memory interrogation. Both processors have access to CPU control core. Thus, data transfer is parallel and a degree of handshaking is implied in mechanization. Once the information is obtained and interpreted by the IOP, it can then establish the necessary linkage with the external devices.

The flight computer I/O design, by contrast, reflects extreme sensitivity to power consumption. All data transfers are serial, register lengths are variable, and transfer times are device-dependent. Once the flight computer I/O design began to crystallize, it became quite obvious that an I/O bottleneck would exist if modeling were limited to the basic micro machine capability. This became painfully true in respect to the timing involved. An overwhelming amount of microprocessing time would be consumed in attempting to maintain the four-channel simulation.

Additional hardware was designed and added to the micro machine to solve the problem. The various timing periods involved were produced via hardware, thereby permitting the data transfers to occur in parallel (at the micro level) upon time out and, consequently, simulate the serial transfer.

The I/O instruction structure also created problems since several fields required decoding in determining instruction intent. This implies a considerable amount of time and core overhead in decoding. Additional hardware modifications were made to reduce the effect, especially in time-sensitive areas.

e. *"Sleep" operation:* Because of power constraints, the flight computer allows a partially powered down mode to be established. It may then "wake up" as a result of external interrupt or termination of a specified time interval. This feature was emulated by suspending instruction execution during the sleep interval while remaining receptive, at the micro level, to those elements corresponding to the "awake" portion of the flight machine.

f. *Timers:* In addition to a sampling clock and the discussed I/O time periods, a 1-ms and a 12-ms timing period were designed into the flight computer. These items were associated with the power conservation and sleep mode. Emulation of these features via the micro code consumed too much core and execution time. The problem was solved by augmenting the hardware to provide the capability.

Although the foregoing items are significant and did have considerable impact on the emulation process, the achievements of the technique are a credit to its flexibility. Modifications were necessary only because of the real-time aspects of the problem.

Table 3-2 is a timing comparison between the real computer and

TABLE 3-2
Emulation timing comparison (μs)

Instruction or Instruction Type	Flight Computer	Emulator
ADD	8.68	7.70
SHIFT	4.34–23.44	8.41–17.34
DOUBLE ADD	13.02	14.52
MULTIPLY	83.33	31.35
DIVIDE	123.26	168.68
STORE	8.68	8.45
INDEXING	4.34	0 (H/W index registers)
INDIRECT ADDRESSING	4.34	1.4 (H/W index registers)
INTERRUPT	8.68	23.62
OUTPUT	8.68	17.15–113.2
INPUT	8.68	10.15–24.5

the emulator. A variety of conditions are evident—from near exactness to a wide variation in both directions.

Input/output and interrupt aspects produced the greatest variation in timing and the poorest results. This was primarily due to two factors: (1) each flight computer I/O instruction was in reality a group of instructions (i.e., several subsets existed for each), thereby requiring an extensive amount of decoding at the microprogram level; and (2) communication linkages between CPU and IOP required servicing time.

Other items, such as multiply, indexing, and indirect addressing, tend to counteract the I/O timing. A reasonable degree of comparison exists for other instructions.

Again, individual instruction time is not the critical factor. The ability to perform the required flight program processing within a sample period is the critical item. For the instruction mix involved, emulation execution time was slightly faster than real computer execution time.

Many features were also implemented in the micro program as an aid to overall system operation. For example, a read and write of flight program reset points was implemented. This feature allowed the user to run for any period of time, stop, and store the machine state. Similarly, any stored reset point could be read and the operation reinitiated. The machine state is determinable and may also be established via micro program, whereas this may be impossible or difficult at a higher level.

4. *Trace emulation:* This microprogram, in association with an IOP program, functioned to provide the user with a printout of the computer state (instruction, location, register content, effective address

and contents, and execution time) after each instruction. Much of the microcode is identical to that of the real-time emulation, but many differences exist. TRACE must store all state conditions and make them available upon request. Also, the time-related aspects have a different connotation than in real time and microcode in these areas differs considerably. TRACE was used for initial program development and in attempts to gain insight into problem areas.

The emulation approach enabled us to obtain reasonable timing and sizing estimates for the spaceborne computer prior to issuing its specifications. This was accomplished through emulation of a hypothetical machine. This approach also accelerated the laboratory system design and mechanization whereby interfaces between the various components, the human–machine interface, etc., were mechanized and operational early in the program. Also, operational runs were made to verify descent algorithms using this language before the computer specifics were known.

After they became known, the hypothetical emulation was phased out as the real time and trace emulation were developed. These items were operational at least a year in advance of real computer availability. Consequently, program development was well under way when the actual machine became available.

Insight and visibility into program operation were possible through the approach, which would not have been possible with the actual machine. Aerospace computers typically have little visibility provided to the user.

One aspect of the approach that proved quite useful as an aid to program debugging was the ability to examine conditions at a lower level than normal machine instruction level—the microcode level. This technique was used many times to "look" at the internal machine state and thereby determine the problem cause.

Emulation also provides the capability to determine and thereby record machine state. Within the system framework, it often became necessary to stop the run after a long period of elapsed time and record all conditions as a reset point so that the exact state could be reestablished later without processing from the initial starting point. This is relatively easy to do at the microcode level but may be extremely difficult at the program level. Indeed, once the real computer became available, a considerable amount of effort was expended in accomplishing the same task.

Emulation offers the user a large degree of flexibility as is illustrated by the changing instruction set of the IOP. As needs develop, changes can be made to accommodate that need. This capability is not realized without some expense as the user must develop his or her software and the personnel at the micro level must be intimately familiar with the machine.

In respect to the microprogramming effort per se, many difficulties were centered around a lack of control store. Both IOP and CPU control store consisted of 2048 18-bit words. The real-time emulation was a constant process of fitting in system real computer design changes without exceeding core or execution-time limitations. IOP control core was completely consumed via emulation of the IOP language. The final version of TRACE (Fast Trace) also consumed the entire CPU control core.

Some additional comments with respect to real-time emulation are warranted. It should be understood that real-time emulation is not automatically attainable. It was possible for Viking because the real computer was a relatively slow machine. The microprogrammable machine must be a basically faster device than the computer to be emulated.

Careful attention should be given to the compatibility of the two computers if at all possible. Otherwise, considerable difficulties may appear as the emulation proceeds. This situation was painfully evident with respect to the real computer real-time emulation. Characteristics of the microprogrammable computer were completely ignored. The result was a series of "find-a-solution" processes, culminating in many instances with hardware modification to the micro machine.

Table 3-3 summarizes the labor time expended in the different Viking microprogramming tasks.

Labor time consumed in the microprogramming effort includes a learning period. With respect to the IOP effort, the figure represents the personnel time consumed over a 5-year project lifetime rather than an amount required to begin utilization of the resource. Basic operation consumed approximately 6 person-months, but as the system developed, additions and changes were made to the instruction set and the operational philosophy. The result was a more-or-less-continual, low-key effort.

Flight computer emulation labor consumption reflects the effort expended in learning associated with the flight computer—an understanding of its operation at the logic design level and in tracking the design and its changes from the conceptual to the developed stage over a 3-year period. As design changes occurred, changes were forced upon the emulation. Further, as previously stated, the micro program involved implementation of system func-

TABLE 3-3
Viking microprogramming labor time

Program	Person-months
Hypothetical computer emulation	4
IOP language microprogram	16
Flight computer real-time emulation	20
Flight computer trace emulation	8
Hardware modifications	10

tions. Probably 70% of the labor would be attributable to emulation of the I/O instructions.

Labor used for trace emulation reflects basic design and checkout and also tracking of changes made to flight computer design.

Hardware modifications relate to those items previously discussed which were incorporated to satisfy I/O requirements.

3.4.4 Facilities and System Test

For some kinds of software development, it is not enough to check out the software. The software is part of a larger system, and the entire system must be checked out, focusing (from the software point of view, at least) on how well the software plays its role in the overall system.

To do this, frequently special facilities—often called laboratories —are needed. In the sections that follow, the activities of system test, and laboratories, are explored.

3.4.4.1 COMPREHENSIVE END-TO-END SYSTEM-LEVEL TESTING (MARTIN-MARIETTA)

A series of integrated tests were performed using the Flight Operations ground data system, a Viking Lander on-board computer and its Flight Software, and the Viking Lander science, telemetry, communications, and power subsystems. Ten different tests, covering the four major mission phases, were completed over a 22-month span to verify compatibility of the various programs and demonstrate representative Viking mission sequences. Approximately 156 software design changes were implemented as a result of this integrated series of tests.

The major factors that dictated this comprehensive testing were: (1) error-free Flight Software was required for the on-board computer; (2) scientific and engineering mission design features had to be accurately translated into uplink commands to the Flight Software, and the effect of these commands on the lander functions had to be predicted with certainty by the uplink programs; and (3) the downlink programs had to provide accurate scientific and engineering data in a timely fashion so that new uplink commands could be generated based on actual conditions encountered at Mars.

The Viking system is a large one with many interrelated software and hardware elements whose mission application required virtually error free performance. Mission success is strongly dependent on comprehensive testing of the critical system elements, where the emphasis is placed on testing mission-level functions and performance requirements on an end-to-end basis. This provides a necessary check and balance against the design requirement testing done by the developers of the individual hardware/software elements of the system. The class of integrated testing described herein was a mandatory part of the Viking development.

The Flight Operations/Flight Software integrated test concept was not part of the original Viking development plans. The concept was recommended by several people on the project and further emphasized by some audit/review committees. As the benefit of the tests became apparent, more were defined and approved for implementation.

Each test involved running a series of the Flight Operations programs in the Viking computer environment at the Jet Propulsion Lab (JPL) in Pasadena to produce uplink commands for the Flight Software in the on-board computer. These commands were transferred to Denver by tape or data line, where they were loaded into the on-board computer via the operational uplink communications port. For tests involving the interplanetary Cruise, Preseparation Checkout, or Landed surface operation mission phases, the Flight Software/on-board computer were run in a test bed composed of a full-up, operational Viking Lander. This nonflight article lander, with its power, telemetry, communications, science, and guidance and control subsystems, was made available after an environmental qualification test program had been completed. For the test involving Descent to the surface of Mars, the Flight Software/on-board computer combination was coupled to a hybrid computer facility programmed to simulate the descent vehicle and Martian environment.

When the Viking Lander or the descent trajectory simulation were run under control of the Flight Software, a lander-level downlink telemetry data stream was recorded. These data were then transferred to JPL by magnetic tape or data line, where it was processed through a series of downlink programs to produce science and/or engineering outputs.

The general test configuration for the four mission phases is shown in Figures 3.4 and 3.5. The 22 individual software programs involved in the integrated testing included:

1. Twelve batch Univac 1108 programs with a total of 147,000 source cards
2. Seven batch IBM 360/75 programs with a total of 88,000 source cards
3. Two real-time IBM 360/75 programs with a total of 230,000 instructions for telemetry and image processing
4. One Flight Software program with a total of 18,432 words

The following mission and spacecraft design constraints had a significant influence on the design and implementation of the integrated tests described herein:

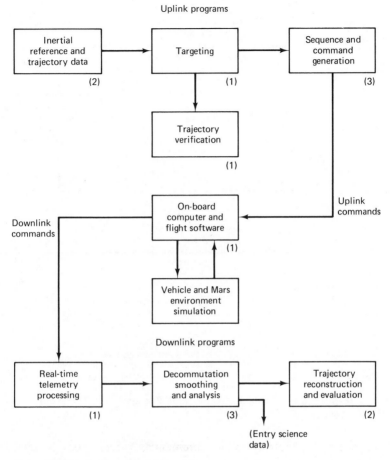

Note : Number of programs shown in parentheses.

Figure 3.4 Descent Test

1. The lander downlinked data to earth, directly and/or relayed through the orbiter, only once a day over a 20-minute one-way light time path.

2. After the lander was separated from the orbiter, the descent program in the on-board computer could not be modified by uplink.

3. During surface operations the lander was in a nearly autonomous operating mode, running a preprogrammed mission in the onboard computer that could be modified by uplink only once every 2 days except in emergency conditions (once a day maximum).

4. The mission was designed to be adaptive and the adaptive reaction time, as measured from on-board downlink data generation to im-

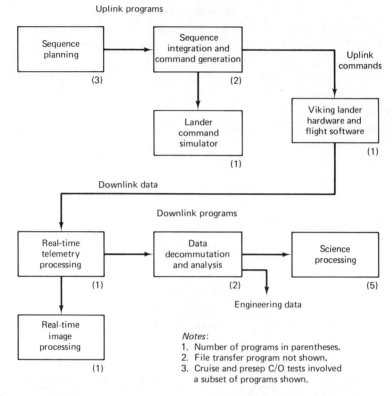

Figure 3.5   Landed, Cruise, and Preseparation Checkout Tests

plemented adaptive uplink commands, varied from 3 days for emergency conditions to a maximum of 21 days.

5.   The on-board computer was the central controlling source for performing, on a time-shared basis, all lander functions, including science control and data acquisition from seven experiments, direct and relay communications to earth, data storage management via tape recorder and core memory, and lander power management.

The qualitative impact of the testing described herein can be summarized as follows:

1.   *Immature software:* In terms of meeting the mission objectives, many of the programs tested were found to be immature. In particular, the three programs that (a) integrated science experiment/engineering subsystem sequences and modeled the various lander functions; (b) generated lander uplink commands; and

(c) simulated Flight Software functions/commands required the majority (i.e., 48%) of the design changes implemented.

2. *Lander "signatures":* Quick-look analysis of the downlink data from the integrated test revealed many anomalies. Extensive analysis indicated that most of these were not caused by any design problem or failure in the hardware or software (i.e., they were signatures of a normal system). The acceptable items were cataloged and the availability of this knowledge during mission operations avoided unnecessary problem solving and delays.

3. *Mission design validation constraints:* The design and implementation of many of the integrated tests were based on various of the Viking mission design strategies; this provided a means to test the validity of each strategy. The testing identified many mission design problems and constraints. As a result, revised strategies were developed and validated in the integrated test series. The accepted constraints were documented and served to guide the development of related mission design strategies.

4. *Flight Team training:* Initially, the integrated tests were performed by a centralized group assigned to the task. Most of the group members were on the Flight Team, but their integrated test assignments were not necessarily related to the functions they were to perform during the mission operations. During the last three tests, tasks such as uplink generation, downlink processing, etc., were performed by the appropriate Flight Team groups. This experience proved a valuable aid in training people for their actual mission assignments with realistic data.

The quantitative impact of the integrated testing described herein can be summarized as follows:

1. Duration of integrated test program: 22 months
2. Programs tested: 22 programs involving approximately 483,000 source cards/instructions
3. Number of tests: 10 tests covering four mission phases
4. Hours of real-time lander (Flight Software) operation: tests ranged from 2 to 419 hours; 1098 hours total time
5. Software design changes derived from test program: approximately 156 changes affecting 20 of 22 programs tested
6. Labor cost: approximately 380 person-months; peak loading 26 to 28 people for a 6-month period

7. Computer cost: Univac 1108 at JPL   275 hours
                     IBM 360/75 at JPL   2300 hours
                     IBM 370/155 at Denver   250 hours
                     CDC 6400 at Denver   40 hours
8. Loss of mission critical data or objectives due to software design
    failures during actual mission: none

3.4.4.2 HARDWARE/SOFTWARE INTEGRATION LABORATORY (MARTIN-MARIETTA)

To assure compatibility and performance between the flight program and the Guidance and Control (G&C) subsystem, an Integration Laboratory was built. It provided capability for stand-alone calibration, diagnostics and test of G&C hardware as well as to operate that hardware with Flight software in a simulated real-time environment. This Integration Laboratory was extremely useful in early identification of system interface problems as well as acting as an independent source to compare hardware build signatures with realistic responsiveness. As a result, the reliability of the system integration process on flight vehicles was greatly increased.

A hardware/software test facility which provides a high degree of visibility and control has usually been implemented only on manned-type missions where a very high reliability is required. In the case of Viking the extremely difficult descent presented an equally complex situation that could not accept the classical approach to hardware/software mating. With the Viking approach to laboratory integration, the hardware was mated and analyzed with the software at each step in the system build.

The Viking Hardware/Software Integration Lab was conceived at the beginning of the Viking project as a G&C subsystem test facility. The Viking G&C system consisted of an Inertial Reference Unit composed of gyros and accelerometers, a Radar Altimeter, a Terminal Descent and Landing Radar, Reaction Control System Thrusters, Terminal Descent Engine Values, Terminal Engine Shutdown Switches, and the Guidance Control and Sequencing Computer. The original intent of the laboratory was to test the hardware and software interfaces of the G&C subsystem. Since the computer delivery was not due until very late in the program and a specific computer had not even been chosen, the IC-7000 microprogrammable computer mentioned earlier was installed in the facility to act as a flight computer for the preliminary G&C subsystem development and integration. As an interface tool the IC-7000 was found to be adequate, but it was soon realized that it had also the potential to support the entire flight software development and test activity. This activity of hardware/software integration and software development was to continue for the entire Viking Lander development.

One IC-7000 processor (the CPU) was used to emulate the real computer, and the second processor (the IOP) became the interfacing I/O to the "environment." The "Environment" was a multitude of possibilities, including an Analog/Hybrid Simulation of the Martian atmospheric condition and flight dynamics with Analog/Hybrid models of the G&C hardware, digital models of the G&C hardware, or the actual G&C hardware. With these capabilities actual hardware performance could be compared to software models and be played against various "worst-case" flight conditions.

In addition to playing hardware controlled by Analog/Hybrid simulations against the flight software, the hardware could be calibrated, tested, and interfaced in a stand-alone condition. With such a configuration, software verification, system validation, and engineering performance testing were all performed within the bounds of the same lab, with closed-loop tests being able to be performed with or without hardware in the loop. Eventually, the lab was connected to a 4.8K-bit high-speed data link with the Viking Mission Control Center at JPL. With such an interface Mission Control could send test data to the lab, a test could be performed, and the results could be sent back to JPL for flight control analysis. All in all, the lab supported the project from inception through operations.

The hardware cost of the lab, excluding G&C Flight hardware was approximately $3 million. The analysis, flight software development, simulation software development, and test and diagnostic software development cost was approximately $7 million. For a $10 million cost, a highly reliable software system was produced for a $1 billion project, which was not an unreasonable percentage of the project cost. Today, the Lab and its development costs would be considerably less, due to the advancements in microprocessors, associated interfaces, and microprogramming skills.

3.4.5 Test Documentation

Documentation permeates all phases of the MPP company software life cycle. Testing is by no means left out of that situation. Typically, there are documents telling in advance how a test will be conducted, and what its results should be, and documents telling after the fact what actually happened. Examples of this approach, especially representative of software delivered to a corporate customer such as the government, are given below.

3.4.5.1 TEST FORMALISM (BCS)

The objectives of test formalism are to ensure that all tests planned are necessary and sufficient, and that their results conclusively prove that the developed capability is complete, correct, and operable. The test specifications identify all the activities required, such as preparing test procedures and test data cases, and determining expected results. Resource requirements for each activity are estimated, and specific task assignments are detailed; these become part of the Program Manager's overall project plan.

Formal test planning is employed to reduce the costs of testing; tests are deliberately planned to take advantage of "live" customer data where possible, and are sequenced to minimize resource expenditures for building test drivers. To ensure repeatability of tests, test procedures and data are placed in a controlled library.

Traditionally, test data are used in one set of tests and then modified to create conditions for the next set of tests. The errors discovered in the first set of tests are corrected and changes introduced into the software must then be retested to assure that the original problems were resolved. In traditional practice, however, recreating the original test conditions is often costly and difficult since the test data themselves have been modified. In the interests of being able to recreate tests (to verify that code changes actually fixed a problem previously encountered) in a cost-effective fashion, the test materials (e.g., test procedures and data) are now constructed and controlled in a more disciplined way.

The software developer identifies at Preliminary Design Review (PDR) the method (e.g., inspection, analysis, simulation, exercise, demonstration) by which each required functional capability will be tested. After securing customer concurrence at PDR on the test methods, the software developer produces a test plan, which identifies (or names) each test that will be conducted.

The developer then proceeds into test design. Given the test method, a design for each test is prepared, which identifies each exercise within the test, relates each exercise to the function(s) it will test, and describes the sequence of exercises. The test design also includes a definition of the type of data and materials required to support each exercise. The software developer also devises a detailed schedule for the construction of test procedures, data, and materials, and for the actual conduct of tests. This schedule is integrated with the Program Manager's construction plan. Test designs and the test schedule are presented at the Critical Design Review for customer concurrence, and to solicit customer participation in testing (e.g., providing test data, reviewing test results).

3.4.5.2   TEST DOCUMENTATION (SPERRY UNIVAC)

Test documentation consisted of test documentation for the Common Program and test documentation for the Navigation Program.

The following test documentation was prepared:

Program Performance Specification for the operating system program
Certification Test Plan

Certification Test Procedure

Certification Test Report

Informal documents for internal testing formed the basis for these formal documents.

3.4.6 Acceptance Test

No matter which direction the informal testing took (top-down or bottom-up), there follows a formal test process in which the soon-to-be user of the software product witnesses and, hopefully, approves the product in action.

This is the acceptance test. It is a demonstration that the product really can do what the customer wants it to do. Usually, it is a major milestone in software product development—acceptance transitions the software into the production and maintenance phase, while rejection turns the life cycle back for a new iteration through the earlier phases.

The test itself is usually defined in the test documentation, and is probably a repetition of some previously completed informal tests in a new setting. Thus, the acceptance test is the culmination of all the previous testing activities.

3.4.6.1 *ACCEPTANCE TESTING (BCS)*

The primary objectives of acceptance testing are to confirm that the delivered capability is ready for operational usage and to show that the software developer has satisfied its contractual obligation.

To prepare for this formal demonstration, the software developer identifies the customer's acceptance test requirements, and prepares and submits an acceptance test plan for customer concurrence. Typically, the formal demonstration plan will include tests for installability, operability, and useability. The test for installability involves actually installing the software on the customer's facility, using installation procedures and materials previously prepared. The test for operability is performed after the capability has been installed, to demonstrate that the software will execute and produce results on the customer's machine. The useability tests include the exercises submitted by the customer, and demonstrate that the software will perform functions which the customer feels are typical of its intended use.

To ensure that the formal on-site demonstration is an orderly process, the software developer typically conducts a "dress rehearsal" of the demonstration at its own facility, using the acceptance test procedure (and materials the developer has prepared) to perform the installability, operability, and useability tests, including the usability exercise devised by the customer. This dress rehearsal is conducted under conditions which are as close as practical to those that will exist at the customer's facility (i.e., the same procedures, materials, hardware configuration, and even individuals with the same skills as the intended users). The software developer packages the results of this dress rehearsal into a set of "control listings" which can then be used to verify that the results obtained during demonstration at the delivery site are as expected.

The dress rehearsal and formal demonstration activities are part of what has traditionally been called System Test. These new practices are employed to avoid what in the past has been a serious problem, both for the customer and the software developer; namely, that the user has not been provided at delivery all the materials needed for operational usage. This situation is damaging to the reputation of the developer, and expensive for the customer, who must bear the additional costs of completing the package for use in its intended environment.

The identification of acceptance test requirements and the preparation of a plan for acceptance testing are activities performed by the software developer prior to the Critical Design Review. At CDR, this plan (identifying tests for installability, operability, and useability) is presented to the customer for concurrence. After CDR, the developer prepares the test procedures and materials for all tests, and the test data to support the installability and operability tests. Later, the developer requests the test exercises which the customer has prepared, so that preparations for the formal demonstration can be completed.

3.5 MAINTENANCE

Maintenance, as is often the case in software development, was given short shrift in the MPP company reports.

Most of what was said about maintenance had to do with controlling the maintained software product. Configuration management, as will be seen later in the section on management practices, was an almost universal concern.

A few things were said about fault detection and fault tolerance, but the content was almost always that of using software to enable hardware fault response.

Almost nothing was said about the techniques for software maintenance. Of course, many of the design/implementation MPPs included maintainability as one of their goals. Maintenance, then, is primarily thought of by the companies as a "do-it-right-the-first-time, then control it" activity.

3.5.1 Change Control

In a huge software system, it is evident from the MPP reports, change control is essential. Perhaps it is the most frequently mentioned modern programming practice.

3.5.1.1 CHANGE CONTROL BOARD (CCB) (BCS)

A Change Control Board is typically constituted of persons (1) knowledgable of the customer's mission and the intended use of the computing system and its software, (2) representing the interests of the user, developer, operator (i.e., facility), and sponsor of the software, and (3) authorized to make commitments on behalf of the organizations they represent. The purpose is to ensure that due consideration is given to all aspects of a proposed change and, if the change is authorized, that all actions needed to implement it will be carried out.

In practice, a software Change Control Board is chaired either by the Program Manager or by a representative of the customer. The Board meets periodically, or as required to review and act on proposed changes. As a rule, the chairman will specify the required participation for each meeting as a function of the implications of the changes to be acted on.

The Change Control Board has two primary responsibilities: to act on change proposals, and to approve distribution of baselined systems. In the former responsibility, it reviews the problems reported and decides the proper disposition of the changes proposed for their resolution.

The problem review must consider a number of factors. The Board must determine whether the problem, if left unresolved, would critically affect the customer's ability to carry out its mission. If so, the Board must determine the priority of the problem relative to any others in this category. (For example, problem A may be crucial to an initial operational capability, whereas problem B may not become significant until a later time.) Also, they must consider the possible side effects of implementing a solution. (The users may already be familiar with the problem and have devised appropriate workarounds; correcting the problem may require substantial retraining, with the result that the solution could cost more than it is worth.) And there is the matter of available funding—whether the change is in-scope or out-of-scope—and whether (or when) the budget can pay for the needed work.

If a proposed change is deemed necessary (i.e., the problem is significant and of sufficiently high priority to warrant correction), the Board will authorize development to proceed. Specifically, they will assign action items to the various organizations that must participate in developing and testing the change, set a schedule for accomplishing the work, and specify funding authority for the effort.

It should be noted here that the Board must also consider possible interactions of changes. That is, two (or more) reported problems may require for their resolution that the same configuration item be changed, perhaps in different ways. Looking ahead to the time that corrections to both problems will be eligible for release, the Board will have to authorize a third change, one that combines the effects of the other two. By this means the Board retains its option to release one change or the other, or both.

After the change has been developed, tested, and submitted to the problem reporter(s) for verification, the Board can act on its second responsibility: approving the distribution of a new baseline. Ordinarily, this action will be taken only at predefined intervals (each 4 months, say) or at times in a customer's mission when release of a system update is appropriate. At these times there will usually be a backlog of verified changes. The Board must determine which of these it is appropriate to release to operational use (considering possible impact on established procedures and the need for retraining).

In practice, the Program Manager will submit, for consideration by the Board, the specifications of one or more baselines he or she feels are suitable combinations of capabilities and changes for release. Where more than one specification is submitted, the Program Manager will provide selection rationale for each. The Board will then act to approve release (of one), setting a schedule for implementation and buy-off and, usually, establishing a fall-back plan should the new package somehow prove inoperable. With the actions assigned by the Board, it is the Program Manager's responsibility to get the updated system into operational use.

3.5.1.2   SOFTWARE CHANGE REQUEST/IMPACT SUMMARY (MARTIN-MARIETTA)

Software change request procedures were well established at Martin-Marietta and JPL prior to the Viking Project. Only minor modifications were needed to adapt them to Viking's needs.

It is well known that hardware wears out with time. It is not too widely known that software wears out with change. Given sufficient change traffic a software system will eventually become inefficient and error-prone. Viking Lander and Orbiter software adapted from existing programs was in general less efficient than Viking software developed from scratch. Any software change process should attempt to protect software efficiency and flexibility when authorizing new requirements to be implemented. A useful technique for accomplishing this is to review and approve the method of implementation separate from the requirements request.

The Systems Engineering Directorate documented the change procedure for software in the Viking Lander Software Plan. It included both a Software Change Request (SCR) form (Figure 3.6) and an Impact Summary form

Page of	SOFTWARE CHANGE REQUEST	SCR/UCN number:

Title of change

Issue date

Change source | **Reference** | **Category**

Change is ☐ Recommended ☐ Mandatory | **Originator** | **Sect/unit** | **Phone**

Software system affected

Yes No	Yes No	Yes No	Yes No	Yes No
☐ ☐ GCSC	☐ ☐ STE	☐ ☐ FLT OPS	☐ ☐ DSN	☐ ☐ OCIS

Software program(s) affected: (name and identification number)

Description of change:

Reason for change:

Anticipated schedule	Date	Originating dept. approval:
Request to initial SCB review		
Request to final SCB review		Software change coordinator approval:
VCS/VCI input		
COD		Software control board approval
Change needed		
Change complete		

Figure 3.6 Software Change Request Form

(Figure 3.7). The primary reason for including the Impact Summary form was to maintain visibility and control over the growth of Flight software.

Any member of the Viking Flight Team could originate a hardware/software requirements change by preparing a change request and taking it to the Project Control Board. Typically, software changes were needed to support

Page of	SOFTWARE CHANGE REQUEST – IMPACT SUMMARY						SCR/UCN number:		
Title:						Date:			
Prepared by:	Sect/unit	Phone	Date	Reviewed by:		Sect/unit	Phone	Date	
Documents affected: (identification number and name)									
Memory sizing impacts: (core memory, drum, disk)									
Program Subsection Δ Words									
Computational timing impacts:									
Program Timing area Δ Time									
Rework impacts: (schedule, man-months, hardware, procedures, etc.)									
Software control board recommendations:									

Figure 3.7   Impact Summary Form

hardware changes. If the Board felt that the change request merited consideration, it was sent to the appropriate hardware and software groups for further assessment. The software group would then prepare a SCR to describe how the change could be implemented and an Impact Summary showing estimated delta impacts to computer resources. The change package was then taken to the Software Change Board (SCB) for review and approval/disapproval.

By contrast, the process used by Flight Operations, whether at MMC or at JPL, rarely allowed management to understand the impact that changes would have on computer loading or program performance. Since the programmers were aware of the constraints on program size and run times, they could merely create a new load module to perform a new task, thereby hiding the impact to the system. Flight Operations managers attempted to control the growth of the system by refusing to authorize any changes other than "make play." Therefore, the only changes that came before them were marked "make play," after which they were invariably approved. Fortunately, many of the changes were designed to improve program performance and reduce computer loading requirements.

That is not to say the Flight Operations change process did not work. In fact, it did. The overriding reason for this was that the as-built software system was extremely large compared to the change traffic that impacted it. If you add a cup of water to a half-filled quart bottle, you will notice the change immediately. If you add a gallon of water to a swimming pool, you won't see the change. In that sense it is unlikely that impact summaries would have served a useful purpose to Flight Operations management.

Typically, a Software Change Request and an Impact Summary could be filled out in an hour or two. Some of the larger changes may have taken from a day to a week to work out. However, this should be viewed as a zero-cost impact, since Viking did not have to add any unplanned personnel to handle the task. Furthermore, most of the work would have had to be done eventually since the vast majority of changes were necessary and were approved.

The time consumed in processing a change fluctuated considerably. No accurate labor estimate can be made for the average change. Most traffic was on the books for 1 to 2 months. Some went through the system in a day. One, which attempted to standardize Viking Orbiter and Lander file headers, took a year to finally resolve (and then no single standard was reached). Keeping the above in mind, the personnel support required to coordinate, respond, review, and approve an SCR is estimated at 1 to 2 weeks.

3.5.1.3 PROGRAM LIBRARY CONTROL (SDC)

The COBRA DANE project had established standards for the Program Library including definition of responsibilities for the System Librarian, for interacting with the library, for controlling change, and for quality assurance.

The standard practices for Program Library operations included the establishment of a System Librarian with specified responsibilities and the definition of rules for interacting with the library.

The System Librarian's responsibilities included:

Generating, updating, and maintaining Program Libraries

Maintaining a software problem status data base

Monitoring update decks submitted by programmers

Producing computer-generated software and software problem status reports

Interaction rules specified that:

1. The System Librarian shall have sole responsibility for maintaining the Program Library. Individual programmers are forbidden, under all circumstances, to directly modify a Test Bed Program Library.
2. The System Librarian shall establish a dummy deck (i.e., a program stub) for every anticipated program. The dummy deck shall include the program ident, an end, and such control information as program status and significant developmental due dates.
3. The programmers shall work from the Test Bed Program Library while coding, all code to be turned over to the System Librarian upon completion as an UPDATE deck.
4. Although the System Librarian may inspect program decks to ensure that programming practices are observed, it is the responsibility of the Chief Programmer to see that the practices are enforced.
5. The System Librarian will perform no quality assurance other than ensuring that control information is correct and that other modules are not inadvertently changed.
6. Once program checkout is complete, the program will be placed under control. That is, no changes may be made to a controlled program without specific authorization.
7. For programs under control:
   a. A list of all known errors and omissions will be kept.
   b. All code must be certified to have been tested (but not necessarily all paths).
   c. Test drivers, if necessary, shall be supplied by the programmer.
   d. The System Librarian will update control information (status, due dates), resequence the program, compile the code, and report errors noted by the compiler.
8. To modify controlled programs:
   a. Submitted changes must be identified by deck control numbers.
   b. Changes must be accompanied by short explanations of what the changes do.

    c. Any errors corrected must be identified.

    d. Relations to other previous or anticipated changes must be noted.

9. Programmers shall prepare properly commented and structured program modules and shall provide proper control cards for library operations.

Library control procedures defined a two-stage interaction: A Unit Test phase prior to placing a module under control and an Integration/Verification phase after the module was placed in the Program Library. Programs coded and unit-tested were submitted to the System Librarian, who gave them an "uncontrolled" status and identification and placed them in the Upfile. The modules were kept in Uncontrolled status in the Upfile until the CCB (Configuration Control Board) authorized inclusion in an Update cycle. While still "Uncontrolled," changes could be made to the module without authorization. Once the Update cycle was run, the problem shifted to "Controlled" status and all changes had to be authorized. Any problems uncovered were described in a Software Problem Report (SPR). The Chief Programmer responsible for the module assigned a control number and initially assessed the urgency of the problem. When completed, the change was added to the Upfile, but was not added to the library until CCB approval was given. The CCB reviewed problem status weekly. A status of "Open" was given to problems filed and being worked on or "Deferred" if filed, but awaiting manpower. A status of Resolved indicated that a solution had been found but was not yet verified and approved by the CCB. A status of "Closed" was assigned to rejected SPRs, to SPRs combined with others, and to those settled by allied changes or later redesign. Changes could remain in the Update file for some time pending CCB approval if their test status was doubtful or if they depended on other changes to be valid. The CCB could also adjust the priorities of changes assigned by the Chief Programmers. Problem Status Reports were limited to those SPRs Open, Deferred, Resolved, and Closed by the current update cycle. Build and modification status accounting was required.

However, as the pressure to produce became acute, the library lead time became very short. The decision on which modules were ready to load rested largely with the Chief Programmers, who comprised the bulk of the CCB. In a pressure situation, whenever there is a choice between risking delivery of a questionable product and the onus of missing a schedule, production-oriented people almost always opt for taking the risk. This undoubtedly happened in COBRA DANE, for programmers reported that programs that were not adequately unit-tested appeared in the System Master library from time to time.

The rule that programmers were to work out of the central library in developing and testing their programs was observed well until tests involving interactions with other program modules were underway. With more than one library update occurring weekly, which resulted in many corrections and changes being made to the master, plus some faulty programs being loaded, the programmers had to work in an unstable environment. That is, a feature checked out one day might not work the next due to changes in other modules. It was deemed less frustrating to work around known errors than to contend with unknown errors and the instability of a constantly changing environment. The programmers created for themselves copies of the library that they could control and maintain. In essence, instead of a single central library, each Chief Programmer Team had its own.

3.5.2   Maintenance Techniques

Little was presented by the MPP companies related to the technical process of maintenance. Only one company dealt with the subject, and then only in passing.

3.5.2.1   PROGRAM MAINTENANCE (SDC)

Programs were in a continual state of change, much of which required revision of data elements to accommodate new parameters or the adjustment of the value of constants. Much reprogramming had to be done to reflect data changes with little guarantee that all affected routines would be detected and maintained. Programs were apt to pass through the hands of a number of programmers (and contractors) for maintenance over the years. It was expected that the COMPOOL (Communications Pool, a concept similar to Fortran's COMMON) would simplify program maintenance by at least:

Substituting recompilation for reprogramming in cases of data modification or restructure

Facilitating the use of symbolic correctors for temporary (or minor semipermanent) program modifications or corrections

These expectations have been successfully realized. Program maintenance is facilitated by:

Using a COMPOOL-sensitive compiler

Well-defined interfaces

Numerous analytic aids

The COMPOOL-sensitive compiler permits updating all programs affected by a data change by redeclaring the data element once in the COMPOOL and recompiling the affected programs. Individual program changes, with attendant opportunity for error, are avoided.

The establishment of standard calling sequences and data interfaces tends to reduce the number of programming choices and make program interactions easier to understand and maintenance simpler. The simpler interfaces have reduced the number of errors.

The analytic aids include both symbolic and disassembled binary COMPOOL listings, listings of the characteristics of a compiled program, system and program set-use tables, environmental listings down to the table-item level, and core maps, if desired, for every dynamic load. These aids make it easy to locate data errors, avoid duplicate data and program names, and understand the structure and operation of the programs.

3.5.3 Fault Detection/Recovery

One application of software, particularly in real-time systems, is fault detection and recovery. This almost always refers to hardware components of the total system, and not to software components.

Because it does not affect the software process, it is really not relevant to discuss here. It is included for only two reasons:

1. It is a unique application of software, with some unique problems.

2. It is often unclear, in the context of discussing fault detection/recovery, that it does *not* apply to software. The reader of this book is put on notice to read carefully any discussion of fault processing that appears at first glance to apply to software.

3.5.3.1 *REAL-TIME AUTOMATIC CASUALTY RECOVERY (SPERRY UNIVAC)*

Real-time automatic casualty recovery processing was provided by software. The developed real-time operating system software provided this capability for third-generation digital equipment, including the AN/UYK-7 computer. This software provided the capability to detect and isolate certain hardware failures, and to automatically recover real-time system operation.

The following paragraphs describe real-time automatic casualty recovery employed on the studied programs, with emphasis placed on recovery from a computer module casualty.

The mission requirements for the central digital system included those that not only specified the normal real-time function of the computer system, but also required that the system be fault-tolerant, in that it:

1. Automatically recover from all first occurrences of singular computer hardware component and peripheral failures

2. Maintain navigation accuracy across computer memory reloads and reconfigurations

3. Recover real-time computer support in less than 4 seconds for any software reload and reconfiguration

4. Maintain system operation support for the mission duration, which was far in excess of the Mean Time Between Failure for any single hardware component

These fault-tolerance requirements were identified as a goal for the digital system design, production, integration, and testing on both the system hardware and operational software. The Navy required that the hardware be selected from third-generation equipment already proven acceptable to operational requirements. Therefore, these fault-tolerance requirements must have been met by the use of equipment not particularly designed for automatic casualty recovery.

Real-time automatic casualty recovery of a computer component failure was the responsibility of special-purpose executive software and processor firmware. This software and firmware included:

1. *On-line, confidence tests:* tests detecting malfunctions.

2. *Isolation tests:* tests run after detection of a suspect failure to identify the failure within a hardware unit.

3. *Error processing:* routines that control fault isolation and operational program recovery for abnormal CPU interrupts.

4. *Memory resume processing:* redundantly stored recovery routines to reconfigure/reinitiate software such that a unit generating the resume was suspended from use by the operational program.

5. *Recovery routines:* routines to provide for reloading of software as necessary, reinitialization of suspended program modules, and recording of the assumed fault condition for later manual maintenance testing and repair.

On-line CPU confidence tests were run periodically in the background mode during dual CPU operation. This program attempted to "halt" any malfunctioning CPU executing the test. This "halt" left the remaining CPU to detect, via software, that it was the only one operating and would then call upon the CPU recovery routine. Other confidence tests that would test memory addressing, control memory, and CPU arithmetic processing were directly executable as subroutines by any program module. For example, either resident control program module of the two application subsystem programs would run these tests before initiating operational use of the tested computer resource. If any test detected a malfunction, it identified the faulty hardware component and called for the appropriate recovery routine.

The key to fault detection was that any "abnormal" interrupt or test-detected malfunction was assumed to indicate a hardware failure. Through testing, the failure was isolated to a hardware component. By recovery, the failed component was deleted from operational use, software was reconfigured, and operation restarted. Finally, a notification was provided to be descriptive of the failure and new operating condition for later manual analysis and repair.

Four

Management Practices

The production of software is a change- and challenge-oriented task. The manager of software production must be prepared to deal with a changing and challenging world. And that puts the manager of industrial software development into a special kind of position. It is sometimes said: "I know how to manage. I can learn software." That may be true, but the manager who sets out to "learn software" must at the outset be geared for the fantastic rate of change of this not-even-middle-aged field.

Fred Brooks said it best in *The Mythical Man-Month:**

> Structuring an organization for change is much harder than designing a system for change. Each man must be assigned to jobs that broaden him, so that the whole force is technically flexible. On a large project the manager needs to keep two or three top programmers as a technical cavalry that can gallop to the rescue wherever the battle is thickest.
>
> Management structures also need to be changed as the system changes. This means that the boss must give a great deal of attention to keeping his managers and his technical people as interchangeable as their talents allow.
>
> The barriers are sociological, and they must be fought with constant vigilance. First, managers themselves often think of senior people as too valuable to use for actual programming. Next, management jobs carry higher prestige. To

---

* Brooks, *Mythical Man-Month Essays on Software Engineering,* © 1975, Addison-Wesley Publishing Company, Inc., Chapter 11, pp. 118–120. Reprinted with permission.

overcome this problem some laboratories, such as Bell Labs, abolish all job titles. Each professional employee is a member of the technical staff. Others, like IBM, maintain a dual ladder of advancement. . . .

Managers need to be sent to technical refresher courses, senior technical people to management training. Project objectives, progress, and management problems must be shared with the whole body of senior people.

Whenever talents permit, senior people must be kept technically and emotionally ready to manage groups or to delight in building programs with their own hands. Doing this surely is a lot of work; but it surely is worth it!

And there lies the challenge for the software manager in the 1980s. It is not enough to manage. It is necessary to manage change.

The MPP material that follows deals with the management of software in three principal areas: ways of achieving visibility and control of software development, ways of organizing for software development, and ways of dealing with the resources involved in software development. The MPP companies, convinced of the vital role management plays in this area, have a great deal to say in this chapter.

4.1 VISIBILITY AND CONTROL

High-technology fields, such as software implementation, are a special challenge to management. It is not enough to manage budget, schedule, and people, although that is important—the manager must also be responsible for the (often obscure!) software product itself.

In this domain, mechanisms for visibility and control are vital. The manager must be able to determine at any moment whether the software ship is veering in roughly the right direction, and if it is not, he or she must be able to grab the tiller and change the course.

Considerable attention was paid to these concerns in the MPP reports. In the large-project world—as most of these projects were—visibility and control are both enormously more important, and enormously more difficult. Ways of achieving visibility and control can be broken down into the categories of planning, reviews and audits, management of the technology itself, and configuration management. Elaboration of those areas, in the words of the MPP companies, follows.

4.1.1 Planning

The planning activity may become quite formal in the large-project world. It is fairly common practice for a "software development plan" to be required before any of the other phases of the life cycle begin.

(It is not unknown, however, for this report to be written after the fact, showing not "what we will do" but "what we should have done!") In the case that follows, the construction of the plan itself consumed a significant amount of project cost and schedule.

4.1.1.1   FLIGHT OPERATIONS SOFTWARE PLAN (MARTIN-MARIETTA)

The Flight Operations Software Plan was the controlling document for Viking operational software development. It established management roles and responsibilities, the software design and development process, and the methods by which management would control and implement the software system.

Development of an integrated software system requires that compatible standards, procedures, and processes be established to minimize interface problems, ambiguous terminology, and communications problems. This was particularly essential to Viking, since several agencies and contractors were responsible for various portions of the software system. A unified plan agreed upon by all parties that clearly and consistently outlined the method by which the software system would be developed and implemented was considered mandatory by the Viking Project. No consideration was given to permitting each operational software developer to manage their development processes independently.

The first step taken in developing a software system should be to write a software plan. The plan should define management roles and responsibilities, specify documentation requirements, establish milestones by which progress can be measured, define configuration management control, and describe the development process to be followed from initial design through system integration. Once a plan has been formalized and agreed upon, management should take appropriate steps to assure that it will be followed. If this is done, schedules and costs can be controlled effectively.

The Viking Project Flight Operations Plan was prepared by an Integration Contractor Software System Engineer. It was concurred upon by Flight Operations managers at the Viking Project Office, the Jet Propulsion Laboratory and Martin-Marietta Corporation. It was approved by the Viking Project Manager, at which time it became the controlling document for the development of the Viking Operational Software System.

Eight minor revisions were made to the plan using the Viking Integration Change Control system. The final revision was incorporated 2 years after its inception.

Copies of the plan were distributed to all Flight Team members, programmers, and engineers.

The plan consisted of five sections and three appendices, organized as follows:

1.0   Introduction
    1.1   Purpose
    1.2   Scope
    1.3   General
    1.4   Acronyms and Abbreviations
    1.5   Definitions of Terms

2.0   Applicable Documents
    2.1   General
    2.2   Reference Documents

3.0   Management of the Flight Operations Software System
    3.1   Introduction
    3.2   Software Subgroup
    3.3   Integration Contractor
    3.4   Design Responsibility

4.0   Software Design and Development Process
    4.1   Introduction
    4.2   Software Functional Description and Integrated Software Functional Design
    4.3   Functional Requirements Document
    4.4   Software Requirements Document
    4.5   Software Data Base Development and Definition
    4.6   General Design Document, Schedule, and Work Plan Development
    4.7   Program Development, Testing, and Release
    4.8   Test Plan Development
    4.9   Testing
    4.10 Project Software Delivery
    4.11 Software Maintenance and Support

5.0   Management Control Method
    5.1   General
    5.2   Milestones
    5.3   Documentation
    5.4   Requirements Definition
    5.5   Design Monitoring
    5.6   Review
    5.7   Approval of Detail Design
    5.8   Software Control Board
    5.9   Software Handling and Labeling
    5.10 Computer Program End Product
    5.11 Software Development Progress Monitoring
    5.12 Programming Guidelines and Conventions
    5.13 Flight Operations S/W Interfaces with On-Board S/W

Appendices

The plan established roles and responsibilities for all the Flight Team members who created or used a particular computer program. The primary responsibilities were to plan, coordinate, and monitor the development of the Operational Software System. Cognizant Engineers were made responsible for program requirements and testing, and their associated documentation. Cognizant Programmers were made responsible for program design and development and their associated documentation. Flight Team members were made responsible to support and review development of program and test requirements.

Documentation requirements were specified relative to organization, responsibility, review, concurrence, approval, and change control. This included program documents (functional, requirements, description, test, and user), the Integrated Software Functional Design, the Software Data Base Document, and the Lander/Orbiter Software Test Plan.

The principal management control methods employed were: establishment of milestones to support schedules; preparation of documentation, monitoring of design response to requirements; formal reviews of documentation, software end products, and test results; approval of detailed design; change management; software handling and labeling; release of software end products; software development progress monitoring; and establishment of programming guidelines and conventions.

The software development progress monitoring required the maintenance and publishing of detailed schedules, and the holding of weekly telecons to discuss progress and resolve problems. The strongest feature of the plan was that it specified the means by which it could be made to work. That was by creating roles and responsibilities for key persons which made them responsible for the development process. The overall plan was successful because it led to an orderly development of the software system.

The principal reasons that programs had to be modified and redelivered were due to new requirements, poor designs, program-to-program interface errors, and errors detected due to the lack of good test data. How the plan treated each of these subjects, and how it might have been improved to lessen the impact of these redeliveries, are discussed in the following paragraphs.

Requirements were written by a cognizant engineer and documented in a Software Requirements Document. The engineer was supported by a cognizant programmer concerning programming techniques, feasibility and I/O formats, and by a system engineer concerning interface requirements.

The plan should have required the reviewers to estimate the Requirements Document completeness in terms of potential new requirements. This would have had the effect of forewarning those programmers who were developing operational software in parallel and dependent on Flight hardware or software that significant change traffic was potential. As such, during the design phase, those programmers would have tended to model requirements as data rather than as part of the program structure, thereby giving up (in some cases) efficiency for flexibility.

Program designs were developed and documented in a General Design Document which was widely reviewed. The deficiency here is that the plan did not take into account the programmer's experience, the fact that the engineer and technical personnel usually will not understand the ramifications of the design relative to the computer system, or the fact that the system engineer had too many responsibilities to be able to give adequate thought to design ramifications. The plan should have specified a criteria for the selection of cognizant programmers, which it did not. It also might have required that one or two outside programmers attend the review to question the cognizant programmer as to how the design was to be implemented, and comment on what they thought of the approach.

The plan identified the Data Base Document as the place to document all interfaces, and required that each interface be tested by Software Integration. The wording here was perfectly adequate. However, the milestones section of the plan should have required interface testing to be conducted as an extension of Users Acceptance Testing, which would have been prior to placing the software under strict change control. This would have forced a top-down approach to integration, wherein programs would be delivered in subsystems, rather than by the "as available/as needed" approach actually used by integration. This would not have reduced the number of errors detected, but would have significantly reduced their impact on redeliveries.

Finally, the plan did not address the subject of test data, other than to mention that a cognizant engineer or programmer was responsible for its generation. The plan should have specified requirements for the development, review, documentation, and approval of test data, stressing the completeness of the data to assure thorough program testing.

The software plan was negotiated and written at a cost of 6 person-months. Beyond that it is difficult to describe it in quantitative terms, other than to state that it contained 99 pages. The true impact of the plan was that it established the basis for successfully developing a million-plus source card software system on schedule.

4.1.2 Reviews and Audits

All the planning in the world will be useless if the plans are not carried out. It is the purpose of reviews and audits to determine whether that is really happening.

The technology of reviews and audits was probably more common among the various MPP companies than any other.

4.1.2.1 MANAGEMENT PROCEDURES (BCS)

It is not sufficient that a person designated as Program Manager merely possess the responsibility and authority required by that position. The PM must also exercise them. That is, he or she must do something to ensure that plans are being followed and that the assignments made in accordance with these plans are being executed. Further, the Program Manager must determine that the results of those plans and assignments are sufficient to meet the goals of the program.

Software developers have traditionally viewed their product simply as a set of machine instructions; the user could then direct the computer to execute those instructions to process data and produce results appropriate to his or her needs. The user now sees that he or she needs not only the instructions, but a variety of other things as well. For example, the contract will now call for delivery of a document describing not only how to direct the computer to execute the software, but also how to prepare the data for processing and how to interpret the results. The contract may specify that the software be coded in a symbolic language that the customer has people trained to understand (in the event the customer should later wish to modify the capability). If several users are to employ the capability, the contract may require delivery of materials that will help train them to use it effectively. And there may be a stipulation that, for the contractual obligation to be considered satisfied, once the software has been installed in a designated computer facility, the developer must demonstrate that correct results are produced when data typical of the intended usage are processed.

Formal reviews are one means by which the customer can ensure that the developers are doing their work in a way that will satisfy the contractual obligations. Typically, there will be three such milestones: a Preliminary Design Review (PDR), a Critical Design Review (CDR), and an audit of the physical and functional configurations of end items (PCA/FCA). Usually, the contractor will convene a formal meeting for each milestone review.

The objective of the Preliminary Design Review is for the developers to present evidence, and obtain customer concurrence, that the requirements to be satisfied by the computing capability have been properly identified and, if formal demonstration at delivery is called for, that suitable means of demonstration have been devised. Working with representatives of the using community, the developer will determine what characteristics—functions, performance, interfaces, and environment—the computing capability must possess, and record these findings in a requirements definition document, supported by a prioritization of requirements according to criticality of need and anticipated benefit.

As further evidence that they understand the intended application, the developers may submit the equivalent of a User Guide, describing what the computing capability will look like to the intended user. This material can serve as a vehicle for showing that the software (in conjunction with the hardware) will in fact satisfy the requirements established for it. In preparing this document the developers will ordinarily have considered also what major software components will be required to implement the capability, and thus will be prepared to discuss how these components can be constructed and integrated. In addition, the developers will have analyzed the costs to satisfy user requirements versus their (criticality and benefit) priorities, and will present information that justifies their recommended design solution based on the contracted price.

Between PDR and the next formal milestone, the Critical Design Review, the developers complete their planning for the work that must be accomplished to meet their contractual obligations. At CDR, then, they should be able to present a list of the identifiable products that will result from their development efforts. They can state the purpose of each (specifically, how it will contribute to meeting the established requirements) and when it will be completed. Besides the software itself (usually identifiable to the level of individual subroutines), this configuration list will include such items as training materials, test procedures, demonstration data cases, installation aids, and operational procedures.

The CDR objective is for the developers to show that there are no critical omissions from this list or, more to the point, that they have planned for everything they will need to complete delivery of the required capability. Once satisfied of the adequacy of the developers' plans, the customer authorizes work to proceed.

The final formal milestone (excepting only delivery, demonstration, and acceptance) is the Physical Configuration Audit/Functional Configuration Audit. The PCA portion of this review consists of noting that all items reported at CDR as planned have actually been produced. Usually, this simply requires that someone has signed for each item listed, indicating that the item is physically in his or her possession or under his or her control. The FCA portion is similar, in that someone acknowledges having inspected or tested each item to determine that it satisfies the function for which it was developed.

The objective of PCA/FCA is for the developers to provide notice that they are, or shortly will be, ready to accomplish delivery and complete the contractual obligations. Further, the customer is given evidence (the signed-off configuration list) of this readiness and need not rely solely on the contractor's judgment for the customer to commit his own resources to accept the product and transition to operational usage.

The effect of imposing formal reviews such as those just described is to substantially restructure the activities of software development. As shown in Section 1.4, traditionally the development effort has consisted of a repetitive, overlapped cycle of designing, coding, and checking subroutines of a software component, followed by a process of integrating these components into an operational whole. The definition of requirements for the total capability was usually performed by the client prior to the start of development, and refined as the details of the design were resolved. The client performed the final testing of the software, largely to be sure that their algorithms had been implemented correctly and that they performed as expected.

It was often at this point in traditional projects that the client became aware that additional work needed to be accomplished if they were to make effective use of their new computing capability. Specifically, they needed training materials, operating and maintenance instructions, usage guidance, and similar materials. Since the software developers had completed their work and were available for reassignment, they constituted a ready, in-place means of getting these new tasks done. BCS now generally recognizes that these "additive" tasks are really part of the software development job, and plans for their accomplishment so that they will be completed at the same time the software itself is. As a result, the overall process—when structured by PDR, CDR, and PCA/FCA milestones—comes to look as shown in Figure 4.1.

The milestone reviews described are typical of military procurements. Similar, not necessarily identical, milestones may be employed in other types of software developments.

4.1.2.2 SOFTWARE DEVELOPMENT MANAGEMENT VISIBILITY (MARTIN-MARIETTA)

Progress was monitored by maintaining five levels of schedules based on a series of significant milestones. Program- and system-level requirements, design, interface, and test documents were reviewed and approved. Software change traffic was closely monitored, widely reviewed, and well documented. Weekly meetings were held to air problems. Open items lists were maintained. Software Systems Engineers were established to monitor the implementation of the software design, development, and testing and to assure that all interfaces, requirements, and schedules were correctly and completely satisfied.

Software systems are frequently delivered late, not documented accurately, contain unidentified risks, overrun costs, are unreliable, and fail to meet mission objectives. This was of particular concern to the Viking Project, since the launch windows were narrow and planetary operations had to be completed during a 4-month period between Mars Orbit Insertion and the conjunction of Mars with the sun. Therefore, not only was a well-defined software development cycle established, but a great deal of emphasis was placed on providing management with sufficient visibility to assure that the plan was carried out.

The need for management visibility into any development process is obviously necessary if costs and schedules are to be controlled. The use of

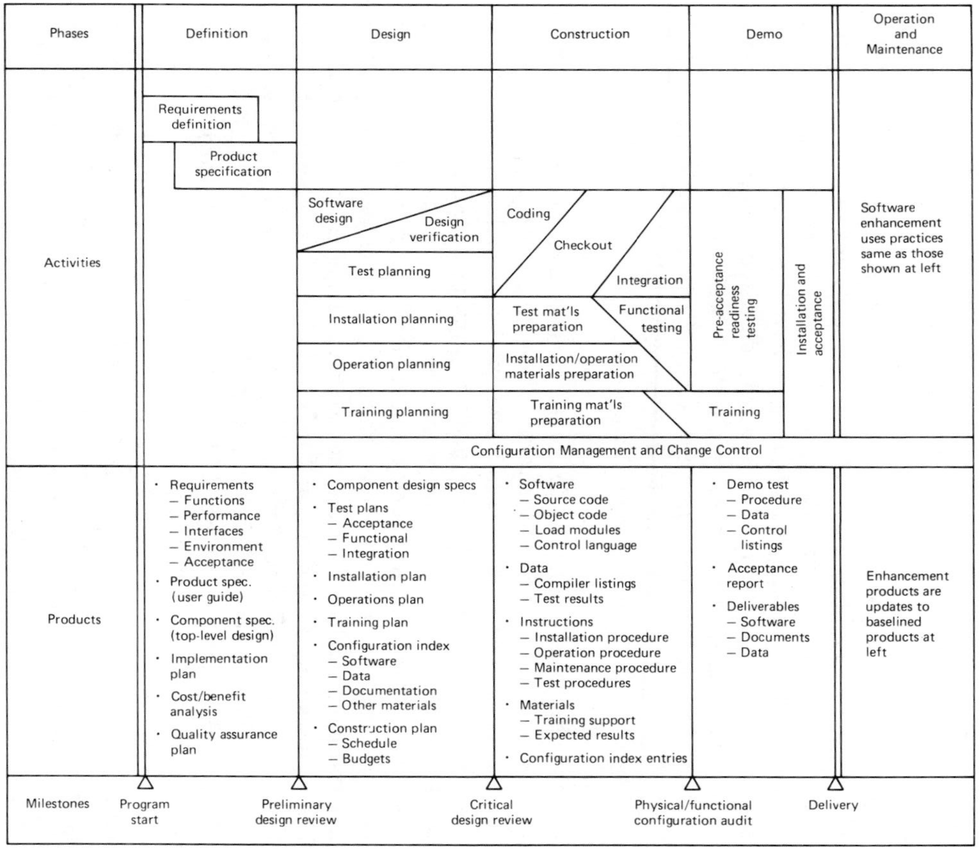

Programming Practices Life Cycle—Modern

	Definition	Design	Construction	Demo	Operation and Maintenance
Phases					
Activities	Requirements definition Product specification	Software design Design verification Test planning Installation planning Operation planning Training planning	Coding Checkout Integration Functional testing Test mat'ls preparation Installation/operation materials preparation Training mat'ls preparation	Pre-acceptance readiness testing Installation and acceptance Training	Software enhancement uses practices same as those shown at left

Products	• Requirements
	  – Functions
	  – Performance
	  – Interfaces
	  – Environment
	  – Acceptance
	• Product spec. (user guide)
	• Component spec. (top-level design)
	• Implementation plan
	• Cost/benefit analysis
	• Quality assurance plan
		• Component design specs
		• Test plans
		  – Acceptance
		  – Functional
		  – Integration
		  – Installation plan
		  – Operations plan
		• Training plan
		• Configuration index
		  – Software
		  – Data
		  – Documentation
		  – Other materials
		• Construction plan
		  – Schedule
		  – Budgets
			• Software
			  – Source code
			  – Object code
			  – Load modules
			  – Control language
			• Data
			  – Compiler listings
			  – Test results
			• Instructions
			  – Installation procedure
			  – Operation procedure
			  – Maintenance procedure
			  – Test procedures
			• Materials
			  – Training support
			  – Expected results
			• Configuration index entries
				• Demo test
				  – Procedure
				  – Data
				  – Control listings
				• Acceptance report
				• Deliverables
				  – Software
				  – Documents
				  – Data
					Enhancement products are updates to baselined products at left

Milestones	Program start Preliminary design review	Critical design review	Physical/functional configuration audit	Delivery	

Configuration Management and Change Control

Figure 4.1 Programming Practices Life Cycle—Modern

documentation, milestones, reviews, presentations, meetings, and change control are necessary but not sufficient to assure that a reliable system which meets the mission objectives will be delivered on schedule. Root-level program schedules and software systems engineers, used effectively, can significantly enhance management visibility.

The degree and type of visibility management had into the Mission Operations software development process varied as a function of the development phase.

During the software system definition phase, visibility was very good. The software plan and the integrated software functional description were carefully reviewed at the director and Project Manager levels. Milestones were well defined, and detailed schedules were developed. The quantity of software to be developed and the results of computer loading studies gave top management visibility to allocate resources on a realistic basis.

This was followed by the requirements phase, wherein management had the least visibility at any point in the development cycle. It was restricted to monitoring schedules and reviewing each Software Requirements Document prior to its release.

Visibility improved during the design and code phases. The Requirements Documents were under rigid change control, so that impacts caused by requirements changes were reflected in weekly updates to schedules. Reallocations in personnel assignments were made to prevent serious schedule slippages. Management could also monitor the development of the Software Data Base Document, which defined interfaces and the common data base, and the Lander/Orbiter Software Test Plan, which showed the system integration process and indicated the resources that would be required to carry it out.

The certification, conversion, and user acceptance test phases permitted the lander, orbiter, and integrating contractor software systems engineers to assess which requirements and constraints had been met in test and which had not. The latter were placed on waiver lists, the resolution of which could be monitored by all levels of management.

The software was now placed under rigid change control, and errors detected during the unit verification and system integration phases were made highly visible by means of a very efficient failure report system. Corrections to these errors could be controlled at the director level and implemented through an Integration Change Control Board.

During the spacecraft compatibility test phase, the failure report system was changed to a Viking Incident Surprise Anomaly system, which gave management the added visibility to assess the projected impact that software errors and requirements changes would have on specific operational phases.

Sixteen milestones were identified to provide management visibility into the development process of each program. In addition, the cognizant engineers for each program were required to keep weekly assessments of percentage completion during the design, code, debug, and programmer test periods.

If the percentage completion estimate was not compatible with the schedule for an ensuing milestone, the cognizant engineer was required to change the projected completion date shown for that milestone to an earlier or a later date, as appropriate. Three columns were maintained for the schedules of each milestone: planned, projected, and actual. Therefore, when a projected schedule date was changed, management could assess the impact it would have relative to the entire software system development process. Labor and resources were reallocated, as required, to maintain a consistent overall schedule.

The impact of software requirements changes was handled by scheduling phased deliveries for programs. Separate schedules were maintained for each phase of program delivery.

The milestones used to monitor Viking program software development progress were:

1. Release of Software Functional Description
2. Functional Requirements Document sign-off complete
3. Software Requirements Document available for review
4. Software Requirements Document sign-off complete
5. General Design Document sign-off complete
6. Program design and initial module code complete
7. Module testing complete
8. Certification Test/Users Acceptance Test Plan available for review
9. Certification Test/Users Acceptance Test Plan sign-off complete
10. Program development complete
11. Certification test complete
12. Acceptance test complete
13. Program delivery for integration
14. Unit Verification test complete
15. Program integration tests complete
16. Project software delivery

The program delivery milestone required delivery of all program documentation, including the Program Description Document and User's Guide, for which no earlier milestones existed. Therefore, projected and actual schedules were maintained for each deliverable item for this milestone.

Weekly meetings were held among upper management, team leaders, and the software systems engineers. Progress, problems, and conflicts were aired at these meetings. Open item lists were issued and monitored.

A Viking Integration Change/Viking Change Summary/Software Change Request system was established to monitor all changes to software requirements. A Project Change Board met weekly to discuss the status of all open change traffic. Representatives from each subsystem were required to attend these meetings to assure that any impact on their subsystem would be recognized and taken into proper account.

Lectures and presentations were held at frequent intervals wherein all programmers and engineers were briefed on management concerns, the development cycle, and items pertinent to the software system and its status.

Preliminary and critical design reviews were held on the integrated software functional description of the software system.

The integrating contractor software systems engineer was required to review and approve the results of all users acceptance tests and provide upper management with written reports of those reviews.

The Software Subworking Group, which was composed of the integration, lander, orbiter, and institutional software systems engineers, was required to issue monthly reports to upper management, stating work accomplished, problems encountered that required resolution, and work planned for the following month.

Changes to the common data base required formal written approval by upper management before they could be implemented.

An Integration Change Control Board met weekly to discuss the status of all programs scheduled to be delivered or redelivered to the software system. The board was chaired by a Project Manager and attended by the software systems engineers and representatives of software programs to be discussed. The need for and impact of changes or waivers were aired at these meetings.

Several documents played a key role in providing management visibility throughout the development stage. The Software Functional Descriptions and Integrated Software Functional Design permitted management to determine which programs were required, how they would interface, what utility programs would be needed, conduct computer program assignments and loading studies, hold a system critical design review, and determine integration requirements. The Lander/Orbiter Software Test Plan proved to be an extremely useful tool to the project. It allowed management to schedule labor and resources, and asssured them that interprogram communications would be thoroughly tested. The Software Data Base Document gave management a single source by which they could be assured that all program interfaces and the common data base would be visible and controlled. This provided the visibility by which management could determine if a change to one program would in any way affect the operation of any other program in the system.

The JPL Mission Build process allowed management to know what software was in the system at all times.

The visibility techniques management employed during the software development process were sufficient to permit a reliable software system that met all mission objectives to be delivered on schedule. The use of documentation, milestones, reviews, presentations, meetings, and change control were standard management visibility tools. The concepts of the root-level schedules and the software systems engineers roles were innovative, and worked well.

A great deal of expense and effort could have been saved had management demanded greater visibility early in the development process. Programmer selection was essentially ignored, assignments being made on an availability basis rather than by experience and computer understanding. Critical reviews were not held to challenge requirements, especially where they affected design. Nor were critical reviews held to challenge the program designs themselves. As such, management control over the design and code phase was limited to monitoring schedules, so that design inadequacies did not become visible to the software systems engineers and systems programmers until the acceptance testing and integration phase. Costly modifications and work-arounds were then required to force the program designs to meet mission timelines and computer constraint requirements. This occurred with about one-third of the programs.

Ten percent of the programming and engineering labor effort was consumed in activities directly related to providing management visibility. The primary efforts of the software system engineers and their staffs were devoted to directing and monitoring the development process and maintaining software schedules, thereby providing management with central sources by which progress and status could be measured. These staffs varied in size during the development stage.

The labor and computer resources that might have been saved had proper attention been paid to programmer selection and critiquing requirements and designs is estimated to be in excess of 3 person-years.

4.1.2.3   TECHNICAL AND MANAGEMENT AUDITS (MARTIN-MARIETTA)

The Viking Project Office formed a group of NASA software managers to review the Viking software development approach and design. Following this, three independent audits were performed by software experts from around the country.

The successful development of any major software system is a considerable task for experienced professionals. Hardly anyone had ever built a system as large as required to support the Viking Mission. Therefore, the desire to have experienced software development managers review and comment on the Viking approach manifested itself in the Viking manager's minds early in the program. During the coding phase of development, managers knew that their visibility into the process would be limited. Technical audits offered them the opportunity to assess progress, thereby enhancing the chances for schedules to be met.

Management is typically reluctant to shift significant amounts of resources to accommodate obviously well intentioned and reasoned recommendations originating from within their working ranks. It is difficult for them to weed out the good ideas from those that are necessary. By bringing in experienced experts from around the country to audit the development process, management can obtain a basis for making such decisions. Equally important is the fact that such audits are likely to produce recommendations concerning areas or concepts that have been overlooked.

In 1971, the Viking Project manager formed the previously mentioned committee of software managers from Johnson Space Center, Goddard Space Flight Center, Ames Research Laboratory, Marshall Space Flight Center, and NASA headquarters. The purpose of this committee was to attend monthly Viking management status reviews and make comments, assessments, and recommendations to the Project manager relative to the Viking approach. The committee stayed in existence for approximately 2 years, monitoring progress up to and including the critical design reviews for Flight and Mission Operations software.

In late 1973, three software managers with different backgrounds were brought in to perform a semiindependent audit of the software development process. This included the head of Systems Data Corporation, an IBM executive, and a member of a software consultant firm.

Shortly thereafter, the Viking Project Office conducted an independent audit of Flight software. For this purpose they brought in experts from both industry and government.

Finally, the Viking Project Office arranged for a group of experts to attend a presentation of the Flight and Mission Operations software development process late in 1974.

In addition to these outside audits, managers held monthly meetings to review progress. This included audits of the major problem areas encountered by the Software System Engineers.

During the tenure of the committee, its members would sit in and passively monitor the proceedings of the Flight Operations Working Group, which consisted of the managers responsible for the software development. In addition, the committee attended the preliminary and critical design reviews for both Flight and Mission Operations software.

An early finding of the committee was that the multiagency Viking managers could not resolve problems among themselves. Month after month the same problems remained unresolved. Furthermore, too many of the problems were technical in nature. One major recommendation made by the committee at this time was that management should concern itself primarily with handling schedules and resources and make the system engineers responsible for the design and development process. In that way, management would only be required to resolve those problems that the system engineers could not resolve, which should greatly reduce their task. A second recommendation was that the multiagency Viking Flight Team be organized immediately in order to develop a working rapport long before it was needed to support the mission. Both recommendations were adopted.

The committee offered numerous suggestions to help resolve interagency problems, influenced the Integrated Software Functional Design, recommended that schedules be carried to several levels of detail (five were adopted by Viking), and pointed out the need for a computer loading study that covered the entire planetary operations phase on a day-by-day basis.

The semiindependent audit in late 1973 led to the decision to reallocate resources to accommodate end-to-end tests for the cruise, descent, and planetary operations of the mission. The auditors flatly told management that there was no way to know whether or not the system would work without such tests, and none had been scheduled. The idea was not new; it had been recommended earlier by software developers. The fact that it was repeated by an accredited outside source provided the straw that broke the camel's back in this area.

The independent auditors brought in to review Flight software saw the need for the Systems Engineering director to place software on an equal basis with hardware.

The spring 1974 audit might have been more fruitful had it occurred a year earlier. It recommended that individual program requirements be constantly reviewed to try and weed out any unnecessary ones. Most of the software had been developed by that time, so it was impractical to make extensive use of the recommendation. Two programs were reviewed with only minor success. Auditors expressed concern over the interagency integration task, but could offer no constructive comments on the subject. Finally, they stated that they believed the programmer, rather than the engineer, knows best how to test a piece of software. Martin-Marietta did not accept this recommendation, since they were concerned primarily with the function the software was to perform, and the engineer knew the functions. They required that the programmers deliver working software to the engineer, who was then required to acceptance-test it.

The final audit came toward the end of the software development process. For that reason it amounted to more of a review than an audit. About all it was able to comment on was that a sound approach had been taken and no major item had been overlooked.

The managers frequently required that the system engineers make semiformal presentations both before them and before the cognizant engineers and programmers. The intent of these presentations effectively made them status and design audits by management. The audience would comment, criticize, and raise questions following each presentation. Action items would be assigned at these presentations to resolve problems.

During the coding phase of operational software programs, the director would notify the cognizant engineer of a program that an audit of the program would be held in 3 days before the Mission Director. At these audits the engineer had to demonstrate what had been accomplished, what remained to be done, and how the schedule would be met. On a few occasions, when the

Mission Director was in Denver, the engineers were given only a 2- or 3-hour notice of such an audit. On some occasions the directors were not satisfied that the schedules supported the work to be done, based either on what had been accomplished or on the amount of new requirements facing the engineer. In these instances the engineer was required to maintain a schedule, which broke the work assignments down to a daily basis over a period of about a month.

The audits were extremely valuable to the Viking Project and contributed directly to the success of the mission. Technical interagency software problems were resolved more easily when the responsibility for handling them was shifted from the managers to the system engineers.

The establishment of the Viking Flight Team early proved to be a sound idea. The members of the team quickly realized that their responsibilities lay within the directorate and group to which they had been assigned even when the group leader or director was from a different agency. By the time the team was needed, responsibilities were well established and understood, which resulted in smooth operations during the mission and quick response to anomalies. The implementation of five levels of schedules played a major role in developing the system on schedule.

The computer loading analysis study led to the realization that the Viking Project would have to install a third 1108 computer at JPL to meet mission timelines. The computer was installed, and subsequent events proved that it was needed.

The scheduling of end-to-end tests for the Flight and Mission Operations software systems may have made the difference between mission success and mission failure. Although management was not convinced that the tests, which were an unscheduled and expensive resource drain, would do more than give them a warm feeling that the system would work, they nevertheless accepted the auditor's recommendation. When the tests were finally conducted, they revealed literally hundreds of incompatibilities, errors, and misunderstandings. Had the audit not been made, the tests would not have been conducted. In that event the problems most likely would not have surfaced until planetary operations, at which time they would have been extremely serious.

By auditing software at the program level, the director was able to reallocate resources to maintain schedules when it was evident that an engineer had underestimated the scope of a task. Such discoveries were made at these audits.

The value of audits by outsiders is that they will feel compelled to find something that you are doing wrong. Therefore, if you conduct such an audit and fail to get any recommendations of significance, the probability that you are on the right track and doing a good job is extremely high.

The direct costs of the outside audits was equivalent to hiring consultants for a few days. The indirect costs of the audits was the time spent to prepare for and conduct them. Preparation was generally easy, because the speakers had merely to discuss their accomplishments, plans, and problems, all of which were very familiar. On some occasions the speakers had to spend 2 or 3 days preparing slides and viewgraphs. Since relatively few audits were held, the total time consumed by them could not have exceeded more than a few person-months.

4.1.2.4   *FORMAL INSPECTION OF DOCUMENTATION AND CODE (TRW)*

These inspections constitute a formal, efficient, and economical method for conducting independent and unbiased assessment of the quality of software documentation and code. They include formal inspection techniques, such as peer-group critiques and walkthroughs, quality assurance reviews and audits, and design reviews. They are discussed from a technical point of view in Section 3.4.1.2.

Independent quality assurance audits are conducted at key intervals during the development and evaluation of software through requirements definition, design, coding, testing, and operation. These quality assurance audits are:

1. *System Requirements Audit:* to determine whether planned testing will ensure satisfaction of requirements and to make sure that requirements are traceable to the next-higher-level specification.

2. *Product Specification Audit:* to determine whether product specifications conform to established standards of format, content, completeness, and level of detail.

3. *Interface Verification Audit:* to examine interface requirements, interface design, and program specifications to identify and resolve interface problems.

4. *Product Specification (Engineering Design Document) Audit:* to examine detailed design specifications and the data base definition to ensure that all routine input/output is properly defined, the design data are current, the structure of flow diagrams conforms with project standards, and explicit traceability exists to higher-level specifications.

5. *Unit Development Folder (UDF) and Code Audit:* to incrementally (a) audit UDFs as they are prepared in verifying that changes to unit requirements, functional design description, and flowchart and interface definitions are current; (b) manually (and with the automated Code Auditor) scan the unit source code for compliance with programming standards; and (c) measure thoroughness of unit level testing and identify, if necessary, additional testing requirements.

6. *Preturnover Audit:* to assess the adequacy of development testing of

products prior to their internal delivery to the independent test group through examination of the products and test results for (a) actual versus expected output; (b) completeness, content, organization and approval status of UDFs; (c) compliance with programming standards; (d) testing thoroughness (e.g., execution of every branch condition); and (e) assurance that all reported discrepancies have been corrected and tested.

7. *Testing Audit:* to supplement formal testing done by the independent test group to ensure that (a) established configuration management procedures are followed, (b) test specifications are maintained current, (c) test reports are properly prepared, (d) test procedures explicitly define tests to be conducted and test results comply with acceptance criteria in the test procedure, and (e) test data package contents are complete and comply with approved formats.

4.1.2.5 MANAGEMENT REPORTING TOOLS (SPERRY UNIVAC)

Cost/Schedule Technical Achievement Reporting System (CSTAR)

CSTAR provides a formal means for planning, scheduling, budgeting, measuring progress, reporting, and controlling a program or a proposal. CSTAR uses a basic approach of definition, schedule, budget, and uses budget dollars as a standard unit of measurement to establish progress. This process is followed for all levels of program effort such as projects, organizations, Work Breakdown Structure elements, cost accounts, or work packages.

CSTAR consists of procedures, charts, documents, and a group of computer programs which not only integrate the planning data, budget tables, and rate and factor tables with actual costs, but also generate computerized output reports.

Program Management Information System (PROMIS)

This support program provides Program Management with a formal planning, budgeting, progress measuring, reporting, and controlling capability regarding a specific program. PROMIS uses the Work Breakdown Structure (WBS) as a tool and concept in maintaining product identification while transmitting information and acquiring data. WBS is the same concept used in the larger and more complex CSTAR system. In fact, PROMIS can be considered a major subset of CSTAR which gives many of CSTAR's advantages. It provides sufficient visibility to monitor program progress in scheduling and cost, while reducing materially the high costs of implementation and maintenance inherent in the larger system.

Like CSTAR, PROMIS consists of procedures, charts, a group of computer programs that integrate the planning data, budget tables, etc., with actual costs and generates computerized output reports.

Management Responsibility Reporting (MRR)

This support program collects, maintains, and reports direct costs that are incurred on efforts. These direct costs are listed by individual responsibility. These periodic management reports are generated for:

Program level
Project level
Control task level
Control task summary
Project detail task

The different level reports are valuable to individuals responsible for costs at the program, project, and control task levels respectively.

Data for generating the reports are available from a direct cost master file of current and cumulative costs. Current open commitments and authorized budget figures are also available for reference.

4.1.3   Management of Technology

When managers are dealing with deeply technical aspects of a software product, they need all the help they can get. The tools and techniques that follow vary considerably from company to company, but all address that generic problem.

4.1.3.1   THREADS (CSC)

The THREADS methodology is discussed in Section 3.1.4.2. The following review material is included to assist in the understanding of the next section, on threads management.

A thread represents a sequence of events that contributes to the satisfaction of a specific system function. This sequence is an internal process and may be defined at any functional level. A single thread demonstrates a discrete series of operational activities from stimulus to response.

In threading the system design, the following is accomplished for each operational process:

1. Isolate inputs available (stimuli).
2. Identify outputs to be produced (response).
3. Determine processing required to produce each output from the inputs (processes).

4. Define the sequential processing path from each stimulus to its response (thread).

A complete set of threads defines all processing required to satisfy all system functional requirements. Thus, threading a system design is a process employing a discipline that is external to the system to verify design consistency relative to requirements. THREADS is a uniquely functional approach to design verification that may be used effectively in other roles, such as test plan development and, in conjunction with the Threads Management System (TMS), management control.

4.1.3.2   THREADS MANAGEMENT SYSTEM (CSC)

The Threads Management System (TMS) serves to automate and simplify the process of creating, updating, interrogating, and reporting Threads information to management. The standard TMS output reports include build status, thread status, thread descriptions, threads schedule, and build summary. Examples of these reports are shown as Figures 4.2 through 4.6.

The TMS could be implemented at any phase of the development cycle. The maximum utilization of this tool is realized by implementing it when the

THREAD MANAGEMENT SYSTEM RETRIEVAL

LEVEL: SUBSYSTEM
RUN DATE: 11/15/72

NAME	DESCRIPTION	REFERENCE	SUBSYSTEM ELEMENTS			
CM01	ATC	3.3.2.2.1.2	CDI	CMS	CSN	
CM02	TD	3.3.2.2.1.2	CDI	CMS	CSS	
CM03	MSS/EC	3.3.2.2.1.2	CDI	CMS	CED	
CM04	SS	3.3.2.2.1.2	CDI	CMS	CTS	
CM05	DT	3.3.2.2.1.2	CDI	CMS	CDT	
CM06	IDLE	3.3.2.2.1.2	CDI	CMS	CIS	
TC07	HOLD CLOCK	3.3.6.2.1.1A1	CDI	CED		
TD08	RUN CLOCK	3.3.6.2.1.1A1	CDI	CED		
TD09	SET CLOCK	3.3.6.2.1.1A1	CDI	CED		
TD10	CRT PRINT	3.3.6.2.1.1A1	CDI	CED	CFX	
TD11	SYS STATE PRINT	3.3.6.2.1.1A1	CDI	CED	CFX	
TD12	ALL SIMUL START	3.3.6.2.1.1A1	CDI	CED	CWI	CMI
TD13	ALL SIMUL STOP	3.3.6.2.1.1A1	CDI	CED	CWI	CMI
TD14	RECORD START	3.3.6.2.1.1A1	CDI	CED	CFX	CWI	CMI
TD15	RECORD STOP	3.3.6.2.1.1A1	CDI	CED	CFX	CWI	CMI
TD16	LOCAL SE8	3.3.6.2.1.1A1	CDI	CED		
AV17	AVAIL STATES	3.3.6.2.1.1A1	CDI	CED	CAS	
AV18	DISPLAY	3.3.6.2.1.1A1	CDI	CAS	CDS	

Figure 4.2   Threads Management System Retrieval Report. This report depicts selected data concerning all the threads at a designated level.

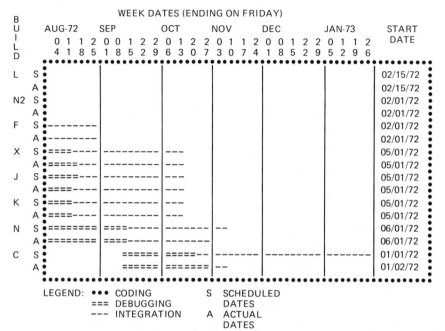

Figure 4.3 Thread Schedule Report. The thread schedule report indicates the status of each build. Both scheduled and actual activities for each development phase are shown. Also included are the build start dates and a legend to assist the reader in understanding the chart.

system is threaded or immediately following detailed system design. The TMS can be an effective tool in all phases of the program life cycle once threads are defined if all capabilities of it are exercised. Project planning, configuration control, monitoring, testing, and verification/validation are all supported by threads. The TMS is also applicable after the development cycle as a configuration management and change impact assessment tool during the maintenance phase.

4.1.3.3 PROGRAM AND DATA BASE INTERFACE MANAGEMENT (MARTIN-MARIETTA)

A common data base was used by all Viking Lander operational programs to access critical tables and constants, such as flight computer turn on times, lander coordinates, and length of a Martian day. Intercomputer file transfer

SUBSYSTEM LEVEL THREAD(S)

PROJECT C, C

SUBFUNCTION	: SPECIAL THREAT SETUP	BUILD	: J
THREAD NAME	: C01-001	STATUS	: 0
		DATE LAST UPDATE	: 09/27

SPEC. PARAGRAPH NOS. 3.3.2.1.2.1A1

STIMULUS : SPCL THR INFO SAB   RESPONSE :   SFCL THT INFO DIS-
                                                   PLAY ON ATC NDS CRT

```
              CDI                          CSN
      ..............              ..............
      .            .              .            .
......:  DISPLAY   :..............:   ATC      :..........
      :  INTERFACE :              :   NDS      :
      :            :              :            :
      :        01  :              :        02  :
      ..............              ..............
```

Figure 4.4   Subsystem-Level Thread Report. The report presents a graphic representation of the subsystem-level threads. The boxes represent the subsystem elements and the processing required within each element. The threads that require more than two boxes would display the additional boxes directly below the two shown.

software permitted user files to be readily available on any computer system, transparent to the users.

Viking Lander operational software was required to be developed from scratch rather than by modifying an existing system. Mission planning, sequence generation, flight path analysis, and spacecraft health and science analysis programs used significant amounts of common tables and constants. These programs operated on two different computer sets and required large amounts of interface data to function correctly. Using tape drives to transfer data between programs during operations would have compromised mission timelines. Coordination of large amounts of data separately used by programs is subject to considerable human error. For these reasons intercomputer transfer and common data base file management software was developed and used by these programs.

It was realized early that the Viking Project would have some unique data base problems. One of the data bases identified as being desirable was the Flight Operations Data Base (the data used and generated by the Flight Operations software). One segment of this data base was named the Common Data Base. This data base would contain data items used by more than one program. The types of data eligible for admission to this data base were tables and constants whose values were not expected to change more than a few times during the mission. This data base was meant to replace data normally compiled within the program as DATA statements or as data input into the program without change each time the program was executed. Having a system of programs operating from a common data base offered many attractive features. It forced consistency of data among the various application programs. That is, all programs used identical values for tables and constants, such as epochs and clock drift tables. A common data base allowed updating of constants to take place simultaneously among all using programs. Data base management procedures allowed control and documentation of values used, and change history information. Operational responsibility for data availability resided with a central data base manager rather than being divided among the operational groups.

Another segment of the Viking data base was the management of inter-

PROJECT C, C		SUBSYSTEM LEVEL THREAD STATUS				PAGE 001	
DATE 12/22/72		FOR BUILD C					
TIME 17:00:00							

THREAD NAME	SUBSYSTEM ELEMENT	DATE OF LAST STATUS CHANGE	DESIGN	CODE	DEBUG	INTE-GRATE
C01–093	CDI	12/04		X		
	CSL	12/04		X		
C90–093	CDI	12/04	X			
	CSL	12/04	X			
C03–025	CDI	9/27	X			
	CSN	9/27	X			
	COS	9/27	X			
C01–378	CDI	9/27			X	
	COS	9/27			X	
	CRI	9/27			X	
	CTC	9/27			X	
E99–007	CCX	04/23				X
	DOX	04/23				X
	COS	04/23				X

Figure 4.5   Subsystem-Level Thread Status Report. The subsystem-level thread status report gives detailed information concerning each individual thread. The report is produced for any designed build. It lists each thread by name and shows the subsystem elements involved in each thread. The date indicates when the TMS data base was last updated for this thread information. The status is shown for each development phase and by subsystem element. It refers to that portion of the element that pertains to the thread shown. In the example, the CDI subsystem element has completed code for the first thread, but has only completed design for the second, and so on.

178   *Four   Management Practices*

PROJECT C, C   SUBSYSTEM LEVEL BUILD STATUS   PAGE 001
DATE 12/22/72
TIME 17:00:00

BUILD	THREADS	DESIGNED	CODED	DEBUG	INTE-GRATED	BUILD STATUS	COMPLETION DATE SCHDL.	ACTUAL
A	10	100%	100%	100%	100%	100%	11/01/71	11/01/72
B	26	100%	100%	100%	100%	100%	1/03/72	1/03/72
D	25	100%	100%	100%	100%	100%	1/14/72	2/01/72
E	23	100%	100%	100%	100%	100%	2/01/72	2/01/72
G	5	100%	100%	100%	100%	100%	2/15/72	2/15/72
H	71	100%	100%	100%	100%	100%	4/04/72	4/04/72
M1	11	100%	100%	100%	100%	100%	5/01/72	5/01/72
PART A SUMMARY	171	100%	100%	100%	100%	100%	6/01/72	6/06/72
L	6	100%	100%	100%	100%	100%	6/01/72	6/06/72
M2	36	100%	100%	100%	100%	100%	7/03/72	7/03/72
F	102	100%	100%	100%	100%	100%	9/01/72	8/24/72
J	66	100%	100%	100%	100%	100%	10/16/72	10/13/72
I	7	100%	100%	100%	100%	100%	10/15/72	10/13/72
K	17	100%	100%	100%	100%	100%	10/15/72	10/13/72
N	42	100%	100%	100%	100%	100%	11/01/72	11/01/72
PART B SUMMARY	276	100%	100%	100%	100%	100%	11/16/72	11/18/72
PART A, B SUMMARY	417	100%	100%	100%	100%	100%	3/15/73	3/15/73

Figure 4.6 Subsystem-Level Build Status Report. This report is designed to provide an overview of the build status. It includes the build name, the number of threads that are identified in each build, and the percentage of completion for each development phase (design, code, debug, and integrate). Each thread has either completed or not completed a particular phase. The overall build status is derived by the use of an algorithm that gives "weights" to each of the development phases. This is necessary since the coding of a thread requires less effort than the debugging phase. A comparison of the scheduled and actual build completion dates will give an indication of the project status. The sample shows a Part A and Part B summary. Each part is a logical collection of builds and represents a significant milestone. The analysis of a particular system would determine whether or not this particular feature is applicable.

program data files. Viking file management was defined to be an automated system that would checkpoint files and transfer files between machines. The checkpointing activity would provide file security and load/off-load on-line mass storage space. File transferral was complicated by the usage of IBM 360 and Univac 1108 computers for the Viking Flight Operation Software System. Programs on one system required files created on the other.

Early attempts at defining methods and operation of a general file checkpoint system were frustrated by lack of agreement among the affected user groups and lack of definition of system usage. As a result, several different methods of checkpointing were eventually used for Viking. The file transfer scheme used seven-track magnetic tape as a universal transfer medium. An electrical interface was established between one computer pair at a time (IBM–Univac).

The file transfer software concept fluctuated wildly during the early systems integration time period. The detailed techniques for translation and the extensive input/output requirements necessitate thorough familiarization with the machines and operating systems. This was initially a problem since the early software development was done in Denver without easy access to the machines that were to use the system. Since file manipulation is dependent on file structure, either great flexibility is required or total definition of file structure must be available. Total definition is impossible until the file generating software is totally defined. For Viking the file transfer algorithms were designed to maximize flexibility and generalize. The design goal was to have greater capacity than required at the time, but excess capacity was continually used up as the systems integration activities progressed. The decision to perform data translation by the file transfer software was contested early in the preliminary design. The alternatives are to design the data files in such a way that translation requirements are reduced (i.e., transfer files in external BCD); to have the programs that use transferred files embed translation within their own structure; or to have specific file translators attached as preprocessors to the using programs.

The Common Data Base on the IBM 360 system used for Viking was based on ISAM (Indexed Sequential Access Method). Subroutines were written which allowed read-only access of data base records by name. The data base could be read directly or sequentially: the subroutines were linked into the application programs. The using programs and the data base were totally insulated from each other. Several programs were written to permit the basic necessary management functions for data base operations. These functions were: load, modify, list, and reorganization. An access method similar to ISAM was developed for the Univac 1108.

There exist lessons to be learned from development and usage of these data base and file transfer schemes. Since the data base is essential to proper development of application programs, data base software and data base techniques should be *thoroughly* debugged and tested before the application program development is started. This was done in parallel with application program development for Viking and resulted in an initial lack of confidence by the application programmers. The confidence gap manifested itself in somewhat poor usage of data base concepts and in invariably assuming it to be responsible for application software anomalies. Gathering the data for insertion into the data base is a monstrous task and requires great cooperation from the suppliers. Data quality and responsibility should be assigned to cognizant groups of people for ongoing maintenance and control. However, all responsibility for manipulation of the physical data base should reside within a single authority.

Changes to data during operations on a common data base must be performed with great care so that all using groups know ahead of time the details of the change. In general, agreement of all using groups should be obtained before changes are done.

The Viking data base access method software and data base utility software required about 4 person-months of programming and checkout effort for both the IBM and Univac systems. The file transfer software development cost was about 1 person-year.

The use of a Common Data Base had a negative impact during development, test, and training. Approximately 1 person-month was lost by users believing software errors were the cause of test repeatability failures, whereas the actual causes were ultimately traced to changes to the common data base. No impact of this type was observed during operations.

4.1.3.4 SOFTWARE DATA BASE DOCUMENT (MARTIN-MARIETTA)

The Software Data Base Document (SDBD) provided central visibility to the Software Systems Engineers, Cognizant Engineers, and Cognizant Programmers of the use of tables, buffers, files, and constants. It provided the means of identifying common data and implementing a common data base internal to the operational software system. After development the SDBD provided centralized documentation and control of all common data and interface files used by the Viking Flight Team.

A considerable amount of data was common to more than one Viking operational program. These data consisted of such items as computer turn-on times, one-way light timetables, Martian parameters, descent parameters, lander coordinates, and antenna-pointing parameters. Coordination of data that would be subject to little or no change was necessary to assure the integrity of the software system. In addition, files interfacing stand-alone software modules required centralized visibility to control their structure and provide a means of assessing system-level impacts caused by changes in individual software modules.

The Flight Operations Software Plan specified that all tables, buffers, files, and constants used by the Flight Operations Software System would be compiled into a single document, entitled the Software Data Base Document. The responsibility for coordinating and maintaining the document was assigned to the Integrating Contractor Software System Engineer. The SDBD was to contain data and files common to multiple programs, common to only one program, and an index of constants established as standards for all programs.

The SDBD was to be placed under the change control system beginning with the milestone for issuing the General Design Documents of each program. In actual practice, each time an interface file description was added to the SDBD it became a baseline and was automatically placed under control. Delivery of these descriptions did not necessarily correspond to the specified milestone.

The software plan emphasized requirements for controlling interface file descriptions, but failed to make references to controlling what it referred to as tables, buffers, and constants. Probably this was the reason why only tables and constants used by Lander programs were incorporated in the SDBD. The Orbiter software system did not include a common data base, and the tables and constants used by each program were documented with that program. The Lander software system required the development of a common data base and associated read-only file management software. Therefore, lander program documentation referenced all keys used to access the common data base. The common data base itself was documented in the SDBD.

The interface file descriptions greatly simplified and facilitated the software system integration process. Despite the fact that every affected engineer and programmer concurred with the structure and content of a file, most interfaces did not work the first time they were tested. The SDBD made it easy to determine the reasons for the failures.

Because of limited labor resources available to develop the SDBD, the document was somewhat lacking in respect to tables and constants contained in the common data base. Multiple entries of constants occurred and not all constants that should have been included were actually included. Some programs accessed tables and constants as input data rather than from the common data base. The potential for error was therefore greater than it should have been during planetary operations.

The fact that the tables and constants were not published until the software system was delivered also caused some problems. During the early stages of program deliveries, the common data base software was not fully tested. As a result some programmers had to build in the option to access common data through either input cards or the common data base in order to meet their acceptance test schedules. Because the data base had not been published, the cognizant technologist team sometimes had to guess at values for constants not yet agreed upon, such as time of separation. Then 6 months later when the test case was repeated to assure the program was still the same as had originally been delivered, the user would discover that the program output was different from that expected. This then led to a failure report, and time and effort would be spent trying to locate the source of the error.

The two shortcomings noted for the SDBD were both in areas where people failed to recognize the importance of the document. The concept is extremely valuable, and should be emphasized, implemented, and enforced in the development of any major software system.

A 4- to 5-person-year level of effort was made to develop and maintain the

SDBD for the life of the project. In order to have assured compliance with the tables and constants portion of the document, an additional 1- to 2-person-year effort would have been required.

The SDBD was issued in two volumes, which combined were about 2 feet thick.

4.1.3.5 PROGRAM LIBRARY (SDC)

The objectives of a program library are largely those of management control and accounting, but a program library also provides some programming efficiency in terms of organization and knowledge of the exact status and content of modules. Keeping program stubs in the library not only provides a "tickler" to tell management where planned elements are missing, but, where a stub simulator is present, will support an artificial environment for testing completed modules.

The managerial objectives of a program library include:

Configuration identification and status accounting

Design change control and accounting

Software problem control and accounting

Program and operating statistics

Historical records of library operations

If the Program Library is initiated as soon as the system design is firm, with program modules represented by program stubs, an identification of all the elements of the system configuration is available and may be displayed for configuration management purposes. This makes the program production process much more visible to management.

As program elements are completed and tested, the module code replaces the program stubs and a record is kept of each change of state of the elements either in manual or machine storage. Part of the configuration identification and accounting is keeping track of the versions and modifications to a program and of the contents of builds, adaptations, and sets of modules of differing baselined or tested status (as Test Masters and System Masters), usually to facilitate the exercise of more stringent levels of control. Version or mod numbers or identifiers may be added to the module ID or separate library sections may be used. In short, this is an inventory control problem with each module of the product separately identified and/or stored.

In addition to keeping track of versions of the system as modified, changes to the modules are themselves controlled. No unapproved changes to controlled modules are permitted, although the stringency of control varies greatly with the status of the modules.

Keeping records of all changes to modules helps identify the contents of the various versions and modifications of the system and, by keeping test records and change status, an accounting of whether and when a change has successfully been accomplished. Changes may either incorporate altered requirements or correct detected errors and deficiencies. The incorporation procedures are quite the same, but with different impacts on status. Separate accounts are normally kept of design changes and error corrections.

All activity in the program library is usually recorded, either by a Program Librarian logging jobs in and out and recording statistics, or by the operating system. Additionally, both source and object program size and operating time statistics may be kept. Although not strictly part of the Program Library system, some Program Library systems have access to analytic programs that can derive quite elaborate statistics on program makeup. For instance, analysis may find that a load module differs significantly in size from the sum of individual member sizes due to additional space for linkages and reductions in space for overlays. Program and operations statistics are useful to management in detecting current overutilization of computer resources, in making future estimates of resource costs for new systems, and similar analytic applications.

The objectives for keeping historical records lie in the evaluation of how well the project did and in the derivation of guidance for future projects. Unfortunately, to date very little use of such data has resulted. Much of the data is stored in manual form so that analysis requires a major effort. It may also require correlation of data from configuration management, resource utilization records, and the program library logs, a correlation made difficult by not recording against the same criteria. A complete program library system simplifies these analyses.

Improving the efficiency of programming operations is the second main objective for program libraries. This is accomplished by:

Improving the convenience and ease of use of the computer and the operating system

Keeping computer programs in readily accessible storage

Providing a backup capability in case of failure of new versions or modifications

Providing access to various analytic aids

Facilitating organization of the programming process

Making other programmers' modules available for interface tests

Providing a simulated environment via stubs for simulation and test runs

Providing information on the state of interfacing modules to programmers and test teams

4.1.3.6 GLOBAL DATA CONTROL (SDC)

The objectives for the control of global data are much the same as for programs: that is, management control and accounting and programming efficiency. However, control and accounting for system resources may also be added: that is, visibility of the structure and logical content of data elements, accountability and control of data changes, ease of access and use of global data, and an organized way of doing business.

To these must be added the desire to control the assignment of computer resources (especially storage capacity) to system elements and operations. The use of efficient data types and structures, the creation of the most efficient data modules to meet required program operations, and the avoidance of redundant data items are the corollaries to this objective.

Since many system elements normally interface through global data elements, changes to data often carry more adverse impact than do changes to programs. In fact, if proper modularization procedures have been followed, most modules will be decoupled and interdependencies isolated and relegated to data and passed parameters.

Standard practices for global data control include:

Data naming conventions (including program and routine names)

Allowable data structures

Commenting requirements

Central control of global data contents and changes to them

Quality inspections for redundancies and duplication

Analytic procedures for ensuring efficiency of data manipulation and storage utilization

Naming conventions often present rules for the formation of mnemonics, for identifying the subelements of files and tables, and for indicating function or usage. Allowable data structures may prohibit the use of various structures and usages. Commentary usually includes a decoding of the mnemonic names and requires a short statement of data element usage. Additional descriptors (such as size, range, etc.) may be added (manually or automatically) to permit editorial checks on data values and the use of analytic routines for reports.

Data Library operations are much like those for Program Libraries, including, if necessary, version and modification identifiers. The most important function is the control of data changes, including the evaluation of the impact of changes in the system and ensuring that each change is communicated to all users of the data element. Efficient data structures are just as important as efficient program structures and may communicate as much understanding of a program or system as does knowledge of the structure and functioning of modules. Control of them is as important as Program Library control.

4.1.4   Configuration Management

The concept of software configuration management was perhaps the most frequently cited MPP "goodness" practice. At the risk of some redundancy, the views of several of the MPP companies on the subject are given below.

The section on change control (Section 3.5.1) is also, of course, relevant to this topic.

4.1.4.1   *SOFTWARE CONFIGURATION MANAGEMENT (CSC)*

Software configuration management (SCM) is the process of controlling a system configuration throughout its life cycle to avoid unauthorized changes after the baseline has been established.

SCM is applied from the time the design document is approved and baselined through the operation and maintenance phase. The benefits of this tool are realized when a change or an enhancement to the system is required. The documented or designed configuration must be the same as the operating configuration in order for the maintenance personnel to determine which portion of the system requires modification. If any part of a system has been "patched" or changed without updating the documentation, a modification or enhancement could affect the system performance by incorrect interface with the patched portion of the system.

This programming practice was applied to the projects reviewed, and varied in relation to the amount of funds available for configuration control. The AEGIS project, the largest of the three studied, had a configuration management section with five personnel to control the large volume of documentation and programs being produced during system development. During the acceptance testing phase this section controlled multiple versions of the system to conform to the various stages of hardware configuration.

The DD-963 project had a one-person configuration control section. This project was smaller than the AEGIS project and control of the baselined system was not as difficult. All changes made to the baselined programs had to be approved by the chief programmer. All changes to the system required approval of the program Configuration Control Board.

The TRIDENT project was also a small project in terms of personnel (20 to 30 technical) and the configuration control was part of the duties of one person. The configuration control on this project was somewhat lax because under the conditions specified by the prime contractor the system was not considered baselined until it was completed. This version of SCM was not as desirable as that used on the other two projects.

The effect of the SCM varied over the three projects in proportion to the amount of control applied through that function within the project. The TRIDENT project, where the smallest amount of resources was expended in controlling the "current" version of the system, encountered some problems. The problems were costly in worker-hours and machine time but were not unsurmountable.

The other two projects, which placed more stringent control on the baselined version of the system, were more effective in controlling changes to the configuration and ensuring that the system performed in accordance with the specifications.

In summary, the effectiveness of any SCM function is determined by the amount of control applied within a given project.

The use of an SCM function is recommended for all projects. The size of this staff function should be determined by the size of the project. The configuration control plan should be developed during the system design phase and the plan should be enforced to ensure the integrity of the system configuration throughout the life cycle of the project.

4.1.4.2   CONFIGURATION MANAGEMENT AND CHANGE CONTROL (BCS)

The practices of software configuration management and change control are becoming both better defined and more effectively applied.

The objective of traditional software configuration management has simply been to prevent changes. Usually the stated objective has been to preclude "unauthorized" or "unexpected" changes, but the traditional method—of "locking up" the code—has most often had the effect of preventing any changes at all.

In practice, this simplistic method has not provided the desired result: a mechanism for orderly, cost-effective introduction of needed changes. Most commonly, during integration when the pressures to meet schedule are most severe, even the pretense of control is cast off, and what little visibility and control of changes may have existed previously is simply lost.

In the realm of cost management, the emphasis is on making sure that the work performed (and the resources expended) is really required to satisfy contractual obligations. In particular, the Program Manager needs to be sure that any changes in the work plan—and hence in the products of that work—are instituted only after due consideration of responsibility. For example, changes to correct coding errors or document "typos" are clearly in-scope modifications, to be implemented at the developer's expense. (The Program Manager will usually have budgeted for this kind of work in the program plan.) However, addition of a new capability to the software, such as a new report format, is obviously out-of-scope; the resources (and schedule and budget) to do work of this nature must be added to the program plan, after the customer has concurred with the need and provided incremental funding.

Although changes like these may be easy to categorize, most product changes will not be quite so obvious. A typical example is the situation where the customer finds an error in one of the algorithms they have supplied, and the developer could repair the problem with a simple change in the code. Most commonly, the developers will make the code change as an accommodation, treating it as in-scope just to save themselves and the customer the paperwork needed to obtain what is probably a small amount of additional funding.

Only in retrospect will the developers and the customer realize that this simple change has propagated through several documents, training materials, and even test cases—with a total cost far greater than that of just the code update. The Program Manager finds that effective cost control requires effective product control. That is, there must be visibility, at the item level, of all of the products of software development and how they relate to providing the specified, required computing capability.

Having recognized the need for comprehensive cost and product control, the Program Manager must face a much more pervasive question: how the need for a change will be identified. Many people have more or less direct involvement with the software: the users, the designers, the programmers, even the computer operators. Any of them may encounter (or anticipate) a problem. If the problem discoverer cannot find a way to report the problem or, having done so, cannot learn what is being done about it, there is potential for real dissatisfaction, even though the software itself may completely meet the approved specifications.

It should be noted here that a "problem" need not necessarily be the result of a fault in the software. Much more often, the "problem" may be symptomatic of a need for additional capability, which the customer and developer did not recognize when requirements were originally defined. Or the problem may be that the documentation implies the existence of a capability (or usage) not intended. Or, as cited earlier, the users may discover that the algorithms they have specified are inappropriate for the application.

Recognizing the need to provide a mechanism by which problems can be reported, it becomes apparent that two additional mechanisms are required. One of these lets the person who has reported a problem review the change developed in response to it, to confirm that the reported problem has been resolved. The other mechanism provides a way of distributing the change to all who will be affected by it.

To meet these changing needs, three practices already common in the engineering world are being applied in the development of software. One of these is the practice of explicitly identifying a software configuration called a baseline. A baseline specification cites a particular configuration of software items which provides a designated set of capabilities. Another practice is the use of problem reporting/resolution systems; to provide a focal point for reporting problems and obtaining reliable information about the status of a computing capability. The third practice is the institution of Change Control Boards, to authorize the development of changes to repair reported problems, and to approve distribution of software packages implementing proven changes.

Baselining

The practice of baselining employs a configuration indexing scheme. Basically, a configuration index is simply a list of all the task results (to be) produced during the construction phase, including the end items (contract deliverables) into which these results are incorporated. This list serves the Program Manager's needs by providing a basis for task scheduling and resource planning; as task results are produced and signed-off, the Program Manager uses this additional information as evidence of task completion, the key indicator in his or her determination of status, progress, and performance against the program plan.

A baseline extends the configuration index by specifically identifying (1) the set of capabilities implemented, (2) the constituent(s) which provide each capability, and (3) the implementation (i.e., configuration item) of each constituent. The capabilities list is extracted from—and references—the requirements definition approved at PDR: it also references the PDR-approved product specification, to indicate which software component (including documentation and other products of the development activity) provides the specified capability.

The constituents list expands on this by abstracting, from the designs and plans approved at CDR, the identifiers of the items to be produced by development tasks. This, of course, is the basic configuration index. To provide information for later use in the event a change becomes necessary, the constituents list also records the planned resource expenditures for each item.

The implementations list, finally, is the configuration index augmented with the information available at PCA. That is, it now lists the controlled repository in which each configuration item has been placed, and the name of the person responsible for its control. The list may also include such additional data as the actual expenditures incurred in development and the date the item was completed/accepted.

The totality of these is a baseline. Simply stated, a baseline is a mechanism for cross-referencing requirements, specifications, designs, plans, and products of the development effort. Given this basic mechanism, a relatively straightforward extension of the identification scheme suffices to accommodate changes.

BCS has adopted fairly standard terminology for the qualifying identifiers of a baseline. They are, in order of precedence:

1. The *system* name, usually an acronym, which connotes a class of applications (such as structural analysis, or financial modeling, or computer performance measurement) the capability package is intended to support.

2. The *version* identifier, which distinguishes systems having the same name and application, but significantly different sets of capabilities

(e.g., performance measurement of Honeywell computers, as distinct from that for Univac machines).

3. The *release* designation, which identifies the set of capabilities/ constituents/implementations currently approved for operational use, and distinguishes between this set and prior releases, or planned future releases.

4. The *revision* code, which designates a particular set of changes to an approved release.

(In some situations, particularly when a software system is to be used in two or more computer facilities having significantly different configurations of equipment and support libraries/facilities, still another qualifier may be employed. The *facility* designation, interposed between *release* and *revision* qualifiers, identifies changes implemented to accommodate local conditions.)

In practice, a baseline is created for each approved combination of system, version, and release qualifiers. That is, the designated configuration items are copied into controlled storage, and all members stored are labeled to indicate the baseline to which they belong. A baseline is not created for each revision (or facility) qualifier, but a configuration index is set up by which a baseline can be created if the decision is made to approve the revision for formal release. This requires that item-naming conventions allow having two or more implementations of a given item in controlled storage, distinguishing among such items by designating the revision to which each belongs.

There is as yet no "standard" practice for baselining software, nor is there much likelihood of such a standard emerging until there has been substantial improvement in the tools used in this practice.

Problem Reporting and Resolution

The primary impetus for implementing a problem reporting and resolution system is to help ensure user satisfaction. As we will see in the following discussion of Change Control Boards, however, such a system is a key element in being able to exercise effective control of project costs.

There are three essential features of a problem reporting and resolution system: (1) a focal point for reporting problems and obtaining status about resolution, (2) positive feedback on the action taken to resolve a problem, and (3) a mechanism for closing out a problem once resolution action has been completed.

Properly speaking, the Program Manager—as the designated person having responsibility for the software development—is always the focal point for reporting problems and obtaining status. In practice, the PM will usually delegate this function to some individual in the organization (or, if the software developers and users are geographically separated, at each using facility). This person is charged with receiving reports of "problems" (with supporting evidence), and assigns to each an identification code for use in tracing the problem through subsequent resolution action. This person has the additional responsibility of receiving information about the actions taken, and disseminating this as appropriate to interested enquirers.

Change Control Board (CCB)

Throughout the preceding discussions of Modern Programming Practices, there has been repeated emphasis on the interaction between the developer and the customer of a computing capability, to define the requirements, to specify the product, and to concur in the work plan. The central issue in this section is that a change in any one of these must ordinarily be reflected by corresponding changes in the other two. It is this fact that traditionally has made both the developer and customer strongly resist any kind of change at all.

This resistance to change has usually been predicated on the difficulty of ensuring that all implications of a change have been adequately considered and accommodated. With the Modern Programming Practices of comprehensive task planning and item identification, tied to requirements by means of baselining, there is much better visibility of the development process. This visibility now makes it feasible to implement the third key mechanism of software configuration management, the Change Control Board.

Traditionally, the implementation of changes has been the foundering point for software project cost control. The modern programming practice of involving a Change Control Board as the focus for deciding on changes provides an opportunity to significantly improve the traditional situation. The reader is referred to Section 3.5.1.1 for a detailed discussion of Change Control Board activities.

4.1.4.3   SOFTWARE CONFIGURATION
MANAGEMENT (TRW)

Software configuration management is the establishment and practice of formal software management principles to set policies and procedures for the review and acceptance of contractual and internal baselines, including (1) configuration identification and documentation, (2) configuration control to monitor changes to the established baseline specification, and (3) configuration status accounting to report discrepancies and record software implementation status.

Configuration management establishes a series of baselines and methods of controlling changes to these baselines throughout the development and test phases. A configuration management plan, addressing the requirements of this practice, is prepared by the project and approved by the project manager prior to the first software design review. This plan specifies:

1. The baseline structure to be used by the project (requirements, design, test, product).
2. The baseline definitions (products, events).
3. The configuration identification ground rules, including the types of products to be controlled and the rules for identifying these products.
4. The configuration control mechanisms, including the definition of change and approved processes for controlled products and the handling of waivers and deviations.
5. The configuration status accounting system, including the records and reports required to assure traceability of changes to controlled products and to provide a basis for communication of configuration information within the project.
6. The configuration verification approach, including periodic audits to assure that products are developed and maintained according to the ground rules defined in the plan.

The configuration management activity:

1. Establishes and operates a product development library in which the controlled products are maintained
2. Establishes and maintains a regular problem/discrepancy reporting system
3. Monitors the issuance, retention, change control, packaging, and delivery of the computer products for conformance to current baselines

4.2 ORGANIZATION

Software organizational techniques are in many ways like that of any other organization. Typically, there is a hierarchy of responsibilities, with the first cut at a responsibility breakdown either by product (a "project-oriented" organization) or by function (a "staff-oriented" organization). Occasionally, both of these approaches are used, with function organization superimposed over project organization, resulting in a "matrix-oriented" organization.

That taxonomy of organizations will not be discussed in this book, since it was not addressed by the MPP companies, and it is amply discussed elsewhere. Of more interest to the software specialist are the software-unique (or semiunique) organizational entities, where the entity exists because of the technology of software development itself.

Here, the MPP companies discussed a variety of approaches. In the first, one company found the need to establish an interdisciplinary overseeing organization, similar to the advisory boards often found on college campuses overseeing computer center activities from an interdepartmental user point of view. Following that, technology-centered organizations are discussed under the "chief programmer team" umbrella; many of the MPP companies used this organizational approach to guarantee a technically aware level of management.

The concern for software product quality stimulated the next organizational discussion, on software quality assurance. QA programs are now required, for example, on most Department of Defense (DoD) software projects.

Finally, the human failing of inability to see one's own errors is attacked by the Independent Verification and Validation entity. IV + V is the approach used by most of the MPP companies on reliability-critical projects.

4.2.1   Interdisciplinary Organization

Software people, eagerly pursuing their own special interests, are all too often ill plugged in to the needs of the outside world. In large or interdisciplinary projects, this failing may be fatal to the software product. Software that is of high quality but solves the wrong problem may well be as useless as no software at all.

The first MPP section that follows discusses this problem from the commercial marketplace point of view. The second discusses a DoD project so large and exotic that interdisciplinary support was essential. In each case, the conclusion is the same—a broader view than that of software alone must underlie software development activities.

4.2.1.1   PROJECT ORGANIZATION (BCS)

The environment in which a Program Manager operates is shown pictorially in Figure 4.7. The Program Manager occupies a position singularly capable of influencing the effectiveness with which resources are used to accomplish a project's goals.

In order for a Program Manager to perform properly, he or she must have commensurate authority to allocate resources and to supervise activities. The PM must have responsibility for meeting cost and schedule commitments, to deliver products and to satisfy quality criteria which he or she has responsibility to negotiate, and for discharging obligations in a way that both satisfies the customer's needs and meets company profit objectives. The Program

Figure 4.7   Program Manager Environment

Manager must be able to secure resources in accordance with his or her plan for the work, and must have supervisory responsibility for making assignments, monitoring and directing task execution, and evaluating performance.

4.2.1.2   FLIGHT OPERATIONS SOFTWARE SUBGROUP (MARTIN-MARIETTA)

The Viking Project placed the responsibility for planning, coordinating, and monitoring the development of the Flight Operations software system in the hands of a multiagency Software Subgroup. This group was composed of four Software Systems Engineers who were individually responsible for Lander software, Orbiter software, Institutional software, and Project software system integration.

The multiagency managers responsible for the operational software system were each members of a Flight Operations Working Group (FOWG). None of them were experienced in resolving technical problems relative to computer science or large data management systems. When it became evident that it would take a significant coordination effort to reach agreements, the FOWG elected to establish the Software Subgroup for that purpose. Only those problems that could not be resolved by the subgroup would then be presented to the FOWG with recommendations.

The resolution of trade-offs between hardware and software requirements and the management of software resources and schedules is frequently handled by non-software-oriented personnel. This will be successful only if management understands the software development process and realizes that software must be treated on an equal basis with hardware. The management of the software development itself requires an ability to resolve technical program-level problems in a manner that will not affect system-level performance. It also requires the ability to foresee potential performance deficiencies early in the development process. For these reasons, experienced software systems engineers should be made responsible for software development at the system level.

It is obvious that a Software Systems Engineer (SSE) should be made responsible for the development process of a relatively small software system. The problem of developing a large multiagency, multifaceted software system is quite different. The Mission Operational Software System contained engineering, telemetry, sequence generation, command generation, flight path analysis, science analysis, and imaging programs for both Lander and Orbiter. In addition, it contained mission planning, tracking data, ground resource, and institutional software. Separate teams were established to develop the software for each of these functions. Cognizant engineers were made responsible for requirements and end product testing, and cognizant programmers were made responsible for design, code, and implementation.

But this left unanswered such questions as what programs were needed, whether redundant functions are being developed, what standards and procedures should be followed, how the system will function, whether the system can be made to operate within available computer resources, how the programs will be integrated to form a system, and what assurance there is that the programs will be adequately developed and tested. To resolve these and associated questions, four SSEs were identified. They were not made responsible for the software itself; rather, they were made responsible to assure that a viable and efficient system would be generated on schedule.

The Flight Operations Software Plan identified the Software Sub Group as follows:

Planning, coordinating, and monitoring of development of the Flight Operations Software System is the responsibility of the Software Sub Group (SWSG) under the direction of the Flight Operations Working Group (FOWG). The SWSG shall provide guidance for the functional design of the system, and shall coordinate, integrate, review, and advise on the design, development, and implementation of the system. The SWSG shall emphasize Lander and Orbiter software integration and shall resolve any software interface problems that may arise. Problems that cannot be resolved by the SWSG shall be presented to the Flight Operations Working Group with recommendations. Specific SWSG responsibilities shall include:

1. Review and coordinate software schedules.
2. Participate in the evaluation and coordination of the Flight Operations functional requirements so that Viking software requirements can be developed.
3. Review the software design generated in response to the Software Functional Descriptions and the Functional Specification.
4. Review the Functional Requirements Document and the Software Requirements Document to assure that the requirements have been defined as necessary for software design.
5. Identify problem areas where analyses are required to design an integrated software system that will meet functional requirements.
6. Provide guidance for software planning, design, and implementation.
7. Evaluate the readiness of the software system for flight operations.
8. Resolve or recommend solutions to software interface problems involving the various agents.
9. Monitor the implementation of the overall software design, development and testing to assure that all interfaces, design requirements, and schedules are correctly and completely satisfied.
10. Evaluate the readiness of the software system for integration into the computer complex.
11. Evaluate the readiness of the Mission Independent Software System to support Project software testing and implementation.
12. Coordinate ground software interfaces with the on-board software and hardware.

The members of the SWSG were then identified to be an Integration Contractor Software System Engineer, a Martin-Marietta Software System Engineer, an Orbiter Software System Engineer, and a Data System Project Engineer.

The accomplishments of the Software Subgroup members played a major role in delivering an efficient operational software system to the Viking Project on schedule. The SSEs resolved numerous interagency disputes and problems, and developed and implemented the Integrated Functional System Design, the Software Data Base Document, the Viking Software Guide, the Lander Orbiter Software Test Plan, and the Data System and Integration Plan. They developed data management requirements; collected, controlled, and enforced interface agreements; assured that software deliveries complied with procedures; supervised certification, conversion, and acceptance testing; negotiated computer time; held audits and reviews; maintained schedules; wrote procedures; resolved computer system problems; and conducted the

Preliminary and Critical Design Reviews. Finally, they gained the confidence of the engineers and programmers, ran the software, coordinated failure reports and redeliveries, and integrated the system.

Whereas the SSEs were given a fair degree of latitude in carrying out their duties, the most significant difficulties they encountered were caused by decision-making policies of the non-software-oriented management directly above them. Four examples will be given to impress upon the reader the importance of management understanding the software process before events unfold rather than after the fact.

Management did not initially understand the limitations of computer systems. As soon as the system design was formulated, the SSEs conducted loading analyses studies which showed that three or four large mainframe computers would be needed. Management held firm to the decision that the system would operate in one real-time 360/75 and one general-purpose 1108. The SSEs were therefore forced to assign programs to computers under these ground rules. The final system included two 360/75 computers, each operating a little more than half the time, for real-time and batch operations, plus two 1108 general-purpose computers operating full time with a third 1108 available for emergencies and peak loads. Had management faced this decision early, more efficient program loading could have been realized.

Management did not always treat software on an equal basis with hardware. The SSEs requested that telemetry formats contain some additional time-tag words required for data analysis. The request was rejected, and complex and inefficient software functions had to be developed to resolve the situation. This increased the running time for the decalibration and decommutation software functions and caused problems beginning with the third week of planetary operations. Some science data were incorrectly time tagged, not because of software errors, but because of the complexity of the requirements for distinguishing old data from new data. The problem was quickly resolved by modifying the requirements and then implementing minor software changes.

Management rushed software development. The SSEs provided schedules that took into account both the software development scope and permitted a top-down approach to system integration. Management directed that several real-time and batch programs would be delivered up to 5 months earlier than shown on the schedules to support Software System One testing. The SSEs argued that the batch programs were not needed (because Flight computer software would at most be only capable of producing a memory dump) and that early program conversion, acceptance testing, and integration efforts would jeopardize final program delivery schedules. This advice was rejected, and the programs were delivered early and on schedule. They were not adaptive, were unreliable, and could only be run in a "canned" fashion, being very limited as to what data could be processed. No Flight software was available for Software System One testing, so not even a memory dump could be taken.

For that reason, no one even bothered to run the batch programs. Management learned from this experience not to rush future software deliveries.

Management did not fully understand the software integration process. The SSEs originally specified in the software plan that Lander/Orbiter interface integration testing would be conducted priur to program delivery. The reason for this was that the SSEs knew that a large number of errors would be uncovered. Management changed the plan to require that program deliveries be made before integration tests could be conducted. There is nothing wrong with this as long as one is willing to accept the fact that most programs will have to be redelivered. But when that happened, management jumped on the SSEs for making too many deliveries; each was costly in resources because of the involved procedures and retesting that had to be followed. The end result was that the SSEs ignored the plan and reverted to their original approach, thereby controlling the number of redeliveries required. It is important to realize that first deliveries were incentive deliveries, and redeliveries were not.

4.2.2 Technology-Centered Organization

The chief programmer has been well known in the software world since the advent of the Structured Programming methodology in the early 1970s.

In this approach, a software-knowledgeable team leader is given prime responsibility for the development of team-produced software. The technique has been the subject of various analogies, from the surgical team of the medical profession (doctor-led) to the flight crew of an aircraft (pilot-led). Whatever the analogy, the essence of the approach is the emphasis on a technically knowledgeable lead person, and subordinates whose function is technology- and team-centered.

Several of the MPP companies explored this approach. Their findings follow.

4.2.2.1 CHIEF PROGRAMMER TEAMS (SDC)

The purpose of any personnel organization is the mobilization of human resources to accomplish a task. The Chief Programmer Team is based on the premise that an experienced programmer supported by a small team of programming assistants can produce a computer program faster than programmers working under a more ordinary line and staff organization.* At a minimum, the team will consist of a backup programmer and a librarian. Other programmers may be added as required, but the team should not exceed 10 members. The Chief Programmer is responsible for all overall design, for

---

* Claims of productivity of more than 10 times the normal rates have been made for this approach.

writing the main program, and for reviewing and critiquing all subprograms designed and written by his or her assistants. The Chief Programmer directs the activities of assistants but may or may not be responsible for personnel administration.

The Backup Programmer is responsible for one or more submodules and for reviewing and critiquing the programs written by the Chief Programmer. He or she acts as an advisor and sounding board for the Chief Programmer and, most important, is in training to take over from the Chief should that become necessary.

The Librarian, in a batch environment, is responsible for receiving and logging of jobs to be submitted to the computing facility and for preparing job control and linkage instructions and submitting jobs to the computing facility. He or she also receives jobs back from the computing facility, logs job statistics, files copies of listings, and distributes the results to programmers. The Librarian also preserves documentation of other kinds. He or she is the custodian of the Program Notebook or Project File and of the Program Library, and may also be the custodian of subroutines, procedures, and macros, making sure that they are documented and that the documentation is disseminated or that the programmers are aware of what is available in the common pool. The Librarian is also responsible for issuing Program Library reports and Run Log reports and is keeper of status information on the Library. In an interactive environment, much of the Librarian's record-keeping functions may be taken over by the operating system, but he or she retains responsibility for reports, library maintenance, configuration records, documents, and files.*

The remaining programmers work under the direction of a Chief Programmer. It is recommended practice that programmers work as pairs to review and critique one another's work and act as backup. Structured walkthroughs are also recommended to get critiques from the whole team on designs. (Customers and other nonteam persons may participate in walkthroughs.)

It has been suggested that the team may also incorporate, or have available to it, technical writers, administrators, system program experts, and even application area and special skills persons.

Although not a feature of the original Chief Programmer Team Concept, it is now recommended that when a project exceeds the capabilities of one or two teams, a Chief Architect be appointed to determine overall designs of the system and to provide technical direction to the team. If all technical control activities are assigned to this person, such as Configuration Management, Program Library Operation, Data Library Operations, Information Control and Quality Assurance, the Chief Architect Team is, in essence, the Program

---

* In actual practice, Librarianship seems to range from being the team secretary and control clerk to a full-fledged operating and support system expert.

Management Office for the project. This concept assures that there is an administrative head and staff in addition to the technical head of the project.

It was proposed that Chief Programmer Teams (CPTs) be used in COBRA DANE. Chief Programmers were appointed and stayed with the project throughout design, code, and test. The approximately 50 project members (not all programmers) were divided into about 10 teams. The COBRA DANE teams varied from the suggested organization in that a central System Librarian and Data Base Coordinator were used rather than Team Librarians.

Chief Programmer Practices

The Chief Programmer was responsible for:

1. An assigned number of subroutines
2. Delegating coding and testing of subroutines to assistants
3. Review of all programs and modifications prior to release to the System Librarian to ensure that fundamentally incompatible modules have not been coded and tested by different people
4. Providing the System Librarian with information concerning:
   a. Software checkout status
   b. Error-correction status
   c. Descriptions of update package contents
5. Conducting design walkthroughs
6. Coordination with the Data Base Coordinator concerning:
   a. Global data definitions
   b. Utilization of computer resources
   c. Utilization of the data manager
7. Ensuring that programming standards were followed in the programs for which he or she was responsible
8. Providing any test cases and test drivers used for testing the programs to the Program Library

Sole authority for directing conformance was vested in the Chief Programmers for ensuring the adequacy of internal annotation and blocking and naming conventions. There were no procedures for review and enforcement of the standard practices outside the line organization.

The chief programmer was also responsible for the normal administrative duties for the programmers working under his or her guidance.

Observance of CPT Practices

It was the stated goal of the COBRA DANE project that all Chief Programmers be working programmers. This was true. The lead programmers assumed personal programming responsibility for the principal subroutines among those allocated to them and performed the design and programming. Other routines were assigned to subordinate programmers.

The Chief Programmers promoted the standard practice rules for the elements of programming style. Since the observance of these rules was quite good, their daily guidance was effective.

The Chief Programmers held and participated in design walkthroughs. This was done very conscientiously at first, but the reviews were decreased as the work load increased.

The evidence would seem to indicate that a similar situation occurred with other review responsibilities of the Chief Programmers. Modules and changes were initially inspected in depth but with less severity as work pressure increased and greater risks were taken to meet delivery schedules. Although the Chief Programmers devoted time to training and advising their subordinates, the amount of time they were able to give diminished as they grew busier.

Software checkout status, error-correction status, and control of Program Library updates were responsibilities that the Chief Programmers were able to discharge very well. It was reported, however, that the configuration status reports were not widely distributed and if the Chief Programmer was not conscientious in informing subordinates of status matters, the team members had to obtain the information through personal contact and as a result of using the Program Library.

Among other responsibilities, the Chief Programmers somewhat later in the project assumed responsibility for controlling the integrity of team copies of the Program Library and for controlling inputs to the Data Base Coordinator.

The greatest complaint expressed by COBRA DANE programmers concerning the Chief Programmers was their neglect of administrative and supervisory duties. All programmers were too engrossed in the technical work to pay heed to administrative matters, but someone must take care of personnel complaints, resolve conflicts, and obtain decisions. When tensions become high, small personal and technical problems loom large.

Impact of CPT Approach on Performance

The impact of having a few highly proficient programmers performing the bulk of the design and coding work is reflected in the high quality of the COBRA DANE software and the excellent productivity of the teams. The Chief Programmers were some of the best at SDC and the overall quality of the team members was high. Although direct comparison of CPT with other approaches is not available, CPTs were effective on COBRA DANE.

Based on interviews with project members, there are several factors that affected the team performance. Among these are:

Overcommitment of the Chief Programmers
Variability in the enforcement of standards

Underemphasis upon training of members
Relaxation of quality assurance measures
Discharge of administrative duties
Team coordination and direction

Overcommitment. There was a tendency for the Chief Programmers to assume responsibility for designing and coding modules at the expense of not discharging supervisory duties as well as they might. Since the Chiefs were expert programmers, this arrangement made maximum use of their programming skills but may have depressed the productivity of team members. There are dozens of minor technical decisions to be made on a programming project that junior people are reluctant to make or need guidance on. Many of the decisions are arbitrary, but some are not and the junior person may not be able to distinguish which are and which are not. Facing a steady stream of decisions that he or she cannot easily make is frustrating and time consuming. Not only is productivity impaired, but the person becomes anxious and irritable as well. Feeling frustrated and inadequate, the person may leave or shirk his or her work or neglect to research decisions adequately.

One of the advantages of having a Chief Programmer is the person's breadth of understanding of the system and the speed with which he or she grasps the essence of a problem. The Chief Programmer is usually able to resolve a question in minutes that would take another team member hours just to acquire the relevant information.

It is part of the Chief Programmer's job to be available to make decisions and to sort out those that do require further investigation from those that do not. Although this was not an intolerable problem for COBRA DANE, all Chief Programmers were overcommitted to some degree. In view of the unexpected growth of the system, this is understandable. However, it is alleged that work of team members was impaired somewhat and that some turnover did occur as a result.

Standards. Although observance of programming standards was generally good, programmers indicated that there were some differences in the emphasis that the Chief Programmers placed on adhering to the standards. This is to be expected, of course, whenever more than one group is involved. However, despite the quality inspections performed by the Program and Data Librarians, the Chief Programmers were almost the sole arbiters of standard enforcement. If the relative emphasis was enough to be noticed by the team members, some reduction in quality of some programs probably resulted. Independent enforcement of standards might have evened out the differences.

Training. As the person with the best grasp of both system requirements and team methodology, the Chief Programmer had a responsibility for indoctrinating and guiding not only new members but all members of the team. Additionally, he or she must arrange assignments so that more experienced members monitor and help the more junior people, and so the junior people can profit experientially from acting as backup to the senior person. Both these techniques were used on COBRA DANE, but the general overcommitment of all programmers, plus some alleged personality conflicts between "buddies," inhibited their overall effectiveness. Although the juniors on COBRA DANE were most productive, quite a few of the modules they produced had rough spots that the Chiefs polished out during integration.

Relaxation of quality assurance. As noted above, both Program Library and design walkthrough quality assurance procedures were relaxed as the workload climbed. This resulted in some additional errors that required later work to isolate and remove. It is also true that some of the "calculated risks" paid off. Whether or not a beneficial trade-off was achieved is not readily assessible. However, evidence which indicates that the later an error is detected the more costly it is to correct militates against such relaxations.

Administration. Administrative details are often irksome to technically oriented people. Nevertheless, for an effective team operation, someone must take care of the "paper-pushing" and the personnel problems. No matter how much of the clerical work is automated or delegated, the decisions on budgets, schedules, vacations, computer time, and salary increases remain with the supervisor. The supervisor must also settle personal problems and conflicts, intercede with management for the staff, and handle relationships with other groups and agencies if he or she is to have an effectively operating team. On COBRA DANE it was alleged that the overcommitted Chief Programmers were reluctant to divert attention from the main programming task to handle administrative details. How much this detracted from performance, if any, is difficult to determine. Some disruption to plans, records, and morale probably occurred.

Coordination. The COBRA DANE Chief Programmers were exceptionally able, technically competent, strong individuals. Unless given firm guidance, they tended to go their own way. They did have the interface document as a coordination point, but it tended to settle immediate problems rather than coordinate activities or maintain an overview of the total system. Several of the project members felt that there should have been an equally strong technical individual separate from the project manager who could serve as Chief Architect for the system. Such a person could maintain an overview of the system, make configuration decisions from a system viewpoint, ensure components are compatible, better control and coordinate modifications, and better monitor computer resource utilization than any single Chief Programmer. In doing applications system work, it is very important that everything works correctly and fits together precisely. In a more research-oriented environment there is more room for experimentation, more tolerance of change and modification, and less necessity of exact interfaces. System failures are not so catastrophic, and incompatible interfaces can be made to make do with some extra attention. In an operational environment, operations cannot depend upon having a super programmer available to solve stoppages or hang things together. Hence, the Chief Architect who sees that all teams are going in the same direction and that incompatibilities are not being introduced could serve a very useful purpose. COBRA DANE had some very technically competent managers, but there seemingly was a need for a person whose sole responsibility was the technical overview of the system who could arbitrate technical disputes and maintain the integrity of the system design.

Summary. Individual productivity, especially of the Chief Programmers, was magnificent. Considering that the final system was three times the size originally estimated and that there was a major redesign of the Mission Support Software as well as numerous changes, each of which resulted in some work being scrapped, productivity was excellent. There is a definite danger in the CPT approach that the Chief Programmer will become overcommitted to coding and not have time to discharge his or her other duties. He or she must have time to advise team members, train them, monitor their work, and care for their personal and administrative problems. A large project can profit from having a Chief Architect to give overall direction to the design, to protect the integrity of the design from the ill effects of modifications, to resolve disputes, and to see that quality standards are enforced evenly across the total system. The Chief Architect would receive major support in this role from a System Librarian and System Data Controller.

4.2.2.2 CHIEF PROGRAMMER (CSC)

The Chief Programmer is the senior technical staff member assigned to a specified organizational level. For a project employing 20 to 30 technical staff members the Chief Programmer may direct the entire software development effort. On the other hand, a project requiring a technical staff of 100 to 150 personnel may use two or three Chief Programmers. The span of control assigned to any Chief Programmer position depends very heavily on the technical and management expertise of the individual selected for the position. A Chief Programmer is the focal point for all software development within the organizational boundary. The person must be expert in his or her mastery of all elements of program development (i.e., computer languages, hardware, JCL, etc.) but is also a manager assigning tasks, monitoring progress, and adjusting resources to maintain schedules. Much of a Chief Programmer's responsibility is compatible with a Section Manager's. But a Chief Programmer fills a position of broader responsibility than a Section Manager, as the most senior or one of the group of most senior technicians on a project.

The Chief Programmer does not function in a team chief role as described in the Structured Programming philosophy. He has a task group of programmers and analysts involved in coordinated subsystem development. There is no group librarian or configuration management function. These requirements are satisfied by project staff personnel who perform these functions for the total development effort. Similarly, quality assurance and testing are project functions and thus outside the group's responsibility.

The two Chief Programmers for the DD-963 project were assigned project staff positions. Their basic responsibilities did not vary appreciably from phase to phase during the project. They were primarily concerned with technical direction for assigned software production. They did lead individual programming teams which were assigned specified builds to develop and test. The department manager provided management support which freed the Chief Programmers to direct software development with minimum distraction. Overall this was an extremely effective project organization. It was successful in part because the project staff was small, so that the span of control for each Chief Programmer (10 to 12 personnel) and the Department Manager was within manageable bounds. Also, the superior professional and technical skill of both Chief Programmers and the Department Manager was a significant contributing factor.

During all phases of system development the Chief Programmers were focal points for software production. This began during the analysis and design phases, when they were deeply involved in preparation of the performance and design specifications. They also participated in the definition of system threads during this phase. Later, during the code and checkout phase, this experience was applied to the production and demonstration of system builds. They assigned specific modules and segments to programmers within their groups and monitored the development and testing of the program code. As leaders of the build development teams they provided technical direction and guidance to team members through demonstration of the build. Throughout the development of this system the Chief Programmers were a key link between the project analysts and programmers, and the management staff.

To recommend using a Chief Programmer team structure one must consider all the factors mentioned in this discussion. There are no definitive guidelines. It is obvious, however, that this organization can be used effectively and can enhance the technical direction and controls applied to a software acquisition project.

4.2.2.3 BUILD LEADER (CSC)

A build leader is a specialized task leader whose sole responsibility is to supervise production of software to support a build capability. As in most task-oriented organizations, the build leader may have other nonrelated or compatible responsibilities.

As an example, Chief Programmers were build leaders for most of the system builds during one project. The build leader directed the efforts of the task group of programmers and analysts assigned to a particular build. This group functioned as a unit until the build was demonstrated. Build leaders were instrumental in timely production of system capabilities, and in the detection and correction of design and code errors.

Build leaders were used only during the Code and Checkout, and Test and Integration phases. They were used with equal effectiveness across both of these phases. Perhaps the greatest benefit to be gained from using build leaders is in having software development teams working with well-defined, limited objectives. Work progress can be readily determined and personnel can be assigned to specific tasks. The build leader and group functioned as an action team within the project staff. Once the build was demonstrated, these people were reassigned to other tasks. In this way, labor becomes a more flexible resource for use within the project. This was true of the way build leaders were employed through both development phases.

If a management staff elects to employ threads and builds to promote phased production and integration of system capabilities, then build leaders are an appropriate technique to assure their effective use. Build leaders can be used on projects of all sizes. The project staff organization must be structured so that the build leader has available the staff support he or she needs to accomplish the assigned tasks. For example, the DD-963 organization included configuration management, quality assurance, and program librarian functions that were common to all task groups. Thus, the build leaders could devote their full attention to program development. The total project staff size was small enough to accommodate this staff organization. Build leaders and their groups were able to have direct and frequent access to support personnel during build production.

4.2.2.4 COGNIZANT ENGINEER/COGNIZANT PROGRAMMER (MARTIN-MARIETTA)

Each Mission Operational software program was assigned a Cognizant Engineer (CE) and a Cognizant Programmer (CP). The CEs were responsible for generating program requirements and testing the program to meet those requirements. The CPs were responsible for designing, implementing, and defining the procedures for operating the programs.

The rationale for adopting this concept was based on the belief that an engineer who understood requirements would not necessarily understand how computer systems could be used to implement them. Once a programmer implemented working software, the engineer would then be in a position to test the software to meet the requirements. The primary reason for assigning a particular programmer to be responsible for the design, development, and implementation process, rather than using a software pool, was to have a second individual become thoroughly familiar with all the requirements for the software function. A secondary purpose was to provide an incentive for pride in workmanship.

Management can increase personnel work incentive by adopting the CE/CP approach to program development. Programmers will generate working software based on their interpretation of requirements, which are not necessarily correct. Requiring the CEs to write the program acceptance test plan provides the balance required to assure that the programs will function to meet the engineering requirements.

The Cognizant Programmer/Cognizant Engineer philosophy was not adopted for Flight or System Test Equipment software development. In those areas, engineers were assigned to write the Software Requirements Documents, after which they were given new assignments. This in part is responsible for the fact that no formal acceptance test plan or equivalent was ever written for parts of the software system.

The lander power program was originally developed by a single engineer who could code in Fortran. The engineer did not understand the scope of the task and thought he could do it by himself. During the coding phase he began slipping his schedule. Management formed a Tiger team to assess the situation, the result of which was to assign a new cognizant engineer plus a cognizant programmer to assure that the program would be delivered on schedule.

The file management program developed to support the common data base and intercomputer file management functions was originally assigned a CE and a CP. However, when the program was taken to Jet Propulsion Lab in December 1973, the CE declined to move to California and dropped off the Viking project. At that time the CP was made both the CE and CP for the function. He was directly supervised by the Integrating Contractor Software Systems Engineer. He was able to handle the task, but was typically delinquent in providing the required support documentation. The result was that members of the Software Integration Group were frequently required to come in at odd hours to show users how to run the program. Eventually, satisfactory documentation was produced.

The quality of the software produced was a function of the relative abilities of both the cognizant engineer and the cognizant programmer. The talent available to the Viking Project ranged from mediocre to excellent in both categories. When either the programmer or the engineer was excellent, the resultant software end product was very good.

The ability for the engineer to clearly and accurately specify requirements was extremely important. In some cases the programmers learned and understood the requirements as well as the engineers.

Some friction developed on a few of the programming teams. This was only partially due to personalities. Management tended to overemphasize the importance of the engineer to the detriment of the programmer. That is, when everything went well the engineer got the credit, but when problems came up they were too often blamed on the programmer. The roles of the CE and CP should be kept in proper perspective by any project adopting this technique.

The prime disadvantage to selecting the CE/CP technique over using an engineering pool/software programming pool is that each programmer must develop every function required by the program. This makes it more difficult for systems engineering and integration to generate a commonality of utility subroutines used by a multiple of programs. However, the improvement in communications available with the CE/CP more than offsets this disadvantage.

This technique did not entail any kind of a cost impact, since the same number of programmers and engineers would have been needed if an engineering pool/software pool had been used. The development effort for the Viking Lander operational software programs broke down as 45% for engineer participation and 55% for programmer participation. Half of the engineering hours were spent on requirements generation and documentation; the other half was spent on test plan generation and test support. Two-thirds of the programmer hours were spent on design and code; the remaining third was spent on testing and maintenance.

4.2.3 Software Quality Assurance

A deepening concern for the quality of software products, coupled with a lack of typical manager capability to evaluate that quality, has led to the introduction of the software quality assurance organization. Delegated here is the responsibility for an independent analysis of the quality of the software produced.

This is a difficult task, made even more difficult in the early days of the concept by the use of software-ignorant, traditional quality assurance personnel. However, increased emphasis on the software quality assurance organizational concept—especially from the Department of Defense—has led to the increasing use of software-skilled quality assurance people, resulting in a more effective organizational result.

This approach is described below by one of the MPP companies.

4.2.3.1 *SOFTWARE QUALITY ASSURANCE (SPERRY UNIVAC)*

Software Quality Assurance (SQA) is a discipline applying technical and administrative direction and control to assure that all software code and documentation delivered meets all specified and contractual requirements. These disciplines include the establishment of a SQA program to cover each phase of software development (planning, analysis, design, production, test, and configuration management).

Sperry Univac management policies for product development include software quality assurance for all items delivered on a contract.

The following paragraphs described SQA as implemented by Sperry Univac. SQA discipline was obtained by implementation of the following controls:

SQA program establishment
Design control
Development control
Testing/certification control
Program records and change controls

The overall objectives of the SQA program were to:

1. Promote the timely delivery of the contracted software and assure full compliance with all design and performance requirements
2. Make timely provisions for the tests, special controls, schedules, and documentation required to assure software quality

Design Control

The SQA group worked independently of the project software development group during software analysis and design. This SQA work specified controls necessary to ensure program design and design documentation to satisfy the program mission. SQA conducted a critical review of the developed interface design specification and the program specifications to remedy discrepancies.

Development Controls

The SQA group ensured that the program was developed in accordance with its governing functional and design specifications, and to ensure that a uniform method was established for controlling the object program during testing.

The objectives of development control were:

1. Identification of any operational baseline (configuration-controlled starting point) source program
2. To provide in-progress inspections and controls to protect source program quality and functional integrity and to verify that execution timing and program sizing were within limits
3. To provide proper changes to baseline module test programs and qualification test programs corresponding to changes specified for the operational baseline source programs

4. To ensure that proper coding procedures were followed as specified in the Project Standards and Conventions documents
5. To ensure that proper compiler and assembler techniques were followed as specified in the Project Standards and Conventions
6. To ensure that program debug/checkout procedures were used
7. To ensure that the program modules were produced by the approved top-down process

Testing/Certification Controls

Software Quality Assurance was incorporated into the computer program software by conducting a series of informal and formal qualification tests. The purpose of the test effort was to certify and demonstrate that the deliverable computer programs successfully fulfilled the requirements set forth in the interface, performance, and design specifications.

The objectives of qualification testing and certification controls were:

1. To determine, as a result of agreement with the customer, the testing to be performed for each level of the developed program
2. To develop and maintain during use the Computer Program Test Plan and Procedure
3. To define all qualification test parameters
4. To conduct qualification tests for each level of produced programs
5. To write formal test reports after completion of the qualification tests

Program Records and Change Controls

The following states the objectives that the SQA group utilized for the various program records and change controls maintained by SQA.

1. Program Test Records
   a. To provide objective evidence (test results) that the coded program complied with the program design document and that both complied with the requirements and criteria of the product specification.
   b. To provide the data necessary for the evaluation and disposition of program problem reports found during testing.
2. Program Software Trouble Reports
   a. To provide a record of all program problems encountered. (These reports were in-house records used to record problems during testing.)

3. Engineering Change Proposals
   a. To communicate changes required to various program modules and documentation.
   b. To document the changes shown by Program Maintenance Logs, which were the baseline source program.
4. Program Maintenance Logs
   a. To ensure adequate recording of program problems with the corrective solutions.
5. Audit Reports
   a. To provide a record of documentation and a record of discrepancies.

Technical Organization Responsibility

Software Quality Assurance, Support Software Development, and Configuration Management (CM) Controls were implemented through a functional, distinct organization, separate from and independent of any related computer program development effort. SQA organization was compatible with, and subject to, all defined standardized management practices and guidelines established within Sperry Univac. Representative organization charts for a functional and a project organization are shown in Figures 4.8 and 4.9. All three groups were under the cognizance of the Program Manager and under the technical direction of the Project Engineer.

Following is a list of the major areas of responsibility of each group.

1. The Software Development group:
   a. Designed, developed, and delivered the Operational Program
   b. Developed and delivered the Operational Program documentation
   c. Provided technical support throughout the test phases
   d. Incorporated all program changes into the Operational Program
2. The SQA group:
   a. Produced, delivered, and carried out the Quality Assurance Plan
   b. Carried out the final review of all project deliverable documentation
   c. Reviewed the development of the Computer Program Test Plan
   d. Produced the Computer Program Test Procedures
   e. Conducted the testing and formal qualification of the developed Operational Program
   f. Recorded all test results and provided adequate testing and qualification reports
   g. Tested all changes made to the baseline program

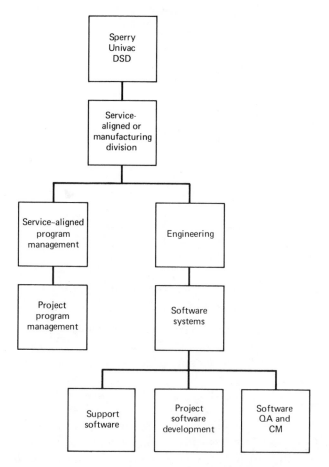

Figure 4.8   Typical Sperry Univac Functional Organization

> h. Provided schedules of all significant events if they were not delineated in the contracted schedule
> i. Produced and maintained records and reports
> j. Processed as defined in the Configuration Management Plan any errors found during Module System Test

3. The Software Configuration Management group:
   a. Developed and carried out a Configuration Management Plan
   b. Placed all deliverable items under formal configuration control
   c. Processed and disseminated all change proposals
4. The Support Software group:
   a. Designed, developed, and maintained all supporting test software

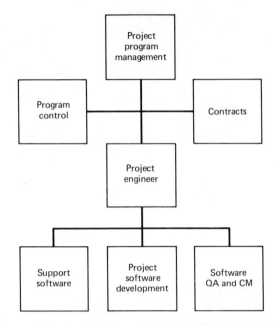

Figure 4.9   Typical Sperry Univac Project Organization

   b. Provided technical support of test software throughout the test phases

   c. Developed and produced all support software documentation

Sperry Univac's policy requires that Software Quality Assurance be proposed on all software developments. The initial implementation of software is a small part of the life-cycle cost of software. SQA applied during development is a most important aspect of producing high-quality operational software. SQA further provides for enforceable configuration management practices well before final software delivery, and enables more easily maintained software over the life cycle.

4.2.4   Independent Verification and Validation

Being blind to our own failings is not a unique software trait. Perhaps, however, the apparent inevitability of failing is. We have not yet learned how to produce error-free software—in spite of now-discredited claims to the contrary.

Acknowledging this problem, one organizational solution is the use of an independent test team. Sometimes also called a "product test" organization, the independent verification and validation group provides the needed role of the relatively unbiased, non-emotionally-invested outside force whose job it is to seek out errors, and not to demonstrate their absence.

IV&V has had some notable successes, particularly in its role in America's space program, where software failures were not only rare but relatively recoverable. The MPP contractors discuss it in what follows.

4.2.4.1 INDEPENDENT VERIFICATION OF ON-BOARD PROGRAMS (MARTIN-MARIETTA)

The on-board computer operations were so critical to mission success that several means were employed to assure error-free software. A separate contract was established to evaluate in detail the algorithms, implementation, and testing of the Lander on-board computer system. The independent verifier performed analyses and tests, using their own tools and interim development products. The overall experience was favorable in helping to identify possible difficulties and in imposing additional discipline on the software development process.

Independent verification means redundant verification, and therefore is usually considered only where software error implies high risks and costs. Redundant activities may include the entire spectrum of development—and, in fact, are considered more effective where this is done. Rederivation of equations; independent scientific simulations; in-depth analysis of concept, design, and code; and finally exercise of developed code and data may all be productive in identifying discrepancies and producing error-free code. The full spectrum of independent verification was employed for the Viking Lander on-board software, beginning with the Software Requirements Definition.

Independent Verification and Validation (IV&V) has long been standard for certain Air Force contracts where software criticality is a prime consideration. Multiple viewpoints throughout evaluation has proven useful in identifying both specific discrepancies and classes of software errors. Improving automated tools and introduction of formalized development disciplines affect IV&V in two ways: (1) the costs associated with the activity are declining, and (2) the probability of initially producing error-free software is increasing.

The Viking Project Office determined that due to the criticality of the Viking Lander Flight Software an IV&V effort would be made. TRW Systems, Redondo Beach, California, was given that contract. The contract included responsibility to verify the Flight Software Requirements, the Command List, the Guidance and Control Analysis, the Analog/Hybrid Vehicle and environmental models, and the Flight Program. The effort lasted for over 3 years on site at NASA Langley under direct NASA supervision.

The independent verification was accomplished in four major areas: Documentation Review, Analysis and Modeling Review, Dynamic Interpretive Simulation of the Descent portion of the Flight program, and static interpretive simulation of the landed and on-orbit flight program functions. The documentation and analysis reviews were performed by senior TRW personnel on-site at NASA Langley. The simulations were performed on the NASA computers at Langley free of charge to the contractor. Although the simulations were accurate, they were extremely time consuming and often took many days to set up and perform a single execution.

Probably the most significant qualitative result of the independent verifier was the confidence it gave to the Project Office that every step that could be taken to assure a correct and error-free flight program would be launched was accomplished. No significant technical problems were uncovered by the independent verifier. Many documentation errors were identified and code problems in preliminary software versions were noted. There were discussions and debates about development and design techniques but all in all no system, software, or operational procedural problems were encountered.

Martin-Marietta believes the cost for independent verification of the flight program was in the neighborhood of $2 to 3 million for the 3-year effort accomplished by TRW.

4.2.4.2   INDEPENDENT TEST AND EVALUATION (CSC)

Independent test and evaluation (IT&E) is a method for conducting software verification and validation. It involves designation of a group or team of technical personnel to form an IT&E unit. These personnel, who must be knowledgeable of system requirements and design, are responsible for conducting all system tests prior to delivering the software to the user. This group operates independent of the system development staff in order to provide an objective and unbiased evaluation of the software. The primary objectives of this group are to prove that the software performs as designed and that the performance meets or exceeds all system requirements. It must establish that the system can be implemented, error-free, consistent with the performance requirements.

To accomplish these objectives the IT&E group performs the following functions:

1. Compares computer program design to system design specifications
2. Develops system test plans and scenarios
3. Evaluates software performance against system performance requirements

To develop an effective test plan, the preparation should begin during the design phase. The test and integration scripts for the AEGIS and DD-963 projects were designed to be executed in conjunction with build demonstrations. The unit testing was done by the individual programmers prior to the demonstrations, and the formal testing was performed by test groups using the test scripts to ensure that the functions designed into a specific build satisfied the requirements for that portion of the system. Using the build concept and integrating each build as it was developed and tested into the baselined system during the programming phase reduced the time required for the final system test phase.

The AEGIS project had a Test and Evaluation Department which reported to the project manager. This group generated the test plans and procedures for all tests, conducted and evaluated the tests, and retested any programs that required corrective action from a previous test. All test plans and procedures were approved by the customer prior to the actual test, and the customer reviewed test results after the test.

The DD-963 project staff had a test group which worked jointly with the Navy in writing the test scenarios from the threads data base. This group reported to the DD-963 department manager. The test scripts were the scenarios used during a build demonstration to ascertain if all functions in the build perform as specified in the requirements document. The results of the test were evaluated and software trouble reports (STRs) were written on any problem detected during the test. The STR was tracked by this group until the error was corrected. The test script was executed again to confirm the correction and ensure that the corrective code did not affect another part of the build. All tests were made with Navy personnel present, and the programs were baselined after the demonstration.

Those involved in directing program development for both AEGIS and DD-963 stated that getting the user involved in the testing process proved to be very successful from two standpoints. First, this provided those developing the software with a firsthand look at how the user intends to use the capabilities. Second, the user becomes more familiar with the product and can provide comments to clarify any operational inconsistencies.

IT&E groups should be used on all software development projects when there are adequate resources to support them. The costs associated with employing an IT&E group can be as high as 10% of the total program costs. Independent test and evaluation is a valuable MPP and should be employed recognizing the following conditions:

1. IT&E personnel disassociated from software development staff.
2. Test plans developed early using requirements documents and then baselined.
3. User involved directly in testing to the extent possible.

4.2.4.3 INDEPENDENT TESTING (TRW)

Independent testing is the performace of formal testing by a team of testing specialists which is organizationally separate from the group responsible for software development. It involves analysis of software requirements;

planning, preparation, and performance of tests; review of test results for satisfaction of requirements; discrepancy reporting; and retesting after discrepancies are resolved and fixes are made. It also includes support to the developers through review of design documentation and designation of distinct functional capabilities to be exercised during development testing.

The independent test group determines whether or not the software works (not how it works), evaluates requirements and design to assure that they are testable, prepares comprehensive test plans, supports quality assurance, and plans the development of test tools. The independence of the test group from the design group is desirable in order to introduce an unbiased and different point of view in the attempt to assess the capability of the developed software.

4.3 RESOURCES

The manager of software projects must contend with a mix of resource problems—budgetary resources, people resources, and technology equipment resources.

In general, the MPP companies spent little time dealing with resource problems. Perhaps the situation is that many of the resource problems are well known, and attackable only with case-specific and sometimes brute-force-type solutions. This is particularly true of budget and people problems.

A scattering of comments were made, however, about technology equipment resources. They follow.

4.3.1 Support Libraries and Facilities (BCS)

It is common practice for software developers to incorporate "standard" elements of software (e.g., subroutine libraries, operating system services, utility programs) into the software capability they are responsible for providing. Use of "standard" software elements has been practiced traditionally to reduce the costs of redeveloping code for common functions, and to improve the reliability of the software capability being produced. Further, it has become virtually imperative that the software developer employ these elements, because of the increasing sophistication of operating systems and hardware. An important objective of this practice is to protect the integrity and, hence, the reliability of the facility on which the developer's software will operate.

The facility characteristics of reliability and integrity are realized, in practice, only on "matured" computer systems. It should be noted that the recent tendency among vendors has been to build new products (hardware and system software) which are less-than-radical departures from that vendor's predecessor systems, thus retaining "matured" elements as much as possible.

Also, recent improvements in higher-order languages and the software libraries and facilities that support them have further reduced the programmer's need to resort to special techniques to achieve sizing and timing requirements, or to avail the programmer of special hardware or system software features.

Even when a new or specialized computer is to be the host for an application, the software developer need not do without "standard" elements. The design of (a subset of) some existing mature operating system can be implemented on the host, and cross-compilers can be used to produce libraries for it by copying software from another, proven system.

New management practices focus on tracking the tangible results of the software development process in order to manage that process more effectively and to control costs. In practice, even for small projects, the sheer number of individual items produced (for each subroutine, a design specification, source code, object code, compiler listing, test data, etc.) is such that a significant clerical burden is imposed. To assess status, the Program Manager needs to know which items have actually been produced and signed off. To assess progress, the Program Manager needs to know what items were planned for completion on a specific date, and whether those items have in fact been completed on schedule. To assess performance, the Program Manager needs to know how expenditures experienced in producing ongoing and completed items compares with his or her plan. Again, the amount of detailed information required to make these assessments precisely makes this practice extraordinarily difficult and costly to implement solely with manual methods. Programming support library aids are being developed which support the recording and controlling of coded items (designs, code, test data, etc.) and assist in modifying these elements. These aids are also providing the visibility needed by management for control purposes.

It should be noted that much remains to be done to fully realize the potential for using the computer to make software design, construction, and control activities more cost effective. In particular, when we surveyed the projects for this study, we found considerable dissatisfaction with the current state of automated aids for Modern Programming Practices, particularly when these aids were compared with traditional (and more mature) support libraries and facilities. The shortfall of newer aids in adequately meeting the real needs discussed above was so apparent that we found it necessary to give equal consideration in our study to the projects' use of manual alternatives in assessing the formality of their MPP implementations.

4.3.2 Resource Utilization (SDC)

The desire to achieve efficient utilization of computer resources was given special impetus by the very limited amount of core storage available in the CDC 3800s. As an index of the success in attaining this objective, it may be noted that the system has grown in size, sophistication, and throughput without a major upgrade in the computer resources available during the period studied.

The analysis of the problems in this area revealed four objectives that could potentially be attained:

1. Control of allocation of storage.
2. Eliminate the need for programs to communicate in a fixed area of core.
3. Eliminate redundant or obsolete data definitions.
4. Control/reduce data environments of programs.

4.3.2.1   STORAGE ALLOCATION

Since all programs, and a limited amount of data were relocatable, core allocation was dynamic for those relocatable elements. Thus, the addition of a program, or the substitution of a modified version, did not require a "link-edit" run. Instead, the executive recomputed the core map whenever a program was to be operated.

The dynamic loading also enables the regular policy of core loads to ensure the elimination of redundant and obsolete data. Core loads for a task may be fitted to the specific needs of the run and not general loads to fit all options for a task. The dynamic loading makes the core reallocations easy and core maps permit monitoring loads for efficient utilization.

4.3.2.2   FIXED INTERCOMMUNICATION LOCATIONS

Jobs run on the CDC 3800 were typically a mixture of programs operating in two different modes. Programs operating under the first mode ran in a core environment that was, to a large extent, fixed, whether the programs required all the tables or not. For instance, depending upon the mode, environments over 6K or 9K, respectively, were dedicated.

The problem presented by the colocation of data tables and control words was described in some of the system documentation:

> Basically, a control word is related to some aggregation of data and contains parameters which govern the use of those data. In this consideration, the simultaneous presence of both control word and data is required. But many control words are set by programs (or options) other than those which will use the data, at least during the particular operational phase. If the control word is embedded in the data an obviously wasteful use of core results during the setting phase.
>
> Examples are legion in the present system: the entire 3140-word Timer File 3 must be brought into core to enter selected events into the 10-word ACMSON

Table; the entire 1548-word Data Block 2 must be brought into core to enter control information into the 50-word Station Requirements Table.

The decision, then, is to disassociate the control words from the data; the former will reside more or less permanently in core, while the latter will enter core only for data manipulation.

The elimination of fixed-address communication, made possible by the COMPOOL definition of data elements, improves the flexibility of operations by:

Making all programs and data relocatable

Permitting dynamic linking and loading

Allowing symbolic correctors

Although the dynamic reallocation of core each time a task is loaded provides great flexibility and gains efficient utilization of storage, it demands a price in computation time. However, if a task is to remain invariant between successive passes, the system provides a push-pull capability that will save and restore an allocation without dynamic address computation.

The symbolic corrector capability may operate during reallocation to make corrections, adjustments, or adaptations to programs to fit current needs.

4.3.2.3   REDUNDANT AND OBSOLETE DATA

The problem of redundantly defined numeric constants was discussed previously. An even greater problem was presented in the identification of obsolete (i.e., unused) data values. The lack of an automated set/use capability meant that only a painstaking, instruction-by-instruction analysis could produce this important program management tool. Even then, of course, it was subject to the human error inherent in the performance of a tedious, repetitive task.

The purging of redundant and obsolete data from the COMPOOL is enhanced by the procedures employed to review and control additions and modifications to the COMPOOL. These procedures include:

Procedures for reviewing proposed changes and maintaining the COMPOOL

Analyses of current content of the COMPOOL

Close review of all COMPOOL changes resulting from adding new programs or modifying existing programs keeps data redundancies to a low level, and ensures the observance of data standards (including the isolation of constant, guaranteed, and transient data) and efficient handling and storage utilization. Considered is the impact of changes on other users, the coordination of changes with users, and the restructuring of the system.

Analytic listings are used to detect redundancies and impacts and to evaluate segmentation and efficiency. The system-set-used listings are specifically used to detect obsolete items, those neither set nor used by the current system.

4.3.2.4 PROGRAM ENVIRONMENTS

The lack of control over the environment of programs often resulted not only in inefficient utilization of storage, but incompatibilities among the programs. For example, a 1598-word output buffer for matrix display was maintained while the program computing the two matrixes to be displayed was limited to processing 21 parameters (i.e., the maximum output could be only 462 words).

4.3.3   Different Development/Integration Sites (Martin-Marietta)

The Viking Lander software subsystem of the Mission Operations Software System was developed at Martin-Marietta on nontarget computers. Programs were unit tested prior to being delivered to JPL.

The forecasts for the loads on the computer sets at JPL indicated that portions of the Viking operational software system could not be developed on them. The Martin-Marietta facility contained CDC 6400, CDC 6500, and IBM 360/75 computer sets, whereas the JPL facility contained Univac 1108 and IBM 360/75 computer sets. The operating systems of the IBM computers at the two facilities were different. No equipment similar to the JPL Univac 1108 system was available in the Denver area. Pathfinder studies indicated that software could be developed on nontarget computers without creating any serious conversion problems.

Great amounts of labor and machine time can be spent converting software. This, coupled with the extra costs of not meeting scheduled delivery dates, can cause software conversion to be an expensive task. Many times much of this labor and machine time and schedule slippages could be reduced by planning, organizing, and controlling the software development activities relative to the conversion process. The principal methods used in the management of the conversion process by Martin-Marietta on the Viking project were: (1) predominant use of a minimal high-order language; (2) education of programmers and engineers on system differences and similarities; (3) emphasis on the fact that the software would eventually reside in another computer system; (4) pathfinder operations to seek out problems that might occur prior to the actual conversion process; (5) establishment of Martin-Marietta computer consultants at JPL to gain familiarity with both the various computer systems and the operational procedures; and (6) the requirement that the software be demonstrated to unit function properly prior to the conversion process.

Prior to initiating software development the Martin-Marietta management examined the need for standards required to develop software on nontarget computers. One output of this analysis was to require the use of Fortran except when individual software requirements represented an actual need for assembly programming. This decision was based on several reasons. Fortran compilers were available on the various computer systems at both JPL and Martin-Marietta. Some of the prototype software for mission operations were already written in Fortran. The programming skills of the Martin-Marietta engineers and programmers were limited in many cases to Fortran.

Once the decision to use Fortran was made, a study was undertaken to determine what differences existed between the various Fortran compilers on the Univac 1108, IBM 360, and CDC 6000 series computers. This study showed that there were variations in permissible number sizes, that some features of Fortran were not available on all the Fortran compilers, and that some implementations went beyond the standard Fortran. A document entitled "Characteristics of Fortran, CDC 6000 Series, IBM System/360, Univac 1108" was written which showed the minimal language that would be used to reduce conversion costs between the development computer and the integration computer. A second reason set forth for the usage of the minimal language was that for some programs the development machine at Martin-Marietta had been determined but the final machine at JPL had not been decided upon. The target computer would be determined at a later date when computer loading studies could be made and analyzed.

The education of the engineers and programmers in the conversion process was undertaken next. Lectures were given which involved discussions regarding the minimal language document and its contents. The minimal language document was incorporated along with JPL documentation on the IBM 360s and the Univac 1108s into a document entitled "Viking Flight Operations Programmer Guide." This was distributed to all programmers and engineers. The primary point stressed during this education process was that by following the minimum language requirements during software development, the conversion efforts of the programmer would be lessened. Other points stressed during this education were that by using the guidelines set forth, together with thorough documentation, changeover between programmers and engineers caused by changes in personnel would be less costly.

The software conversion task was done on schedule, although not without some problems. Many of the problems that did occur had to do with the altering of the engineers and programmers normal work habits. This occurred in the IBM 360 conversion effort. Due to the operational procedures at JPL, in order to receive the necessary turnaround time to do program conversion and testing, blocks of computer time had to be scheduled. These blocks of time were usually 4 to 6 hours in duration during the week, starting at 9:00 P.M. to 4:00 A.M., and up to 48 hours' duration on the weekends. The pressures of trying to make as many runs as possible and meet delivery schedules forced many extra errors into the software. Instead of doing a detailed analysis of the code and the dump of the program, the programmer or engineer would shot-gun many runs to try to fix errors. During longer block-time stretches many engineers and programmers would work until, because of physical and mental exhaustion, they introduced new errors. This altering of normal work habits did not occur on the 1108 conversion effort. The turnaround was excellent and the machine was available for use during normal working hours. Blocks of time were required only in very special cases and were planned by the engineer and programmer so that the use of the time was optimized. In short, the conversion process requires good computer turnaround during normal working hours to be efficient.

The Martin-Marietta (MMC) IBM 370 to JPL IBM 360 conversion effort had some problems that were not foreseen. The JPL version of OS was a real-time system with standard OS features but was a different release than the MMC IBM OS. This caused problems in the conversion effort. In one instance the difference in Fortran compilers between MMC IBM and JPL IBM caused schedule slippages due to errors in the target compiler that were not discovered until the conversion process began. This problem happened early in the conversion process and two steps were taken to help solve the problems: (1) the release of the JPL compiler was installed at MMC for use by the software still in development, and (2) the release of the MMC compiler was installed at JPL for use when needed.

One other problem that occurred should be reported. This was an internal conversion effort done at MMC on the CDC. The operating system was changed during the period in which the software was being developed. This change caused many schedule impacts in the Viking software development. Much time was spent by the development programmers changing their job control cards, their file naming conventions, their file structures, and in learning how the system worked. This coupled with extra downtime and running of two operating systems caused much confusion. The conclusion is that any operating system change should not be allowed concurrent with a major software development activity.

The software should have been maintained at JPL after its initial delivery to JPL. Deliveries of the software were scheduled to include various programs and subsets of the programs required for test and training operations which were carried on throughout the spacecraft compatibility test phase. When a program was delivered to support such a test, the programmers and engineers would take the final converted program back to MMC, convert back to the MMC computer, and then do the development required for the next delivery. This was an extra task that should never be required.

It should be stressed that by following the concepts discussed herein, the conversion of the MMC-developed Viking mission operations software was done on schedule within budget, and successfully supported two Viking missions.

Total personnel for cognizant engineers and programmer activities involved in developing, testing, and documenting Viking lander operational software produced an average of 7 lines of code per day. Individual programs varied from a low of 3.3 lines of code per day to a high of 12.4 lines of code per day. These figures are reasonably within the industry norm for software developed on target computers, indicating that the impact of conversion was relatively low. One program was delivered 2 months late because of differences in compilers, which was a conversion problem. All other programs were converted on schedule. The conversion process represented approximately 5% of the development effort for 1108 programs, and approximately 10% of the development effort for 360 programs.

4.3.4 Computer Loading Prediction Analyses (Martin-Marietta)

Two types of computer loading prediction analyses were conducted for the Viking Mission. They included hand analyses of predicted CPU requirements and use of the General Purpose Simulation System (GPSS) program. Both indicated that the planned Mission timelines could not be met. The Viking Flight Team conducted a full-scale test that verified the findings of the loading analyses. The key decisions resulting from these efforts included changing the Mission Design from two parallel to two serial landed missions, acquiring an additional 1108 computer set to support operations, and decreasing the planned frequency for commanding the vehicles.

Operations analyses of timelines and computer loading analyses are applicable to software systems supporting missions subject to environmental surprises, such as Viking. On the other hand, if the software system is being developed for use in a steady-state environment, a computer loading analysis made for any point in time should be sufficient. Two techniques for accomplishing the loading analyses are available. One approach is to use a complex computer program such as GPSS to model the throughput of each computer used by the system. The second approach is to perform hand analyses of requirements versus capabilities for basic parameters such as CPU time.

Computer loading analyses are a proven useful tool to software managers. Two areas should be concentrated upon independent of the technique selected; (1) the quality of the inputs will determine the accuracy of the output, and (2) careful interpretation of the output is required if correct conclusions are to be drawn.

During 1973, management was developing the Viking Mission design. The key factors of concern were the Mars encounter dates, the landing dates, and the frequency and duration of the biological investigations. At that time the planned nominal sequence was as follows:

1. Viking I encounters Mars.
2. VL-1 lands 12 days later.

3. VL-1 initiates biological investigations 4 days later.
4. Viking II encounters Mars 8 days later.
5. VL-2 lands 12 days later.
6. VL-2 initiates biological investigations 4 days later.
7. VL-1 terminates biological investigations 60 days later.
8. VL-2 terminates biological investigations 24 days later.

The prime Viking landed missions were each planned to have 90-day durations, with about 65 days of overlap. Shortly after the mission was established, the Integrating Contractor Software System Engineer made a hand computer loading analysis based on Mariner 9 experience and proposed 7-day look-ahead for lander planning. The analysis indicated that the computer complex at JPL would not be adequate for Viking.

Management therefore directed that an analysis of a 2-day mission period should be conducted. The fifth and sixth days after the Viking II landing were selected. Representatives from each Viking Flight Team defined the products they would produce, the inputs they would require, and the computer runs they would need. After these data were gathered, a cursory timeline/computer loading analysis was made that indicated that the computers could not support the events planned for these days; people were both waiting to use computers and not ready to use them when they were available. As a result of this analysis the Mission Design was changed to the following sequence:

1. Viking I encounters Mars.
2. VL-1 lands 19 days later.
3. VL-1 initiates biological investigation 7 days later.
4. Viking II encounters Mars 21 days later.
5. VL-1 terminates biological investigation 27 days later.
6. VL-2 lands 3 days later.
7. VL-2 initiates biological investigation 7 days later.

It is emphasized that the decision to slow down the pace and go to a serial mission could have been made from either an operations analysis of people overload or a computer loading analysis that demonstrated computer overload. Furthermore, the decision to go to a serial mission was made when the software system was less than half finished, so that only rough estimates of the characteristics of the programs were known.

At this time the Viking Project issued a separate contract to develop a General Purpose Simulation System Model for the Mission Control and Computing Center system. This was a joint effort by MMC and JPL personnel, using the IBM GPSS as the basis for the model. A Critical Period Analysis covering a 12-day period of the serial mission was conducted in parallel with the development. The purpose of the analysis was to study timelines and computer loading in more detail and to prepare for VFT test and training activities. By this time more software was developed, allowing better inputs for the computer loading analysis.

Because the Model had not yet been verified, a hand analysis was again made. The results of the analysis indicated that more Univac 1108 capability would be needed to avoid another mission simplification. Since lead time for purchasing an 1108 prior to planetary operations was becoming tight, the time saved by hand analysis was quite beneficial.

At this time the Viking Project and JPL faced the choice of purchasing or leasing a third 1108 or of adding a second Central Processing Unit to each of the two existing 1108s. In order to make this decision, a full-scale test was scheduled to be conducted during the 3-day Memorial weekend in May of 1975. Prior to the test both the Model and hand analyses were used to predict the outcome of the test. The test confirmed both analyses, and was the tool that verified the accuracy of the GPSS model. The results of the test led to the decision to purchase a third 1108.

It was not that Viking needed three 1108s but rather that Viking plus the non-Viking JPL users would require that capacity. The decision to add a third 1108 rather than increase the CPU capability was based on the fact that it would result in less sharing between Viking and non-Viking users.

Early in 1976, test and training exercises were conducted in a series of tests using the simplified Mission design, the extra 1108, and modified operational strategies based on the results of computer loading analyses. The tests demonstrated that the system could operate to support the mission timelines.

The processes used to conduct the computer loading analyses were as follows.

Programmers estimated program run characteristics, such as CPU time, I/O time, core usage, disk space, and tape drives. Each program could be used for different tasks having different characteristics. Data were gathered for every case.

Engineers then estimated when, how, and why they would use the programs in each mode. Each team would indicate what time or times during the day each program mode would need to be run to satisfy mission objectives. Estimates of how long it would take to analyze the results of a computer run before the next run could be made were also included.

The hand computer analyses were then based on adding up the CPU time required for each computer during each team's shift and matching it with the inputs supplied by the programmers and engineers. A subjective judgment factor then had to be applied. During any 8-hour period, CPU requirements in excess of 4 hours for the 360/75 or 5 hours for the 1108 indicated that insufficient computer capacity was available. The early analyses indicated that 8 hours CPU time on the 1108 would be required, stressing the need for an additional computer.

The GPSS modeled all the inputs obtained from the engineers and programmers. The program modeled both 1108 and 360/75 operations. The characteristics included core capacity, CPU rate, I/O rate, tape drives, and delays caused by human beings examining computer runs. The model would not allow runs to begin when core or tape drives were unavailable, nor would it allow a program to begin if it required input from another program that had not been completed. As such, the model did not overload the computers. Rather, it would indicate that one day's work required two days to complete if insufficient computer power was available.

The GPSS modeled the scatter load feature of the IBM 360/75, but did not model the core-swapping feature of the UNIVAC 1108. It accounted for print and plot times, but not for system outages. The model is now a standard tool used by JPL as a scheduling tool and for the purpose of estimating potential system performance improvement.

Sufficient evidence for the potential usefulness of computer loading analyses to managers of software development has been presented. A few important aspects are worth noting.

The primary error source of the analysis is the quality of the input. Since the quality of the output is limited by the quality of the input, the cheaper and faster hand analysis offers advantages over a complex simulation model, which would have to be validated before it could be relied upon. In cases where most runs can be executed overnight, one-day granularity is sufficient to achieve an understanding of the problem. In a mission operations environment where a sequence of runs needs to be accomplished during a working-day shift, a granularity of 4 or 8 hours should be used.

Most participants felt that the hand analyses were adequate and the GPSS was an expensive luxury, although a significant number did not hold this point of view. The use of the GPSS did have two generally agreed upon side benefits. People generating inputs for analysis tended to be more careful and thorough when they knew their data would be used in GPSS rather than for a hand analysis. Also, management was more impressed with GPSS results and paid more attention to the implications, regardless of whether or not they understood how the GPSS worked.

The Memorial Day test to verify the GPSS provided additional guidance concerning operational procedures and file management problems. These areas were ignored by the hand analyses and treated inadequately by GPSS.

One final point should be made relative to the computer loading analyses. They only reflected how the team thought the mission would be run. They did not account for the 16-day delay in finding a satisfactory landing site for Viking I, nor for the additional Mission Planning activities for both Vikings I and II (neither Viking was set down at its originally planned landing site). They did not account for maintaining a reduced Viking I mission during the primary Viking II mission. Finally, they did not account for the data rate changes resulting from the scientists analyzing data and then trying experiments that were not originally planned. Their primary value was to determine the level of activity that could be supported, which allowed management to realistically assess how much could be accomplished.

Since the computer loading analyses were conducted in conjunction with operations timeline study analyses, it is difficult to determine their specific costs. Probably 1 person-year was spent to generate inputs. Less than 1 person-year was spent on hand analyses. About 3 person-years were required to develop the GPSS model. An additional 1 to 2 person-years were required to maintain the model.

Approximately 200 members of the team supported the 3-day Memorial weekend tests used to validate the GPSS. Had it not been for the computer loading studies, that test probably would not have been scheduled.

Five

Evaluation Methods

If there was variance in the definition of Modern Programming Practices among the participating companies, that variance was minor when contrasted with the variance in methods used to evaluate the MPP.

Several of the companies simply presented their MPPs, talked about their usage, emphasized their strengths (and, occasionally, their weaknesses), and concluded by recommending them.

A few of the companies conducted a more elaborate study. BCS, for example, used a questionnaire and interviews to gather data on the value of the MPPs, using Program Managers and key technical contributors. Cost performance of MPP use in practice supplemented those opinions with somewhat more objective data.

CSC used "all available information sources—project, personnel, documentation, reports, products, etc." The objective framework superimposed over these data was error incidence performance of the MPPs.

TRW performed the most elaborate study of MPP value. Although reliance was placed on the same kinds of information sources as CSC, the data were refined and massaged more thoroughly than the other companies. The result is the most definitive set of conclusions and recommendations of the six participating companies.

Methodologies used by the MPP companies to perform the evaluation are described both in the material that follows (an overview of the evaluation) and in Appendix A (the details of the evaluation). It will be obvious to the reader that (1) there is no uniformity of approach to the problem of programming practice evaluation, and (2) this dilemma is exacerbated by the unavailability of the kinds of data needed to perform the evaluations. Clearly, these problems must be addressed before any more serious studies can be undertaken.

5.1 STUDY APPROACH (BCS)

The fundamental hypothesis of this study is that software development (definition, design, construction) rules, if rigorously defined and applied and supported by modern techniques and tools, make possible the production of higher-quality software at lower-than-customary cost.

We began our study by defining the set of Modern Programming Practices being employed within BCS, and contrasting these with traditional software development approaches. For each Modern Programming Practice, we determined what tangible evidence would indicate formal implementation of the practice by a software project. We then postulated what qualitative effects these MPP could be expected to have on the software development cycle. This resulted in a rationale predicting the effects of the various practices.

From the prediction of effects, specific hypotheses were formulated for testing and study. These hypotheses, the defined MPP indicators, and the parameters necessary to determine project costs formed the basis for a questionnaire that was used to collect the data for this study (see Appendix A-1). The questionnaire was used in a series of interviews with the Program Managers and key individuals on five BCS software development projects.

Once the data-gathering interviews were completed, the development costs for the five projects were predicted. We based our predictions on estimating techniques currently in use within BCS which presume that traditional approaches to software development are used. We then compared predicted costs for the projects versus the actual costs they experienced, to determine if the projects enjoyed particular benefits from employing MPP.

Since all the projects surveyed did not employ all of the MPP being investigated, the next step was to correlate practices actually implemented on each project with that project's cost benefits. The result of this correlation was a set of MPP determined to have high leverage in reducing software development costs.

5.2 OVERVIEW (CSC)

Each project was carefully researched to isolate the modern programming practices used. In some cases the project managers had adapted specific practices to meet unique requirements. These variants were also identified and defined. Using each complete list of project MPPs as a guide, the individual projects were carefully examined in depth. All available information sources were used. This included project personnel, documentation, reports, products, etc. This research was directed toward assessing the impact of the programming practices on the conduct and completion of the system development.

Once the assessment had been completed, the programming practices identified were compared with the structured programming technology (SPT) techniques discussed in the IBM Structured Programming Series. Before the two could be compared it was necessary to develop a format and criteria for completing the comparison. There was not a one-to-one correspondence of MPP to SPT techniques except in a few instances. In some cases, terminology was different where actual activities were the same or very nearly alike. In these instances the practice and technique were identified by their similarities. In every instance possible, correspondence between individual MPP and SPT techniques was established for comparison purposes. The comparison process was completed for each applicable computer program life-cycle phase, and to the extent possible, was based upon quantifiable factors common to the activities under study. Where correspondence was not established, the activity was evaluated and compared to other MPP and SPT techniques within appropriate phases.

Following the comparison of MPP and SPT techniques, a composite set of standard practices was identified. These standard practices were selected because of their positive effect on the acquisition process and their utility within the various types of system development environments. The factors influencing the selection of these practices are discussed, together with techniques for their use. This set of modern programming practices represents an optimum array of management and technical aids to be applied throughout the complete life cycle. However, these practices are not representative of the entire spectrum of available management and technical aids. They were selected from only these projects and the Structured Programming Series. It must be emphasized that there are other practices that should be evaluated to produce a more definitive analysis.

The MPP research was hampered during its conduct by adverse circumstances which had some effect on the results. This is not to say that the conclusions drawn are necessarily invalid. It is simply to point out that for conclusive proof that the research findings are true, more comprehensive and extensive research is necessary. The most significant problems encountered in this research project were twofold. First, none of the three projects' management controls or reporting produced the types of data necessary for a thorough analysis of the programming practices effectiveness. The data required for complete analysis must be defined at the project outset and then collected and verified throughout the life of the project. The performance measurement and reporting required for this goes far beyond that necessary for routine project management and will, in all likelihood, increase overhead costs considerably. Second, by beginning this study when the projects were completed or in the final development phases, much of the information sought was not readily available. Key project personnel often had transferred, substantiating resource data were occasionally missing, and some reports were difficult to analyze.

MPP data collection can only be effective if it is structured as a coordinated project task which is an integral part of the software development. This approach to software data collection offers significant benefits over that used for this study. First, by initially defining data collection requirements and procedures there is more assurance that they will be less disruptive of the software development process and will produce more definitive and accurate data. It is extremely important that data collection not inhibit the normal production cycle. Data accuracy must be maintained throughout the collection process to ensure the validity of research findings. Next, software data collection must be carried out by an independent research group. To the maximum extent possible members of this group should maintain a disinterested status relative to the project to prevent any bias from appearing in the research report. This approach will be costly in terms of personnel required in excess of that required exclusively for program development.

5.2.1 Comparison Process

A methodology for comparing the practices and techniques has been devised. This methodology is founded upon the percent of time specific error types exist and the probability of detection or reduction of that error type by the practices and techniques within each life-cycle phase. Using these data and statistical analysis techniques, each practice or technique can be assigned an effectiveness value for each life-cycle phase. These values will be used later to support the selection of MPP that will be proposed as standards for Air Force software engineering projects.

CSC's comparison methodology is a stepwise process proceeding from identification of programming practices and techniques to calculation of their individual effectiveness values. The fundamental premise upon which this methodology rests is that the timely production of error-free computer programs is the goal of software acquisition projects. Computer program errors are defined to include not only processing faults, but also failure to satisfy system performance requirements. This broad definition is meant to be inclusive of all aspects of computer program performance.

In developing the comparison methodology, four major assumptions were made. First, practices and techniques that promote the detection or reduction of computer program errors can be ranked according to their effectiveness with regard to that capability. Second, each practice or technique included in this study has been used to further the timely production of error-free software. Third, it is possible to define an inclusive set of software error types that can be readily identified during any software development. Fourth, data can be collected that will support definition of probability of error-type existence and probability of error-type detection or reduction.

In the following discussions, values that are used in the matrices and in the calculations are not universally supported by project research data. There are several reasons for this. The Software Production Data project involved research of only three CSC software acquisition projects and the IBM Structured Programming Series. This meant that available data points to support conclusions were limited or nonexistent. Much of the available resource material was not designed to support research of this type. In many cases the material could not be substantiated or expanded because project personnel had transferred or left the Company. To counter these conditions, the research staff used statistical techniques and CSC management staff surveys. Through these aids a consistent and reasonable data analysis was completed, although CSC admits that these data are by no means complete. It is felt that enough of a data base exists to make a first-cut rough estimate—at least to the extent of trying to prove the usefulness of the methodology. It is important that, in the following discussions, the comparison methodology itself be given consideration equal to that of the comparison results. The methodology comprises these activities:

1. Identification of practice or technique life-cycle phase applicability
2. Definition of software error types
3. Establishment of percentages of error-type existence
4. Establishment of error-type detection or reduction probability
5. Calculation of practice or technique effectiveness values

For a detailed discussion of these activities, see Appendix A.2.

5.3   OBJECTIVE, SCOPE, AND PROBLEMS OF MPP STUDY (TRW)

The primary objectives of the study were to:

1. Assess the impact of modern programming practices (MPP) applied to the TRW STP software development activity
2. Develop a methodology for comparison of STP MPP with alternative MPP implementations used on other projects by other contractors

To fully achieve these objectives we needed to obtain valuable insights into the relative merits of individual practices and to devise and demonstrate a technique to evaluate the combined effectiveness of selected practices when applied to projects of varying type, size, and complexity.

In attempting to carry out this task, TRW was faced with several formidable problems. First, the hypothesis, as stated above, is extremely general and ambiguous. The state-of-the-art of software engineering has not yet produced a useful definition of "higher-quality software," and, although much has been done recently toward development of software cost estimation methods, the emerging cost models are as yet imprecise, awkward to use, and limited in scope of application. As a result, there is not yet a commonly understood and accepted meaning of "higher-quality software" and "usual cost" upon which a test of the hypothesis can be based.

The second major problem has to do with the availability of relevant data to be used in testing the hypothesis. Although a great many data on the STP software development activity were collected and available to support the MPP study, the identification of truly relevant data and translation into credible evidence concerning the hypothesis was seen to be a costly and probably imprecise and inconclusive task unless planned and approached in a highly selective fashion.

In striving to overcome the possible adverse effects of the above-mentioned problems, TRW defined and implemented an innovative MPP impact assessment approach which included:

1. Formulation of many more definitive subhypotheses involving the impact of individual practices on characteristics of software and the software development process
2. Accomplishment of a modified Delphi exercise, including several surveys of STP personnel to permit both relative quantification and testing of the subhypotheses
3. Highly selective examination of STP records and documentation for further testing of certain subhypotheses
4. Evaluation of the overall hypothesis through combination of subhypothesis test results

Each of the surveys was designed to achieve a balance of:

1. Desired objectivity in formulation and testing of the hypotheses.
2. Essential reliance on actual experience and use of qualified engineering judgment in evaluating MPP impact.

For a detailed discussion of these activities, see Sections A.3 and A.4.

Six

Conclusions
and
Recommendations

The culmination of this discussion of Modern Programming Practices is the so-called "bottom line"—given all the verbiage of description, which, in fact, are the real gems among the MPP candidates?

To some extent, the conclusions are anticlimactic. Most of the MPP companies simply said, in essence: "Our MPP are all good MPP." This is not a surprising conclusion—for one thing, industry is unlikely to use a methodology if it has no payoff, and thus the MPP were in a sense "prescreened"; and for another, it is human nature to advocate relatively uncritically the processes we utilize.

However, this is a mildly disappointing conclusion, since a large quantity of MPP have been presented, and it would be nice to present a short summary of the "best of the best MPP" as a conclusion to this book.

Fortunately, one of the MPP companies did, in fact, rank the methodologies which they studied. These rankings came out of an elaborate technologist survey which is described earlier in this book and in Appendix A.

TRW's ranked conclusions are therefore listed first in the conclusions and recommendations that follow. The remaining MPP company conclusions are then presented.

6.1 CONCLUSIONS AND RECOMMENDATIONS (TRW)

6.1.1 Conclusions

Of the more than 30 candidate Modern Programming Practices considered during this study, the following four were determined to have the strongest positive impact on software quality and productivity:

1. Requirements Analysis and Validation
2. Baselining of Requirements Specification
3. Complete Preliminary Design
4. Process Design

This outcome is consistent with data available from other projects indicating that increased rigor and engineering discipline in the requirements definition and design phases have the highest leverage on improving software production.

The following three MPP were determined to have the next highest impact:

5. Incremental Development
6. Unit Development Folders
7. Software Development Tools

The following four MPP completed the list of the highest-impact practices:

8. Independent Testing
9. Enforced Programming Standards
10. Software Configuration Management
11. Formal Inspection of Documentation and Code

All eleven of these MPP were determined to have a generally positive impact on attaining desirable qualities of software and achieving more productive developer effort through elimination of typical software production problems. A special survey and analysis of the impact of 18 detailed programming standards on 30 specific software qualities showed a generally positive impact on software quality and a mixed impact on software development productivity. Noting, however, that improved software quality strongly correlates with long-range benefits such as easier software maintenance, the net result is an overall positive impact of the standards on software life-cycle productivity.

6.1.2   Discussion of Conclusions

It should not be surprising that the overall evaluation of the STP MPP turned out to be positive, mainly because STP was never intended to be a trial experiment with a set of practices having unknown effect. Indeed, a major emphasis of the project was to evolve an improving set of practices to eliminate a wide range of software production problems, to enhance specific software qualities and to reduce the life-cycle cost of the software.

This evolutionary approach has had several effects. The first and most obvious is that an evaluation of any set of relatively mature practices will almost certainly produce a positive impact rating, because, in general, the practices are designed, applied, examined, and refined with that goal in mind. Another more subtle but important observation concerns the evaluated impact of individual practices.

Before a newly implemented practice becomes mature (i.e., during its initial application), its value is strongly governed by two competing phenomena: the Hawthorne effect,* and a resistance to change/learning curve effect. The first results in emphasizing (often overemphasizing) the strengths of the practice while resistance to change has generally the opposite effect. This competition is healthy since it leads to steady improvement of the practice through refinements that maximize the strengths and minimize the weaknesses. The evolutionary process involves many people, however, and it is sometimes painful and usually slow. Thus, the premature evaluation of a practice, if objective, will often be mixed, having positive impact in some areas, negative impact in others. In some areas the impact may be inconclusive (i.e., neither clearly positive nor negative) due to differing experiences, and insufficient data.

The best example of the latter phenomenon occurred in the evolution of the structured coding requirement. It was the most recently adopted STP standard programming practice. The evaluated impact of the structured coding practice was either negative or inconclusive with respect to one-third of the desirable qualities of software and the development process. Among the factors that also influenced the structured programming requirement were:

1. The formal requirement for structured coding was established 2 years after the start of the project, after a large amount of code had been developed.

2. The structuring standard was imposed on coding in either Fortran or assembly language, neither of which easily support writing structured programs.

3. The phase of the project during which the major benefits of structured programming are expected to be reaped (i.e., during operations and maintenance) has not yet begun.

* The tendency to perform well when being observed.

Another important feature of the study results is the grouping of the 11 MPP into three broad categories. The four highest-ranked practices (Requirements Analysis and Validation, Baselining of Requirements Specifications, Complete Preliminary Design, and Process Design) fell into one group; the three middle-ranked practices (Incremental Development, Unit Development Folders, and Software Development Tools) in another; and the four lowest-ranked practices (Formal Inspection of Documentation and Code, Software Configuration Management, Independent Testing, and Enforced Programming Standards) fell in the bottom group. The significant point to be noted is that the highest-ranked group contains practices that are generally applied at the front end of the software development activity, the middle-ranked group applies to the middle stages of development, while the lowest-ranked group applies mostly to the latter stages.

Notice also that the first group, and, to some extent, the second group of practices are viewed as providing assistance to the human performance of tasks generally thought of as complex, thought-provoking, and highly creative. The last group, on the other hand, is more often viewed as the implementation of policing functions aimed at checking up on developers and pointing out their mistakes. It is likely that a practice popularity poll would correlate well with the actual ranking of the groups according to their relative positive impact on software development.

The relative impact ranking of the groups of practices was also strongly influenced by their history of application in the STP chronology. In particular, the software development activity has been influenced by the first group of practices for the longest period of time, and those practices, therefore, have had more opportunity to make their positive impact felt. This observation is consistent with recent software engineering research findings which point out (1) the large fraction (as high as 70%) of total software problems that occur early in the development cycle, and (2) the unusually high value of practices that help find problems as early as possible, before they propagate confusion, additional work, and expense throughout subsequent project phases.

Another important conclusion of the study is that the isolation of the effect and evaluation of impact of any given practice within a large, complex, and dynamic project environment can be exceedingly difficult. Fortunately, this conclusion was anticipated at the outset of the study, and great care was taken to identify a select subset of the many STP practices such that:

1. The number of practices was small enough to permit thorough study of each.

2. Each practice was generic enough (i.e., not strongly oriented toward unique features of STP) to permit relatively straightforward inclusion in Air Force development guidelines with broad applicability.

3. Each practice had been used extensively enough to ensure a

reasonable base of project data and experience to support impact evaluation.

4. The set of practices, in combined application, spanned the development process and addressed each major development phase.

The careful selection of MPP limited the number of practices a lot and limited their scope a little, but it permitted sufficient depth of the impact analyses and sufficient effort for comparison methodology development to make it possible to ultimately conclude:

1. The STP MPP (and some practices in particular) contribute significantly to enhancement of important qualities of software, and generally the investment required to implement and apply MPP pays off in overall life-cycle cost reductions.

2. There are significant differences among MPP in both the areas to which they contribute and the magnitude of the contributions they make.

3. It has been demonstrated that a methodology can be developed and used to obtain a comparative evaluation of alternative MPP implementations.

4. The MPP comparison methodology (including the support tools developed for this study) can be used to both select and evaluate candidate combinations of MPP for projects of varying type, size, and complexity.

6.1.3   Recommendations

The overall objective of the MPP study was to assess the effects of MPP on a large DoD system software development so that those practices determined to have a favorable effect could be recommended to and considered by the Air Force for adoption on future developments. In light of this goal and owing to the determination of positive impact for all 11 of the STP MPP, it is reasonable to recommend that all be considered for inclusion in Air Force software development guidelines, procurement practices, and policy initiatives. Of these MPP, the four most highly ranked should receive especially strong consideration in view of the pressing need for improved methods for defining, expressing, and allocating software requirements and for maintaining their traceability throughout the development process. On the other hand, it is clear that not all software development activities are alike, and few systems compare with the size, complexity, and real-time performance requirements of the software being developed by TRW on the Systems Technology Program.

Based in part on the above consideration as well as on the detailed MPP study findings documented fully in this report, it is recommended that the Air Force:

1. Continue to emphasize those high-impact MPP listed above which are now covered or will be covered in existing and new Air Force and DoD policies.

2. Emphasize the following additional high-impact MPP in future Air Force policy initiatives:
   a. Incremental Development
   b. Unit Development Folders
   c. Software Development Tools (especially those with demonstrated capability and broad applicability)

3. Promote research to formalize and generalize other high-impact MPP:
   a. Process Design
   b. Software Development Tools (especially requirements definition and design aids, higher-order languages and diagnostic language processors, and advanced test tools)

4. Support continued investigation necessary for further confirmation of the results of this study and comparison with other results on other projects.

5. Develop standardized definitions and measures (e.g., productivity, modularity, cost) critical to accurate and comparable assessments of impact of alternative MPP.

6. Pursue evaluation of MPP used by other contractors on other projects and build upon the impact evaluation/comparison framework using the tools and data base developed in this study.

7. Establish ground rules and a methodology for relating software qualities to software operations and maintenance costs to support better assessment of life-cycle MPP impact.

8. Initiate research and development of techniques for selecting an appropriate subset of high-impact practices commensurate with the type, size, complexity, and available resources of planned software procurements.

6.1.4 The Overall Message

The overall message appears to confirm some of our earlier findings, and prompt new ones, namely:

1. The proper handling (i.e., baselining and controlling changes) of software requirements is of critical importance with respect to software quality, cost, and schedule, and MPP that encourage and sup-

port proper handling (such as Baselining of Requirements Specification and Requirements Analysis and Validation) are most needed and have most beneficial impact.

2. Although there is substantial agreement on the overall beneficial impact of the 11 STP MPP, there is clearly room for improvement, especially regarding the four least highly ranked MPP (Independent Testing, Enforced Programming Standards, Software Configuration Management, and Formal Inspection of Documentation and Code). This is consistent with the MPP Impact Evaluation summary, which generally indicates higher positive MPP impact (in the theoretical case) than that reported in the actual STP software development to date.

3. Most of the positive attitude toward and general acceptance of MPP is expressed in terms of positive impact on software quality (particularly reliability and maintainability), while it is apparently felt that MPP contribute less directly to software development cost and schedule. Furthermore, if MPP are introduced late in the development process, or if they are poorly defined or poorly understood and inconsistently applied, they can adversely effect rework, productivity, and personnel motivation with possible negative impact on cost and schedule.

6.2 RECOMMENDATIONS (MARTIN-MARIETTA)

Each of the techniques described in this report are applicable to specific situations that can arise during the development of a software system. The following recommendations are made relative to software management functions:

1. Follow a top-down development cycle that includes the following phases
   a. Mission definition
   b. System requirements
   c. System design
   d. Module requirements
   e. Module design
   f. Code and debug
   g. Module test
   h. Subsystem integration
   i. System integration
   j. Mission test

2. Write a software management plan that defines and can control the development cycle from requirements through final system delivery. The plan should be geared to the software task at hand. At a

minimum it should specify management roles/responsibilities, documentation requirements, developmental milestones, any standards that will be imposed, reviews that will be required, baselines that will be established, the software control process, the change control procedure, the level of testing that will be required, and delivery procedures for the software end product.

3. Establish meaningful milestones that can be measured. Items such as documentation release, approvals, reviews, baselines, deliveries, and tests are useful in this context.

4. Do not wait until the test and integration phase to find out if the software system will support the mission. Determine as early as possible if operational problems will exist. Computer loading and operational analyses can be used to support this function.

5. Stress the importance of requirements to be complete, accurate, and precise. They should go beyond the technical needs for the software and address such items as all known constraints, human engineering problems, and test considerations.

6. Establish baselines to control requirements, design, and end products.

7. Place requirements under control and do not permit changes to them to be approved until their impact on costs, schedules, and resources is understood.

8. Stress the importance of designing to meet the requirements. Also stress the importance of designing to take advantage of the target computer characteristics.

9. Do not permit coding to begin until the design has been approved.

10. Establish an independent test and integration team to test the software against requirements. Let the programmers test the software against its design.

11. Maintain central sources for requirements and data.

12. Gear configuration management to bringing software under control as soon as practical. Do not begin formal integration until the software is under control (i.e., out of the hands of the programmers).

13. Stress the importance of test data. Begin the effort to collect it early in the development cycle. Avoid the use of scaffolds (i.e., fake, hand-generated type data) wherever possible. If they are necessary, have them developed independent of the programmer responsible for the software that will process them.

14. Plan on uncovering errors during every phase of test and integration. Greater emphasis on the requirements/design phase should reduce the number and seriousness of errors.

In addition to the above it is recommended that procurers of large software systems adopt a policy of hiring independent software experts to audit the development approach and problems faced by contractors responsible for building large and/or complex software systems. The auditors should have experience in developing similar systems, and the same auditors should not be used over and over again. The audit report should be made available both to the procurer and to the contractor.

No recommendation is offered relative to which is best—the Chief Programmer approach, the Software Chief approach, the Cognizant Engineer/Cognizant Programmer approach, or the software pool approach. The size and/or nature of the software system will influence most contractors as to which approach is most appropriate. In any event, each of these approaches is sound, and the selection of the particular approach should be left up to the software developer.

Since Viking did not require structured programming techniques be followed, no recommendation can be made relative to their value. However, some techniques associated with structured programming were followed. These included modular design, in-line procedures, minimizing the use of unconditional transfers, and code walkthroughs. All of these features tended to improve software reliability.

6.3   STUDY FINDINGS (SPERRY UNIVAC)

The following major findings resulted from this study:

1. Generally, each program required the apportionment of personnel according to: 10% for analysis, 30% for design, 35% for coding and debugging, and 25% for testing.

2. Top-down development of programs 3 and 4 showed a 15% savings over conventional development of programs 1 and 2.

3. Software tools, especially those hosted on the Univac 1108, were found to be effective and viable for use by management, engineers, and programmers during program development.

4. Automated testing involved scenario control, real-time simulation, data recording, and data reduction using target equipments and established real-time operability of each surveyed program.

5. Although different documentation standards were employed on the surveyed programs, in each case the ratio of lines of source code per number of pages to describe design and testing was about 23:1.

6. Sperry Univac prepared software development guidelines for use during design, coding, and maintenance of each surveyed program.

7. Software quality assurance and configuration management were

employed on each surveyed program to assure product quality, controlled development, and compatibility with system management established by the customer.

8. Real-time, on-line casualty recovery and on-line maintenance testing were provided through system design and implemented in the operating system software to effectively maintain continuous system operation.

The study resulted in the following recommendations, which would enhance the introduction of MPP into project utilization:

1. *Top-down programming:* Establish the requirement that any new software development utilize the top-down program development method.
2. *Software verification through simulation:* Develop a policy that includes simulation as a method for verifying (testing) software.
3. *Fault tolerance:* Implement a standard that provides for failure detection, failure isolation, and failure recovery as a part of the operational system design.
4. *Software tools:* Standardize a policy that allows for development and application of software tools.
5. *Application of MPP:* Further analysis and evaluation is needed in the application of modern programming practices.

6.4 RECOMMENDED MPP (CSC)

Selection of the programming practices to be recommended as standards for Air Force software engineering projects is the culmination of this MPP comparison process. This process, which began with research of three CSC software engineering projects, has led to the identification and description of all programming practices that were used. These programming practices include both management and technical disciplines applied in all phases of computer program development. A comparison methodology has been defined that permits unbiased and definitive comparison of the programming practices. The comparison methodology has been employed to establish a basis for analyses of CSC programming practices and IBM SPT (Structured Programming) techniques. Application of the comparison methodology as described in this report has produced a quantitative assessment of each practice and technique in the form of phase effectiveness values for the Code and Checkout phase. Now, MPP selection procedures will be used to identify those practices and techniques that will be recommended.

It is important that the functional similarities of programming practices be

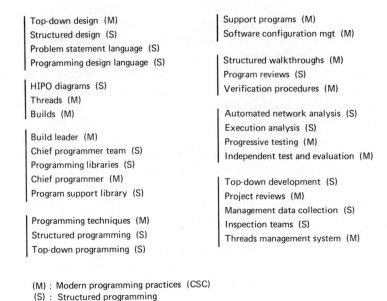

Top-down design (M)
Structured design (S)
Problem statement language (S)
Programming design language (S)

HIPO diagrams (S)
Threads (M)
Builds (M)

Build leader (M)
Chief programmer team (S)
Programming libraries (S)
Chief programmer (M)
Program support library (S)

Programming techniques (M)
Structured programming (S)
Top-down programming (S)

Support programs (M)
Software configuration mgt (M)

Structured walkthroughs (M)
Program reviews (S)
Verification procedures (M)

Automated network analysis (S)
Execution analysis (S)
Progressive testing (M)
Independent test and evaluation (M)

Top-down development (S)
Project reviews (M)
Management data collection (S)
Inspection teams (S)
Threads management system (M)

(M) : Modern programming practices (CSC)
(S) : Structured programming

Figure 6.1 Functionally Similar Practices

considered. Functional similarity refers to the employment and performance characteristics of certain programming practices that make them functionally similar. For instance, top-down design and structured design are both employed to perform the same design function and their effect on the design process is essentially the same. HIPO diagrams and threads also fit this description. In each case one of those practices may do the job better than the other, but in any case no one would consider using both practices on the same project, so functional similarities among the programming practices are identified to aid in the selection process. Figure 6.1 shows the programming practices defined in this research project with the functionally similar subsets indicated by vertical bars.

A standard set of MPPs that would be applicable to all software engineering projects cannot be developed with the current data available. Each project must be analyzed in view of its characteristics and development environment, then a proper set of MPPs could be established based on the effectiveness of those MPPs throughout the project life cycle. However, based on the data collected during this project, the following set of MPPs would be applicable to most software development projects:

Top-down design
Threads
Builds

Chief programmer

Programming techniques

Support programs

Software configuration management

Program reviews

Independent test and evaluation

Project reviews

Threads management system

6.5 CONCLUSIONS AND RECOMMENDATIONS (SDC)

The general conclusions to be drawn from this study are:

1. Observing standard programming practices does contribute to software quality.
2. Observing standard software management practices does organize and regulate the software development process, making decisions easier and better and reducing effort and confusion.
3. Environmental factors such as working conditions and availability and power of tools and facilities does affect the difficulty and efficiency of the software development process.

6.5.1 Elements of Programming Style

It is concluded that the elements of programming style such as rules for commentary, naming, paragraphing, and modularization contribute to the ease of understanding and maintainability of software.

6.5.1.1 COMMENTARY

Based on statements from the specification writers, commentary greatly improved the understandability of the COBRA DANE programs. The modules that gave the writers most difficulty were those few where data annotations were deficient, especially in the description of flags and registers of bits passed as flags.

It has been estimated that, for small modules, lines of commentary ought to equal lines of code. Composing proper commentary takes some thought and care, but its performance requires only a small proportion of the total coding and debugging task. It is estimated that commenting the code took less than 5% of the code and checkout time.

6.5.1.2 NAMING CONVENTIONS

Naming conventions provided help in organizing and classifying program elements. The names reported by the specification writers as giving difficulty were those in which the organizing elements were missing, such as table items that were not identified as elements of a specific table or file. The naming system decreases debugging and diagnostic time by making items easy to find and understand.

Following a consistent set of naming conventions adds no significant increment to programming time. Enforcement of the standard via quality inspections by program and data control personnel does entail a small cost, perhaps as much as 20% of the librarian's time. The contribution to better communication and to improved maintainability totally justifies the effort required.

6.5.1.3 PARAGRAPHING

Except for providing lines of special characters (asterisks) to set off blocks of code or blocks of commentary, programmers reported that no special effort was required to follow paragraphing rules. That is, it became habitual and automatic, and was as useful in debugging as in later legibility. The impact on readability of the programs was excellent. The specification writers universally reported no difficulties in following the overall organization and flow of programs.

6.5.1.4 MODULARIZATION

Modularization broke the programs into simple, easily understood units. Single entrance and exits and restrictions on calls outside the parent module's area of control kept flows simple and easy to follow. Where exceptions to program length, entry points, and simplicity of flow did occur, both specification writers and test personnel noted that these modules were harder to understand and to maintain. Inversions in flow due to Fortran IFs not falling through into the main flow resulted in jumping about in the code, but that is a recognized Fortran structured programming deficiency.

6.5.1.5 RECOMMENDATIONS

Although standard practice rules for writing programs are becoming more generally accepted, a minimum acceptable set needs to be extracted and stated as verifiable standards. Although the principles involved are better established than they once were, detailed implementation remains a problem. That is, technical proficiency is required to either perform or to evaluate skilled technical tasks such as modularizing a program or annotating code well. Additional formulation is required for the principles, and additional development of technical implementation guides is needed, if enforcement of the standard practices is to be based on other than expert judgment of conformance.

However, adopting rules for using the elements of programming style is beneficial no matter how unsophisticated they may currently be.

6.5.2 Program Library Operations

Instituting a well-controlled Program Library operation provides a nexus of coordination for a programming project. It provides configuration control and status information as well as a vehicle to control and account for program corrections and changes. Some of the elements to consider are:

The nature of the Program Librarian
Library structure and maintenance procedures
Change control procedures
Quality assurance provisions
Integrity of builds and versions

6.5.2.1 SYSTEM LIBRARIAN

A System Librarian seems a viable alternative to Team Librarians, but a System Librarian must be a skilled and forceful person if he or she is to enforce programming and library interaction rules and gain the support and cooperation of the programming teams.

6.5.2.2 LIBRARY MAINTENANCE

Although COBRA DANE suffered no ill effects from not initializing the Program Library with a full set of program stubs, it is believed that management visibility goals would be better served if that had been done. Firm procedures for interacting with the Program Library, including access rules and lead times for submitting materials, help regulate and organize programming as well as library operations. Regular maintenance and strong control has a stabilizing effect on the project. Where access rules were relaxed, inefficiencies were seen to occur in COBRA DANE operations.

6.5.2.3 CHANGE CONTROL

One of the principal advantages of Program Library operations is the opportunity it affords for placing a completed module under control so that no unauthorized or unverified change is made to it. The change control procedures worked very well for COBRA DANE. COBRA DANE managers felt strongly that program change control was one of the most beneficial practices of the project. It prevented unnecessary change and ensured that all proven errors were corrected. Control of changes has high impact on project performance and upon program quality. Program Library procedures contribute significantly to this control.

6.5.2.4   QUALITY ASSURANCE

Program Library operations offer a unique opportunity for verifying the observance of programming standards and the adequacy of unit testing. Further, the quality of controlled software is assured by the change procedures.

6.5.2.5   BUILD INTEGRITY

The build approach used in COBRA DANE was very effective in meeting the requirements of the project. Build deliveries keep the motivation to produce at a high level by providing short-range goals with a high specific content. The approach helps organize the work and established priorities. However, COBRA DANE experience indicates the need to protect the integrity of the delivered builds. Both programming and integration personnel need a stable environment to work within. Instability in the programs, whether the change corrects or creates an error, was really the impetus for the Chief Programmers making copies of the Program Library that they could control.

It must be concluded that providing a stable and known software environment during an evolving software development situation presents a problem. A means of protecting and guaranteeing the integrity of a build or version or modification of the system when these configurations must support other activities is highly desirable.

6.5.2.6   RECOMMENDATIONS

It is recommended that some sort of Program Library operation be instituted on every project to store the software product representation, protect it from unauthorized change, ensure the quality of the delivered product, and support configuration status accounting and reporting.

A wide range of Program Library operations running from almost completely manual to highly automated systems have been discussed and tried. Expansion of the Program Library operation to incorporate project monitor functions (schedules, budgets, and personnel records as well as a software inventory) has been suggested, plus a variety of support and analytic tools. Obviously, small projects cannot afford highly complex and powerful Program Library support programs unless there is a high volume of such projects using the library. To achieve some balance in standard practices for Program Libraries, a minimum set of functional requirements needs to be established.

Additional functions may be suggested, but not required. It is not judged feasible at this time to develop a standard tool, but standard operations seem essential.

It is suggested that the standard functions include:

1. Separate accountability for delivered and controlled versions, builds, and modifications.
2. Accountability for configurations in differing stages of development. (At a minimum, "master," "fall-back," and "test" or "developmental" versions should be maintained.)
3. Program change accountability for any controlled program. (It is suggested that status accounting records cross-reference every program change to authorization for making the change.)
4. Library activity logs.
5. Program Library configuration status reports and program change status reports.
6. Program Librarian responsibility definitions. (Note that "team" Librarian should have responsibilities and authority different from "System" Librarians.)

6.5.3 Global Data Control

Instituting a good system data control operation is just as important as that for programs. Although COBRA DANE began with relaxed system data controls, by the end of the project, stringent control was implemented.

6.5.3.1 DATA BASE COORDINATOR

If the Data Base Coordinator is to enforce programming standards for data naming conventions and data structures, prevent redundancies in definitions, consult on the efficiency of data structure and handling, and monitor the utilization of computer resources, a skilled and forceful person is required. The coordinator and the data control procedures must have strong management support. Initially on COBRA DANE, the Data Base Coordinator operated on a clerical level and exercised no control over the content or operation of the global data definitions. Before the project was over, the Chief Programmers assumed responsibility for the integrity of data in their areas of purview.

6.5.3.2 MAINTENANCE

The same access and update criterion applied to the Program Library need to be applied to the System Data Library. Regular updating and firm control procedures contribute to efficient programming. Where control was not exercised in COBRA DANE, uncoordinated data changes caused unexpected program failures that interfered with program testing and equipment checkouts.

6.5.3.3 CHANGE CONTROL

Data change control procedures that parallel program change control procedures should be instituted. Ensuring evaluation of changes to detect all "ripple" effects and to ensure data efficiencies is a valuable service. Not having data change status accounting may be one reason the effects of data change were not always well coordinated or communicated in COBRA DANE.

6.5.3.4 QUALITY ASSURANCE

Quality inspections are part of the access and change control procedures. Changes to data ought to be checked as thoroughly as changes to programs. Although not a high percentage, violations of naming conventions and usage did create some difficulty in understandability of the COBRA DANE programs. The specification writers thought good annotation of data more important than the annotation of instructional statements.

6.5.3.5 RESOURCE ACCOUNTING

Tracking resource utilization is especially important in real-time programs. Not having adequate advance warning of overutilization of computer storage and channel capacity aggravated the redesign crisis when this occurred for COBRA DANE. Although not as crucial for non-real-time systems, resource budgets and accounts are desirable, if not essential, records for all systems.

6.5.3.6 RECOMMENDATIONS

It is recommended that the same level of control be exercised over globally defined data and data base structures as is exercised over program modules and software system configuration.

In operation it is suggested that the file of global data definitions should be one of the Program Library files and any tools provided for maintaining and analyzing the data definition file should be part of the Program Library support repertoire. Although it may not be necessary to have as highly automated and controlled a system as that enjoyed by the SCF COMPOOL-sensitive system, the control procedures used there and some of the environmental analysis tools such as system set used and memory maps are desirable tools for tracking the impacts of change and monitoring resource utilization.

As a minimum set of functional requirements, system data control should include:

1. The same level of control and accounting for versions and other structurally or developmentally defined data elements as for program elements
2. Enforcement of data definition standard practices (including programming standards, avoidance of redundancies, and efficiency of data manipulation standards)
3. Accountability for data changes equivalent to the accountability and control of program changes
4. System data control coordinator responsibility definitions
5. Data configuration and change status reporting

It is suggested that one of the data files described in the data definitions be the file of program modules and its members, and that accounts be kept of computer resource utilization.

6.5.4 Configuration Management

The intangibility of the software product, the degree to which software incorporates the operational procedures of the using organization, and the apparent relative ease of modifying software, all make configuration management particularly important for command, control, and communication systems. The objectives of configuration management are to achieve a firm, complete, baseline of the system, to control and account for all approved changes, and to provide management visibility into system composition and developmental status. Although COBRA DANE had the machinery in the Joint and Internal Configuration Control Boards that partially satisfied these aims, the failure on the project level to institute formal configuration definition, change control, accounting, and document maintenance procedures undoubtedly affected project performance.

6.5.4.1 *CONFIGURATION IDENTIFICATION*

Although all planned program and program test documentation was produced, frequent change not reflected in the documents impaired their usefulness. Internal control over the Program Library representation of the system helped offset the lack. However, the impact of not having a firm configuration definition can pervade all aspects of software development. A firm basis for evaluating the impacts of change is not provided. Uncertainty concerning the responsiveness and firmness of designs and test criteria must follow. To some degree, all these effects were experienced in COBRA DANE.

6.5.4.2 CONFIGURATION AUTHENTICATION

Not baselining or otherwise authenticating the specifications for COBRA DANE, and thus bringing the performance requirements under as tight a control as the Program Library, was felt by many observers to be the most serious factor in the difficulty of controlling and accounting for changes in COBRA DANE and the confusions and uncertainties that accompanied development to some degree. Without an authenticated specification it is difficult to differentiate between a "clarification" and a "modification," and it is difficult to verify or prove that a specified level of performance has been attained.

6.5.4.3 CONFIGURATION CONTROL

The effects of change and more specifically uncontrolled change have been frequently declared to be the most serious cause of schedule slippages and cost overruns. Having formal configuration change procedures might not prevent change, but it makes the changes and their impacts visible. Changes did impact COBRA DANE performance. The project did have configuration control procedures, but probably could have profited from having more formal procedures to make the impacts of changes more obvious.*

In contradistinction to control over functional requirements change, internal control over change to the software product once it entered the "system master"-controlled portion of the Program Library was very tight and observance of the rules was excellent. Control of change in the Program Library contributed a great deal to the organization and stability of the developing software.

It must be concluded that although formal change control procedures do not prevent change, they make the reasons for change and the costs of making changes apparent and indeed provide a rational basis for rejecting less cost effective or important changes.

6.5.4.4 CONFIGURATION ACCOUNTING

It is through configuration and change status reports that the configuration identification and changes to it are made visible to management. The volumes of proposed changes and suspected problems are indicators of potential difficulty. Without these indicators, management decisions are hampered. There is no doubt that configuration accounting does contribute to project efficiency.

---

* Just evaluating proposed changes represents a significant expenditure of resources and usually some lost time on the principal tasks. Formal procedures should make these costs as well as direct revision costs apparent.

6.5.4.5 RECOMMENDATIONS

Whether the software is acquired directly or through a prime, it is recommended that configuration management procedures, which may be used for both external and internal control, be established for all software systems.

Although configuration management practices are normally performed manually, it is suggested that consideration be given to the definition of a software monitor system to be used both for external and internal configuration accounting and reporting. It is possible to combine the software monitor with Program Library operations or to share responsibility with the library.

At a minimum, it is suggested that the configuration management practices ought to provide:

1. Complete, firmly baselined, configuration identifications, especially at the functional requirement or Software Development Specification level.

2. Configuration control for changes to baselined specifications or controlled software configurations. These should include formal procedures for requesting, evaluating, and disposing of modifications to requirements, designs, or controlled products for any reasons that arise either externally or internally to the project.

3. Configuration accounting records and status reports to provide visibility to software configurations as amended by approved changes, and the status of suggested changes. Separate accountability should be provided, as appropriate, for builds and versions of the system.

6.5.5 Chief Programmer Teams (CPT)

The impact of having a few highly proficient programmers performing the bulk of the design and coding work is reflected in the high quality of the COBRA DANE software and the excellent productivity of the teams. However, since there were substantial differences between the way the COBRA DANE teams were organized and the organization recommended in the literature, strong support for CPT is inhibited. COBRA DANE project members did make recommendations for a Chief Architect, a concept that is gaining favor in the literature.

The use of a System Librarian and a System Data Controller, which is the principal way in which the COBRA DANE CPTs differed from the organization suggested in the literature, is deemed a viable alternative to Team Librarians. This is especially true if these controllers are in direct support of the Chief Architect.

No recommendation is made concerning adoption of CPTs as a required management technique.

It is recommended that projects have a "Chief Architect," "Configuration Management," or "Principal Software Engineer" charged with final authority for making technical decisions and commitments and responsible for the overall structure and design of the system. The most efficient software development organizational structure depends very much on the individual company and individual system requirements and should not be dictated by the procuring organization. Whether or not those charged with technical software engineering decisions should also be charged with administration of the project is a moot question, but the chief technical person should be charged with work sizing and scheduling estimates whether or not he or she administers these aspects.

6.6 RECOMMENDATIONS (BCS)

The conclusions of this study lead us to recommend that Air Force software procurements should be structured to encourage the use of certain beneficial Modern Programming Practices. Specifically, we recommend that particular emphasis be given to management planning and visibility, to disciplined testing, to configuration management and change control, and to disciplined top-down design. However, care must be taken to preserve those aspects of the procurement environment that foster competition.

Although certain software development practices may have a beneficial effect on costs, schedule risk, and product quality, it must remain the developers' responsibility to choose and employ the practices they believe will be most cost effective. For a specific software procurement, several developers may be qualified to do the work, by reason of their past experience and knowledge of the customer's application. These developers may also have the necessary equipment, facilities, tools, and data to perform the work. What distinguishes among them are the methods, techniques, and disciplines each imposes on the software development process to maximize cost benefits. For this reason, we believe that it is inappropriate for the customer to specify what methods, techniques, and disciplines must be employed. On the other hand, we believe that it is both appropriate and necessary that the customer specify desired qualities and characteristics of the end items to be produced. In doing so, the customer can encourage the use of beneficial practices.

The emphasis discernable in the Modern Programming Practices investigated in this study is on focus; software development activities are focused and identifiable. As a result, they are more manageable (i.e., controllable). Key to achieving that focus is the concentration of software development responsibility. We feel it is critical that the developer be required to focus the responsibility for software development with functions and duties similar to those we described for a Program Manager.

An additional factor that ensures the appropriate focus on software development activities is the identification (and detailed planning for the development) of those specific products that result from the activities. Focusing on tangible results permits improved management and customer visibility of the development process, and allows a more objective evaluation of status, progress, and performance.

Seven

Research Needs

The MPP view is essentially a backwards view—here are the Modern Programming Practices we have used, and here is what we think about them.

That is not, of course, enough. The effectiveness of these and other MPP is dependent on their being (1) found successful, and (2) integrated into existing software development environments. To some extent, that theme has also been developed in the earlier sections of this book. MPP companies dealt honestly with the failures as well as the successes of the MPP experience.

But looking further into the future, what of the utilization of MPP? Several of the MPP companies, in the material that follows, suggest areas where more needs to be known. These areas are candidates for future research.

7.1 RECOMMENDATIONS FOR FURTHER STUDY AND ANALYSIS (MARTIN-MARIETTA)

1. The data-driven design concepts used for the flight and test software systems proved operationally to be extremely practical. Modifications to lander hardware components could easily be tested by

merely changing data base items. Significant and safe changes to landed operations were available to the Viking flight team, who uplinked 60,000 words of code controlling data modifications to each of the Viking Landers. It is therefore recommended that the Air Force study the influence that designing requirements to be data rather than code has on system reliability, schedules, and costs.

2. The issues involved with software portability need further study. Emphasis should be placed on systems as well as programs. Topics that should be addressed include programmer education, pathfinder studies, design standards, language choices, phases of testing, data base management, interface requirements, translation techniques, and methods that can maintain near optimal performance across differing computer capabilities.

3. The concept of attempting to write a User's Guide as part of the requirements phase should be studied from human engineering and software reliability points of view. Such a technique could prove to be cost-effective from a software change point of view.

4. The relative values of software documentation should be studied. This would include establishing minimal documentation requirements, concepts for reducing the amount of documentation and increasing reliability through centralization, determining how long documents should be maintained by type, and setting standards for the content, control, and organization of the documents.

5. A study to determine the value of a Chief Programmer approach as a function of the size and scope of the software task, especially as it relates to software only or software/hardware development, should be made. Particular emphasis should be placed on determining its impact on management visibility during the development phase. Methods for improving the ability of the software developers to understand technical and human engineering requirements should be addressed.

6. A study should be conducted to determine aids, mechanisms, tools, and procedures that can be used to provide for early software control to improve system reliability.

7. A trade-off study on the types of functions where assembly language is cost-effective over HOL should be made. The average assembly language programmer is of higher quality than the average HOL programmer. In all probability, the bit manipulating Viking Lander decalibration and decommutation program would have been better designed, smaller, and more efficient if the original requirement had been to write it in assembly language rather than Fortran.

7.2 IMPLICATIONS FOR FURTHER RESEARCH (SPERRY UNIVAC)

The efforts performed on this study led to additional topics that involve further work and study. These topics are identified and summarized for discussions:

1. *Should operational software continue to be developed on operational (target) hardware environments?* A study should be performed on at least three projects that utilize the target hardware environment for developing the operational software. A personnel survey should be taken to access the strengths and weaknesses in programmer productivity. The survey should show the management and customer visibility and control when the target hardware is located at the customer site or located at developer facilities. The study should also provide insight into the continued desirability of support software (compilers, etc.) for execution on target hardware environments.

2. *When is it the right time to apply testing during software development, and how much testing is necessary to arrive at reliable software?* A study should be performed that would attest to the statement; "Design more and test less." This study should provide insight into cost-effective approaches to test software.

3. *What documentation is necessary and sufficient to adequately describe software?* The study should ascertain and differentiate between documentation for complete software systems and components of a complete system. This documentation study should evaluate present standards versus documentation that would more adequately take advantage of modern programming practices.

4. *What is the effect on tools if they are required as deliverables?* A survey of management and technical personnel should be performed.

5. *What, if any, tools should be emphasized to assist system definition, system analysis, and system decomposition?* A survey could be performed that would describe tools of this form. A tool could be singled out, and a prototype could be implemented for evaluation.

6. *Can structure diagrams be utilized through automation that will provide verification of design after the program has been coded?* Presently, structured diagrams are being used to document program design before program coding. Automation of structured diagrams from code and automated comparisons could provide this verification. A prototype of this automation should be implemented for evaluation.

7. *Can programming guidelines become a standard?* A skeletal model of a programming guideline document should be produced. This model could be circulated throughout several development groups for their assessment and evaluation.

8. *Can fault tolerance be predicted and accomplished through software using existing, off-the-shelf, militarized equipment?* A model should be developed as a "strawman" and analyzed for determining the methods of evaluating fault tolerance.

7.3 RECOMMENDATIONS FOR FURTHER STUDY (BCS)

As a result of this study, several areas have been identified where further investigation or development seems appropriate. Specific recommendations are detailed in the following paragraphs.

7.3.1 Management Guidance on MPP Application

The significance of management's role in achieving maximum benefits from the application of Modern Programming Practices implies that specific guidance for managers of software development is needed. Command media should be developed to address how appropriate MPP can be chosen based on project objectives and activities. The management disciplines associated with planning, task assignment, and monitoring within a project employing MPP should be examined and formalized into improved specifications and guidelines for software development.

7.3.2 MPP Impact on Product Quality

Although this study did not directly address the issue of quality of the delivered software product, Modern Programming Practices stress the concept of quality, particularly as it is reflected in demonstrated responsiveness to user requirements. The impact of MPP on software product quality should be determined, perhaps by studying the activity of a system from the completion of design through operational use. Such a study should consider change history in terms of repairs and enhancements, measures of customer satisfaction, and benefits expected and realized during the production life.

7.3.3 MPP Impact on Schedule Risk

The impact of Modern Programming Practices on schedule risk can be inferred from an examination of the resource expenditure data gathered in this study. Largely as a result of deliberate preplanning, testing and other construction activities performed late in the development cycle appear to be both more manageable and less prone to schedule slippage. Directed study should be conducted to determine conclusively whether MPP-using projects incur less schedule risk than do software projects that use traditional methods.

7.3.4 MPP Impact on Life-cycle Costs

This study considers the effects of Modern Programming Practices on software development costs; there remains the larger question of how MPP affect software life-cycle costs. Specifically, the costs of operation, maintenance, and enhancement of a system originally developed using MPP may show considerable benefit. Those MPP whose impact is relatively minor during system development may have a more significant impact during the production life of a delivered system.

7.3.5 Cost Estimating for MPP

The development cost benefits attributable to Modern Programming Practices are significant enough that software cost estimating techniques currently in use throughout the industry are no longer completely valid. This study shows that projects employing MPP spend less resources, and spend them differently, than what traditional estimating guidelines forecast. The algorithms that the software industry uses to estimate development costs need to be adjusted by new parameters which account for the influences of specific MPP.

7.3.6 Customer Training in MPP

The changing role of the customer and the software developer, and the new practices that the developers are using to fulfill their obligations, must be understood by those offices responsible for software procurements. Specific training for procurement-office personnel in such areas as the objectives and conduct of formal reviews and the customer's participation in definition, design, and testing activities should be encouraged.

7.3.7 Support Tools for MPP

The opinions expressed by our projects regarding the tools currently available to support Modern Programming Practices leads us to conclude that tools are needed, but that their capabilities must be significantly expanded beyond the level of support currently provided. An automated design aid should be developed which alleviates the dependence on the structured walkthrough for design verification; more sophisticated logic analysis and interface consistency checking capabilities should be provided. A Programming Support Library aid that provides extensive management visibility information could effectively support the Program Manager's assessment of status, progress, and performance. Compilers that directly support structured logic formulations would alleviate a project's dependence on manual peer code reviews.

Appendix A

Detailed Evaluation Methods

Chapter 5 of this book is an overview of the methods used by the MPP companies to perform their evaluations. This appendix contains detailed descriptions in support of the earlier material. It should not be read as a stand-alone section, but rather in conjunction with the prefacing material of Chapter 5.

A.1 PROJECT SURVEY QUESTIONNAIRE (BCS)

I. Background Information (contractual)

1. Which of the Modern Program Practices given below are used in your software development project? (Check those that apply.)

   _____ Program Manager Authority—both technical and administrative responsibility for project.

   _____ Reviews—formal milestone reviews with customer participation at the end of each phase.

   _____ Unit Development Folders—capture of working materials for each identified item to facilitate end item development, testing, documentation.

_____ Design Discipline and Verification—top-down design, formal design representation, completion of design, and deliberate verification of design prior to code.

_____ Program Modularity—definitions/restrictions on data interfaces between modules, adherence to parent/child relationships between modules.

_____ Naming Conventions—structured names for modules and/or data items.

_____ Structured Forms—use of Dijkstra forms as supportable in your programming language.

_____ Code Verification—deliberate peer reviews of code for each module.

_____ Support Libraries and Facilities—use of automated or proceduralized design, coding, and configuration management aids.

_____ Phased Testing—defined and formalized unit, functional, and acceptance testing.

_____ Configuration Management/Change Control—creation and control of baselines (requirements, design, implementation) and procedures for problem reporting and resolution.

2. For each practice checked, supply the date of adoption of the practice and the associated software development phase and/or milestone at which it was adopted.

3. For each practice checked, provide a brief rationale that tells why the practice was adopted for your software development project. For each practice checked, indicate the degree of success expected or achieved in the project by its adoption.

4. List the computing hardware (including the host and target machines) used by your project and their relationship.

5. List the operating system(s) and compilers/assemblers and utility software used by your project.

6. Indicate the method(s) of access to the hardware and the software. (Check those which apply.)

_____ Batch

_____ Remote job entry

_____ Time sharing

_____ Stand-alone

7. Describe the availability of hardware/software: the time schedule

for computer accessibility and the existence of any restricted or experimental software/hardware used by the project.

8. Indicate the number and type of personnel for your project. (Enter number that applies.)

_____ Full time, report to Program Manager

_____ Full time, report outside Program Manager's organization

_____ Full time, outside contract

_____ Part time, report to Program Manager

_____ Part time, report outside Program Manager's organization (e.g., consultants)

_____ Part time, outside contractor

9. Provide personnel résumés that detail experience and training, both prior to and also during this project development.

10. Indicate the percentage of personnel turnover expected/experienced on your project. Was this turnover planned for? Did it have a detrimental effect on project performance?

11. Characterize your project in terms of magnitude, complexity, and software type (e.g., real time, utility, application) performed by the resultant software. When did your project begin?

12. In what phase of the software development is your project currently? (Check only one.)

_____ Requirements Definition

_____ Design

_____ Coding

_____ Checkout and Unit Testing

_____ Integration and Testing

_____ System Testing and Delivery

_____ In Production (Operation and Maintenance)

II. Software Estimating Guidelines

1. Estimate how much of the total deliverable software is of each of the following types:

Mathematical Operations   _____

Report Generation   _____

Logic Operations   _____

Signal Processing/Data Reduction   _____

Real Time/Executive/Avionics Interfaces   _____

How many independent programs does this represent?

2. Estimate the total number of deliverable source statements, excluding commentary. (If this is an enhancement or reimplementation, do not include statements that do not have to be recoded.)

3. Is this development a reimplementation of an existing software design? Is this development a conversion of an existing software system?

4. Is this a follow-on contract with your current customer (e.g., major enhancement)?

5. How many designers/programmers support this development?

    _____ 1–2   _____ 6–10

    _____ More than 20

    _____ 3–5   _____ 11–20

6. Is a higher-order language being used?

    _____ not at all   _____ exclusively   _____ partially

7. Does the source language used provide a macro capability?

    _____ not at all   _____ yes

8. Do you have documentation forms to aid in expression of designs, tests, data structures, etc.?

    _____ not at all   _____ yes

9. Does the computer system used allow for on-line programming activities?

    _____ not at all   _____ yes, code/data entry
    _____ yes, debugging

10. Does the computer system provide debugging tools?

    _____ dumps only   _____ other (specify)

11. What is the designer/programmer experience with the engineering or technical discipline of application? (Insert ∇.)

    Entry level   Moderate   High

12. What is the actual number of months (or person-hours) expended (by phase) on this software development to date? What is the actual dollar cost of this labor expense (by phase) to date?

13. What is the actual amount of CRUs expended (by phase) by this software development to date? What is the actual dollar cost of this machine expense (by phase) to date?

14. What is the milestone schedule? What percent of the total flow time is scheduled for the following phases?

Requirements definition	_____
Design	_____
Code	_____
Checkout	_____
Integration and functional test	_____
System testing and acceptance	_____

15. What percent of the total (estimated) personnel required is planned to be (has been) used in each phase?

III. Indicators of Modern Programming Practice

1. What is the responsibility of the Program Manager?

    _____ Technical (product quality, reliability)
    _____ Make task assignments
    _____ Administrative (budgetary)
    _____ Evaluate performance of personnel

2. Are formal task assignments provided by the Program Manager to project personnel?

3. Are formal phase reviews scheduled and conducted?

    _____ Pertinent items identified and available at each review
    _____ Review objectives specified and understood by participants
    _____ Results of review followed up
    _____ Project and customer representatives participate in each review
    _____ The objectives and procedures for this activity were stated in advance
    _____ This activity was performed according to these objectives and procedures

4. Is project documentation pertinent?

    _____ Document schedule exists for review and completion
    _____ Purpose of each document stated and justified
    _____ Documents are scheduled so that the project can use each completed document as source material for next phase's activities
    _____ Each document is reviewed by its intended audience

_____ Appropriate user content and language are determined for and contained in each document

_____ Project control of documentation so that it "tracks" with requirements/design/implementation changes

_____ The objectives and procedures for this activity were stated in advance

_____ This activity was performed according to these objectives and procedures

5. **Are Unit Development Folders (UDF) used by the project?**

_____ "Working papers" for each item are captured as they are created

_____ Project procedures establish form and content of the UDFs

_____ Their contents are utilized for developing other items, completing other tests

_____ Project controls the access/use of UDFs

_____ The objectives and procedures for this activity were stated in advance

_____ This activity was performed according to these objectives and procedures

6. **Does the project employ design discipline?**

_____ Top-down design approach specified

_____ Formal design analysis and representation techniques used:

    _____ Static design representation (design trees)

    _____ Dynamic design representation (transition diagrams)

    _____ Other (explain)

_____ Design refinement methods are used to adapt the abstract design model to the computing environment

_____ Design completeness criteria are developed and specified. What are they?

_____ The objectives and procedures for this activity were stated in advance

_____ This activity was performed according to these objectives and procedures

7. **Is the design verified?**

_____ Peer reviews (structured walkthroughs) of design are conducted

_____ The objectives and method of conducting peer reviews are stated in advance

_____ Design reachability and connectivity analyses procedurized and used

_____ Design modularity analyses procedurized and used

_____ Mechanical evaluation method used

_____ Project control (compliance methods and verification) over the process of design verification exists

_____ The objectives and procedures for this activity were stated in advance

_____ This activity was performed according to these objectives and procedures

8. Is the completed design utilized to discipline the code construction process?

_____ Standard definition for design and program documentation is established

_____ Code construction plan is prepared and used

_____ Formal design review involving customer is held prior to start of coding

_____ The objectives and procedures for this activity were stated in advance

_____ This activity was performed according to these objectives and procedures

9. Is program modularity practiced?

_____ Content and format of program specifications are established

_____ Modularity criteria specified and adhered to

_____ The objectives and procedures for this activity were stated in advance

_____ The activity was performed according to these objectives and procedures

10. Are structured forms used in the code?

_____ Block structures used

_____ Permissible logic statements defined, used, and controlled

_____ Project compliance and verification procedures control the use of structured forms

_____ The objectives and procedures for this activity were stated in advance

_____ This activity was performed according to these objectives and procedures

11. Are formal coding conventions being followed?

_____ Syntactical forms defined that are (dis)allowed for each programming language

_____ Procedures for accessing external data and handling error conditions

_____ Naming conventions for units of code and data variables

_____ Project control procedures for code organization and comments

_____ The objectives and procedures for this activity were stated in advance

_____ This activity was performed according to these objectives and procedures

12. Is the code verifiable?

_____ The required testing and examination for each unit of code are documented

_____ Peer reviews of the code are procedurized and conducted

_____ The objectives and procedures for this activity were stated in advance

_____ This activity was performed according to these objectives and procedures

13. Are design aids to support the software development used?

_____ Formal design language used in completing the design

_____ Manual aids used (specify)

_____ Automated aids used (specify)

_____ The objectives and procedures for this activity were stated in advance

_____ This activity was performed according to these objectives and procedures

14. Are code construction aids to support the software development used?

_____ Structured programming practices used to complete the code

_____ Manual aids used (specify)

_____ Automated aids used (e.g., precompiler) (specify)

_____ The objectives and procedures for this activity were stated in advance

_____ This activity was performed according to these objectives and procedures

15. Are configuration management aids to support the software development used?

_____ Baselined end items are identified and controlled. Indicate at what milestone/phase baseline control was established.
_____ Manual aids used (specify)
_____ Automated aids used (specify)
_____ The objectives and procedures for this activity were stated in advance
_____ This activity was performed according to these objectives and procedures

16. Does the project perform unit/integration software testing?

_____ Unit/integration testing is defined in a formal test plan
_____ There are expected results and pass/fail criteria defined
_____ The software correctly implements the design when this testing is complete
_____ There is a problem/error reporting system
_____ The project uses compliance and verification methods to control this testing phase
_____ The objectives and procedures for this activity were stated in advance
_____ This activity was performed according to these objectives and procedures

17. Does the project perform functional software testing?

_____ An internal review of items is held to judge their quality and completeness prior to functional testing
_____ A handover of items into a controlled configuration is made formally by the developers
_____ An independent agency performs functional testing
_____ The project produces and executes formal test plans and procedures for functional testing
_____ There are expected results and pass/fail criteria defined
_____ A realistic dress rehearsal of the acceptance test is performed as the final functional test
_____ The software correctly satisfies the requirements when this testing is complete
_____ There is a problem/error reporting system

_____ The project uses compliance and verification methods to control this testing phase

_____ The objectives and procedures for this activity were stated in advance

_____ This activity was performed according to these objectives and procedures

18. Does the project perform acceptance testing?

_____ Acceptance test requirements are part of the project's requirements baseline

_____ Formal acceptance test plan and procedures are developed and user concurrence is obtained

_____ There are procedures that allow review of the quality and completeness of the deliverables

_____ Project and customer are asked if ready to begin acceptance testing

_____ There is a formal deliverables baseline and a committed schedule for acceptance testing as a result of a formal review

_____ There is an acceptance test report attesting to the satisfactory conclusion or conditional acceptance

_____ The report is signed by the customer

_____ The objectives and procedures for this activity were stated in advance

_____ This activity was performed according to these objectives and procedures

19. Does the project use controlled end item baselines?

_____ Project end items by phase are identifiable based on written procedural mechanisms

_____ Controlled, review-established requirements, design and implementation baselines exist with written procedures

_____ There are mechanisms for updating and distributing established baselines

_____ The objectives and procedures for this activity were stated in advance

_____ This activity was performed according to these objectives and procedures

20. Does the project utilize a problem reporting system?

_____ There are formal procedures for reporting problems, errors, desired improvements

_____ There are formal procedures for identifying, processing, and tracking problem reports

_____ There are formal procedures for obtaining or distributing problem report status information

_____ A file of completed or in progress problem reports exists

_____ The objectives and procedures for this activity were stated in advance

_____ This activity was performed according to these objectives and procedures

21. Are baseline change control boards used by the project?

_____ The board represents project management and customers

_____ They have discretionary and budgetary authority to control changes to the baseline

_____ They assess proposed changes, and resolve reported problems by assigning action items

_____ They prioritize and control the changes to be implemented

_____ They authorize baseline updates and distribution

_____ The objectives and procedures for this activity were stated in advance

_____ This activity was performed according to these objectives and procedures

A.2   COMPARISON PROCESS (CSC)

A.2.1   Phase Applicability

The CSC comparison methodology is a life-cycle, phase-dependent process. Each life-cycle phase will be a basis for conducting the complete comparison process. Only programming practices and techniques that are actively applied in a given phase are compared in that phase. Therefore, it is essential that the phase applicability of each practice and technique be established.

Phase applicability of the practices and techniques is graphically portrayed in Figure A2.1. Practices and techniques are merged into one listing under the column heading of Programming Practices. Their applicability through the life-cycle phases is shown on the bar graph. The programming practices have been grouped into two subsets: technical and management. This differentiation will be significant later in the comparison process, as will the ordering of the practices and techniques in the list. The Design phase of the computer program life cycle has been divided into Functional and Detailed subphases. This has been done to better define the phase applicability of some programming practices.

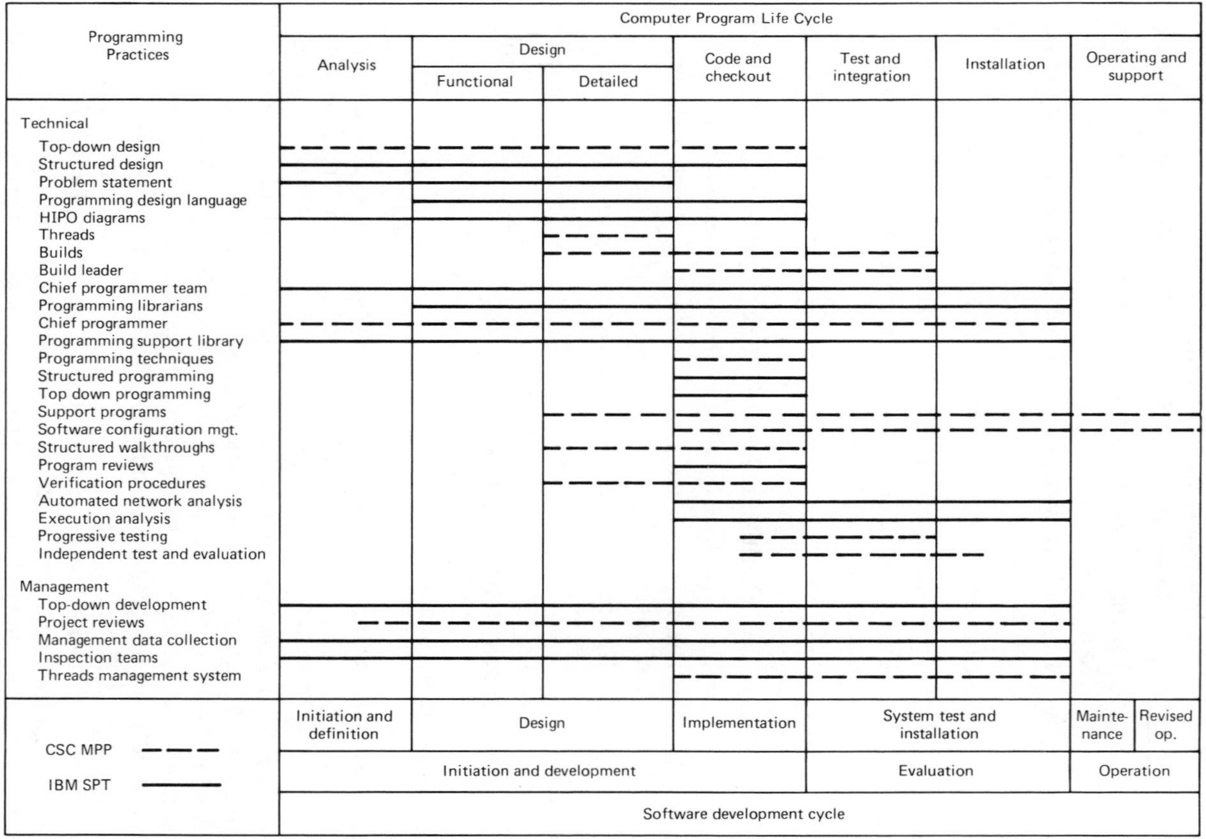

Figure A2.1 Programming Practices Applicability

Programming Practices

Computer Program Life Cycle

	Analysis	Design — Functional	Design — Detailed	Code and checkout	Test and integration	Installation	Operating and support

Technical
- Top-down design
- Structured design
- Problem statement
- Programming design language
- HIPO diagrams
- Threads
- Builds
- Build leader
- Chief programmer team
- Programming librarians
- Chief programmer
- Programming support library
- Programming techniques
- Structured programming
- Top down programming
- Support programs
- Software configuration mgt.
- Structured walkthroughs
- Program reviews
- Verification procedures
- Automated network analysis
- Execution analysis
- Progressive testing
- Independent test and evaluation

Management
- Top-down development
- Project reviews
- Management data collection
- Inspection teams
- Threads management system

Initiation and definition	Design		Implementation	System test and installation		
				Evaluation	Operation — Mainte-nance	Revised op.

Initiation and development — Design and development

Software development cycle

CSC MPP - - - -
IBM SPT ——

A.2.2   Error Types

The universe of software errors may be grouped into discrete subsets based on characteristics unique to the errors in each subset. These subsets, or error types, have been variously defined by different industry studies. The error types established for this study are adapted from those defined by TRW Systems Group for RADC and published in a Software Reliability Study report, RADC-TR-74-250, dated October 1974. The type definitions used during the MPP research are generally more inclusive than those in the TRW report. This has been done so that the number of error types is more manageable. An additional error type was also introduced in this study. Timing errors were isolated as a subset because of their critical significance to real-time software development projects such as those studied during this research task.

The error-type definitions that follow have been used throughout this study to establish MPP effectiveness values.

Computational: inaccurate mathematical operations. Errors in this category occur when a wrong equation or convention is used, causing erroneous mathematical output within a routine or program.

Logic: faulty routine or program decision flow. Included in this category are errors caused by incorrect condition tests, status checks, model definition, and data storage references.

Input/output: improper data reception or transmission. These errors related to data format, field size, position, completeness, and control.

Data handling: incorrect data manipulation within a routine or program. Errors made in reading, writing, moving, storing, and modifying data items internal to a routine or program.

Operating or utility systems: all errors attributed to these systems.

Configuration: incompatibility of applications and operating system software. This category includes the catastrophic errors and unexplainable program halts caused when applications programs violate operating system conventions.

Software interface: incompatible data flow across routine or program boundaries. These errors result from inconsistent data transmission protocols between software components.

Hardware interface: incompatible hardware/software interaction. Any error that may be attributed to data flow between hardware and software.

User interface: incompatible dependent manual/automated functions. Errors at the user interface, including the machine operator, manual or data card inputs, tape inputs, etc.

Data interface: incompatibility between data base structure and using routine or program.

Timing: failure to maintain normal program execution or system operation due to data manipulation timing. Errors caused by the inconsistent operation of time-sensitive processing components.

Requirements compliance: failure to provide a capability specified in the requirements document.

For the purpose of completing this research it was assumed that all software errors could be characterized as one of the foregoing types. Certainly, there are errors that do fit more than one of the preceding type definitions. In the broadest sense it can be hypothesized that the error types defined above will include all known software errors. These type definitions are sufficient to support implementation of this comparison methodology. It is possible that more extensive research would result in refinement or addition to these types.

A.2.3   Error Existence

Throughout the computer program life cycle, as any software system is being developed, programming errors are generated and corrected by the development staff. There errors occur and are removed at rates that are dependent upon factors such as complexity and size of the software system being developed, and size, skill, and organization of the development staff. The relationships among all factors (even their positive identification) and the error rates have not been clearly defined. There simply are not enough empirical data to support definition of those relationships.

Information gathered during research of the three CSC projects was not definitive enough to substantiate any hypothesis relative to the rate of error occurrence or removal. However, through project staff interviews and surveys, the MPP research team gathered information that led to definition of a prototype, error-existence matrix. This matrix, shown as Figure A2.2, incorporates error-type occurrence and removal rates in one set of values representing the percentage of all error types existing across the life-cycle phases. The values reflect percentage of time that a given error type will be generated in a specific phase and remain in the software through subsequent phases. Matrix values for each phase (matrix column) will sum to 1.00, indicating that the error percentages are inclusive of all errors for each phase. The values in this matrix are representative of error-type existence from the three CSC projects studied.

A.2.4   Error Detection or Reduction

Programming practices, in general, function to improve development staff performance, assure adherence to the production schedule, and ensure maintenance of programmed production costs. Software error occurrence and removal represent a common denominator for practice performance measure-

Error Types	Computer Program Life Cycle						
	Analysis	Design		Code and checkout	Test and integration	Installation	Operating and support
		Functional	Detailed				
Computational	0.03	0.03	0.10	0.11	0.05	0.03	0.04
Logic	0.08	0.13	0.19	0.22	0.10	0.05	0.08
Input/output	0.02	0.04	0.05	0.08	0.11	0.09	0.04
Data handling	0.04	0.07	0.13	0.17	0.11	0.08	0.09
Operating or utility systems	0.02	0.05	0.04	0.06	0.03	0.02	0.03
Configuration	0.05	0.06	0.06	0.05	0.06	0.04	0.04
Software interface	0.04	0.11	0.09	0.06	0.10	0.06	0.09
Hardware interface	0.04	0.08	0.07	0.07	0.09	0.11	0.05
User interface	0.06	0.07	0.06	0.05	0.11	0.17	0.17
Data interface	0.03	0.07	0.06	0.05	0.08	0.06	0.03
Requirements compliance	0.54	0.21	0.10	0.03	0.05	0.11	0.16
Timing	0.05	0.08	0.05	0.05	0.11	0.18	0.18

Figure A2.2 Percentaged-Error Type Existing in Each Phase

ment among the three practice functions. Performance, schedule, and cost are affected by the presence or absence of software errors throughout the development process. Therefore, practice effectiveness in all functional areas is related to the detection or reduction of software errors. The operative relationship between practice performance and error detection or reduction has not been explicitly determined. However, a realistic characterization of the relationship can be hypothesized. This may be done by establishing probability values for the detection or reduction of error types by each programming practice in each of the life-cycle phases.

A matrix containing probability values for the detection or reduction of error types by all programming practices is shown as Figure A2.3. The values in this matrix have been developed for the Code and Checkout phase as indicated at the top of the figure. Because of the life-cycle-phase dependency of programming practice performance, values such as these must be defined for

| Code and Checkout Phase | | | | | | | | | | | | |
Programming Practices \ Error Types	Computational	Logic	Input/output	Data handling	Operating or utility systems	Configuration	Software interface	Hardware interface	User interface	Data interface	Requirements compliance	Timing
Technical												
Top-down design	0.05	0.10	0.01	0.05	0.05	0.15	0.65	0.20	0.20	0.50	0.40	0.01
Structured design	0.05	0.10	0.01	0.10	0.05	0.20	0.45	0.05	0.25	0.40	0.40	0.01
Programming design language	0.05	0.05	0.05	0.10	0.05	0.10	0.05	0.01	0.25	0.15	0.45	0.01
Builds	0.03	0.05	0.05	0.01	0.05	0.25	0.45	0.05	0.20	0.35	0.30	0.01
Build leader	0.70	0.60	0.30	0.05	0.05	0.30	0.70	0.15	0.35	0.50	0.55	0.10
Chief programmer team	0.80	0.50	0.40	0.40	0.05	0.60	0.70	0.25	0.35	0.60	0.60	0.50
Programming librarians	0.01	0.01	0.01	0.01	0.01	0.01	0.01	0.01	0.01	0.05	0.05	0.01
Chief programmer	0.80	0.50	0.40	0.45	0.05	0.65	0.75	0.50	0.50	0.60	0.70	0.50
Programming support library	0.01	0.01	0.05	0.05	0.01	0.10	0.20	0.01	0.05	0.01	0.05	0.01
Programming techniques	0.15	0.35	0.25	0.25	0.01	0.50	0.35	0.05	0.10	0.35	0.10	0.05
Structured programming	0.15	0.35	0.25	0.25	0.01	0.50	0.20	0.05	0.10	0.40	0.15	0.05
Top-down programming	0.15	0.30	0.20	0.25	0.01	0.45	0.45	0.01	0.10	0.35	0.10	0.05
Support programs	0.30	0.25	0.15	0.20	0.05	0.10	0.15	0.20	0.35	0.20	0.10	0.10
Software configuration management	0.01	0.01	0.05	0.01	0.01	0.01	0.10	0.01	0.05	0.01	0.05	0.01
Structured walkthroughs	0.85	0.50	0.25	0.30	0.05	0.20	0.80	0.65	0.70	0.15	0.25	0.50
Program reviews	0.75	0.65	0.55	0.70	0.01	0.15	0.70	0.50	0.65	0.50	0.50	0.40
Verification procedures	0.35	0.20	0.30	0.20	0.05	0.25	0.45	0.25	0.35	0.40	0.35	0.20
Automated network analysis	0.10	0.05	0.25	0.10	0.05	0.10	0.20	0.10	0.20	0.25	0.01	0.20
Execution analysis	0.65	0.50	0.50	0.20	0.01	0.15	0.35	0.15	0.10	0.15	0.05	0.50
Progressive testing	0.55	0.40	0.60	0.50	0.05	0.25	0.40	0.20	0.15	0.25	0.05	0.35
Independent test and evaluation	0.55	0.45	0.50	0.50	0.05	0.30	0.40	0.20	0.15	0.30	0.10	0.40
Management												
Top-down development	0.30	0.20	0.20	0.15	0.05	0.10	0.25	0.25	0.20	0.30	0.70	0.01
Project reviews	0.10	0.01	0.05	0.10	0.01	0.05	0.10	0.30	0.35	0.45	0.75	0.15
Management data collection	0.10	0.01	0.05	0.05	0.01	0.15	0.15	0.10	0.20	0.15	0.50	0.01
Inspection teams	0.25	0.05	0.10	0.15	0.05	0.15	0.15	0.20	0.20	0.40	0.65	0.10
Threads management system	0.05	0.05	0.05	0.01	0.01	0.05	0.25	0.05	0.05	0.40	0.40	0.01

Figure A2.3   Probability of Error Detection or Reduction

each phase. Therefore, a unique detection or reduction probability matrix will be necessary for each phase. This report will deal with only the Code and Checkout phase in presenting research findings and developing the comparison methodology. There are two reasons for this decision. First, the Code and Checkout phase activities involve use of more programming practices than any other phase. This means that values for most programming practices appear in the matrices. Second, the resource material for this phase was more comprehensive than for any of the other phases. It should be pointed out that the values in the matrix were qualitatively extracted from the CSC projects reviewed.

Using Figure A2.3, the probability of error detection or reduction by any programming practice in the Code and Checkout phase can be determined.

For instance, top-down design has a 5% probability of reducing computational errors in this phase.

A.2.5 Effectiveness Values

Programming practice effectiveness values may be defined for each practice relative to all error types within each applicable phase. Thus, effectiveness values are a function of the percentage of time error types exist and the probability of practice detection or reduction of those error types. The purpose of mathematical manipulation of the two values is to define a figure of merit or effectiveness value that can be derived for all programming practices. Using this value, programming practices can be compared quantitatively within or across all life-cycle phases. Naturally, the effectiveness values are only as accurate as the probability values. The probability values presented in Figures A2.2 and A2.3 are not based on quantitative measurement. They represent a consensus of experienced assessment by CSC staff members. However, given adequate source material and research tools the actual probability values could be derived. In any case, CSC's comparison methodology does offer a viable approach to programming practice evaluation and comparison. The values shown in Figures A2.2 and A2.3 are valid for the three CSC projects studied. Therefore, they support the comparison process to be described in the following discussions.

Development of effectiveness value is a two-part process. First, the practice effectiveness values are calculated for each life-cycle phase. Next, these practice effectiveness values are used to develop phase effectiveness values for each practice across all life-cycle phases. In the following subsections each of these activities is described using probability values for the Code and Checkout phase.

A.2.5.1 PRACTICE EFFECTIVENESS VALUES

Practice effectiveness values are calculated using the percentage of error types existing and error-type detection or reduction probabilities. The calculation involves selecting a programming practice, error type, and life-cycle phase. Then, the percentage of error-type existence is multiplied by the probability of error-type detection or reduction. That product is multiplied by 100 to normalize the value. As an example, using top-down design programming practice and the computational error type in the Code and Checkout phase, the effectiveness value calculated would be:

Existence Percentage		Detection/Reduction Probability				Effectiveness Value
	$\times$		$\times$	100	=	
0.11	$\times$	0.05	$\times$	100	=	0.55

Completing the calculations for all practices and error types in the Code and Checkout phase will produce the matrix shown as Figure A2.4. Practice effectiveness against any error type may be found by reference to the matrix. The values are significant only through comparison with other practice effectiveness values. The Total Effectiveness column in Figure A2.4 represents the sum of values for each row or programming practice. These totals will be used later in the comparison process. Completion of these calculations for all life-cycle phases will result in a series of matrices that may be used in a life-cycle comparison process.

| Code and Checkout Phase | | | | | | | | | | | | | |
Programming Practices \ Error Types	Computational	Logic	Input/output	Data handling	Operating or utility systems	Configuration	Software interface	Hardware interface	User interface	Data interface	Requirements compliance	Timing	Total effectiveness
Technical													
Top-down design	0.55	2.20	0.08	0.85	0.30	0.75	3.00	1.40	1.00	2.50	1.20	0.05	11.78
Structured design	0.55	2.20	0.08	1.70	0.30	1.00	2.70	0.35	1.25	2.00	1.20	0.05	13.38
Programming design language	0.55	1.10	0.40	0.70	1.20	0.50	0.30	0.07	1.25	0.75	1.35	0.05	8.32
Builds	0.55	1.10	0.40	0.17	0.30	1.25	2.70	0.35	1.00	1.75	1.50	0.05	11.12
Build leader	7.70	13.2	2.40	0.85	0.30	1.50	1.20	1.05	1.75	2.50	1.65	0.50	37.60
Chief programmer team	8.80	11.0	3.20	6.80	0.30	3.00	4.20	1.75	1.75	3.00	1.80	2.50	18.10
Programming librarians	0.11	0.22	0.08	0.17	0.06	0.05	0.06	0.07	0.05	0.25	0.15	0.05	1.32
Chief programmer	8.80	11.0	3.20	7.65	0.30	3.25	4.50	3.50	2.50	3.00	2.10	2.50	52.30
Programming support library	0.11	0.22	0.40	0.85	0.06	0.50	1.20	0.07	0.25	0.05	0.15	0.05	3.91
Programming techniques	1.65	7.70	2.00	4.25	0.06	2.50	2.10	0.35	0.50	1.75	0.30	0.25	23.41
Structured programming	1.65	7.70	2.00	4.25	0.06	2.50	1.20	0.35	0.50	2.00	0.15	0.25	22.91
Top-down programming	1.65	6.60	1.60	4.25	0.06	2.25	2.70	0.07	0.50	1.75	0.30	0.25	21.98
Support programs	3.30	5.50	1.20	3.40	0.30	0.50	0.90	1.40	1.75	1.00	0.30	0.50	20.05
Software configuration management	0.11	0.22	0.40	0.17	0.06	0.05	0.60	0.07	0.25	0.05	0.15	0.05	2.18
Structured walkthroughs	9.35	11.0	2.00	5.10	0.30	1.00	4.80	1.55	3.50	0.75	0.75	2.50	15.60
Program reviews	8.25	14.3	4.40	11.9	0.06	0.75	4.20	3.58	3.25	2.50	1.50	2.00	56.61
Verification procedures	3.85	4.40	2.40	3.40	0.30	1.25	2.70	1.75	1.75	2.00	1.05	1.00	25.85
Automated network analysis	1.10	1.10	2.00	1.70	0.30	0.50	1.20	0.70	1.00	1.25	0.03	1.00	11.85
Execution analysis	7.15	11.0	4.00	3.40	0.06	0.75	2.10	1.05	0.50	0.75	0.15	2.50	33.41
Progressive testing	6.05	8.80	4.80	8.50	0.30	1.25	2.40	1.40	0.75	1.25	0.15	1.75	37.40
Independent test and evaluation	6.05	9.90	4.00	8.50	0.30	1.50	2.40	1.40	0.75	1.50	0.30	2.00	38.60
Management													
Top-down development	3.30	4.40	1.60	2.55	0.30	0.50	1.50	1.75	1.00	1.50	2.10	0.05	20.55
Project reviews	1.10	0.22	0.40	1.70	0.06	0.25	0.60	2.10	1.75	2.25	2.25	0.75	13.43
Management data collection	1.10	0.22	0.40	0.85	0.06	0.75	0.90	0.70	1.00	0.75	1.50	0.05	8.28
Inspection teams	2.75	1.10	0.80	2.55	0.30	0.75	0.90	1.40	1.00	2.00	1.95	0.50	16.00
Threads management system	0.55	1.10	0.40	0.17	0.06	0.25	1.50	0.35	0.25	2.00	1.20	0.05	7.88

Figure A2.4   Practice Effectiveness

A.2.5.2 PHASE EFFECTIVENESS VALUES

Phase effectiveness values are designed to provide quantitative, comprehensive values that represent a measure of programming practice performance against individual error types. These values will serve as inputs to the process of developing phase effectiveness values. An algorithm has been defined that uses practice effectiveness values to produce a value that defines practice utility within a phase. These phase effectiveness values may be used to compare practices in an unbiased fashion.

In developing the phase effectiveness algorithm, consideration was given to certain aspects of the practice comparison process and some assumptions were made. First, the probability of error existence matrix was considered to have established the relative distribution of error types across the life cycle. It represents an indirect statement about the volume of errors by type that will exist in any phase. This is an important factor when evaluating practice performance. Next, the phase effectiveness values, when calculated, must account for error types that practices are most and least effective against. In addition, the relative volume of those particular errors on a phase-by-phase basis is important. Finally, the goal for development of the algorithm was to create a procedure that would promote selection of an optimum mix of practices for use across all life-cycle phases. It was assumed that all error types are of equal significance to the software development process. That is, a logic error is just as significant as a timing error. Error types were not given weighting factors. It was also assumed that practice effectiveness against the most and least frequently encountered errors in a phase does reflect the quality of that practice.

The phase effectiveness algorithm uses the following input data: practice effectiveness value for the error type with the greatest percentage of existence (labeled a), practice effectiveness value for the error type with the least probability of existence (labeled b), practice total effectiveness value (labeled c), and the number of error types (labeled d). The algorithm is expressed as follows:

$$(a + b) \frac{c}{d}$$

To demonstrate its use, given the top-down design programming practice and the Code and Checkout phase, the following data would be input:
Practice Effectiveness Values:

Logic Errors (encountered most often) = 2.20
Requirements Compliance (encountered least often) = 1.20
Total Effectiveness Value = 14.78
Number of Error Types = 12

The algorithm would then be executed as follows to calculate the phase effectiveness value:

$$(2.20 + 1.20) \ \frac{14.78}{12} \ = 4.19$$

This calculation sequence is repeated for each programming practice in the Code and Checkout phase. The resulting values are shown in Figure A2.5. Only the Code and Checkout column is completed because input data for the other phases have not been defined. These values establish the relative merit of the programming practices within the Code and Checkout phase.

A.2.5.3 EFFECTIVENESS VALUE BENEFITS

Certain benefits are realized through the use of effectiveness values in the programming practice comparison process. The most obvious benefit is the capability to develop discrete measures of practice performance through a consistent and comprehensive series of operations. The practice effectiveness value matrices permit the determination of programming practice voids, specific instances where no practice is effective against a particular error type. This situation would indicate an endemic deficiency within the program development process. The phase effectiveness value matrix provides the vehicle for optimization of error detection through identification of the minimum number of programming practices that generate a maximum set of values. Analysis of the phase and practice effectiveness values could provide a global measure of anticipated product reliability. By adding cost-to-detect and cost-to-fix data to these matrices it would be possible to develop minimum-cost approaches to program development.

A.3 MPP IMPACT EVALUATION APPROACH
AND RESULTS (TRW)

A.3.1 Detailed Technical Approach

TRW defined and followed the MPP study approach described below as a sequence of tasks. The tasks, in combination, provided necessary engineering analyses to (1) accomplish an in-depth evaluation of the effectiveness of MPP in the STP software development environment, and (2) develop and demonstrate a methodology for comparative evaluation of alternative MPP implementations. Figure A3.1 illustrates the approximate sequencing of project activities and demonstrates the high interconnectivity of the tasks described on p. 282.

Programming Practices	Computer Program Life-cycle Phases						
	Analysis	Functional design	Detailed design	Code and checkout	Test and integration	Installation	Operating and support
Technical							
Top-down design				4.19			
Structured design				3.79			
Programming design language				1.70			
Builds				2.41			
Build leader				46.53			
Chief programmer team				51.31			
Programming librarians				0.04			
Chief programmer				57.09			
Programming support library				0.12			
Programming techniques				15.61			
Structured programming				15.56			
Top-down programming				12.64			
Support programs				9.69			
Software configuration management				0.07			
Structured walkthroughs				44.65			
Program reviews				74.54			
Verification procedures				11.74			
Automated network analysis				1.12			
Execution analysis				31.04			
Progressive testing				27.89			
Independent test and evaluation				32.81			
Management							
Top-down development				11.13			
Project reviews				2.76			
Management data collection				1.19			
Inspection teams				4.07			
Threads management system				1.51			

Figure A2.5 Phase Effectiveness Values

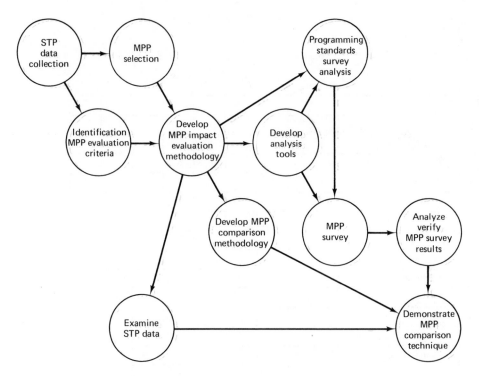

Figure A3.1   MPP Project Activity Network

Task 1: STP MPP Evaluation

This task included: identification of candidate practices and selection and definition of a final set of practices to be included in the impact evaluation study; collection, organization, and analysis of pertinent STP data and reconstruction of the chronology of major milestones in the project development cycle; development of definitions for project terminology; development of a description of the STP software development environment; and detailed analysis to determine the effects of adopting specific programming practices.

Task 2: MPP Comparison Methodology Development

This task included: development and demonstration of a methodology for comparative evaluation of alternative MPP implementations; and preparation and oral presentation of a project status and comparison methodology definition briefing to RADC.

Task 3: Technical Report Preparation

This task included all activities necessary for preparation of this technical report.

A.3.2 Selection of MPP

The term Modern Programming Practices (MPP) generally refers to standard programming practices, software design, construction, test and documentation techniques, and management methods used in the production of software for the purpose of enhancing certain qualities of the software and/or reducing, eliminating, or circumventing known software production difficulties. Clearly, a review of almost any large software development activity could be expected to uncover some practices that easily qualify as MPP. Because of the highly critical nature of the STP software development, it is not surprising to find that the set of such practices employed at various stages of the project is large indeed. Given the primary objective of the MPP study (i.e., to evaluate and quantify the impact of MPP on the STP development) and given limited time and funding to complete the task, it was clearly necessary to choose a reasonably small number of MPP to be studied so that sufficient attention could be given to each.

Our approach to obtaining a final list of MPP was straightforward and involved the following:

1. Identify a baseline set of practices through extensive interviews with key STP personnel.
2. Survey a cross section of STP and non-STP personnel to obtain a relative-importance ranking of the MPP and to identify additions to the baseline set.
3. Analyze the expanded list of MPP, delete those of low rank and those highly peculiar to STP, and, where appropriate, combine several related individual practices into one more general practice.

Through iterative application of the steps above, we progressed from the original list of 14 candidate practices to the final set of 11 MPP as illustrated by Figure A3.2.

It is important to note that we sought not only a manageable number of MPP upon which to concentrate the impact analyses but also a representative collection of practices that spanned the major phases of STP development. Of the set of 11 MPP; four practices apply mainly to the requirements definition/preliminary design phases of software development:

1. Requirement Analysis and Validation
2. Baselining of Requirements Specification
3. Complete Preliminary Design
4. Process Design

Three practices apply mainly to the detail design and coding phases:

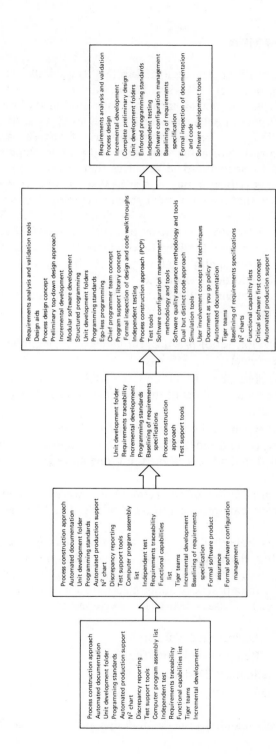

Figure A3.2 MPP Selection

1. Enforced Programming Standards
2. Incremental Development
3. Unit Development Folders

Two practices apply mainly to the test phase:

1. Independent Testing
2. Formal Inspection of Documentation and Code

Two practices apply to all phases of software development:

1. Software Development Tools
2. Software Configuration Management

A.3.3 Impact Evaluation Study

A primary objective of the Impact of MPP on System Development project was to obtain a quantified assessment of the nature and extent of the effect of modern practices applied to the TRW STP software development. Doing so was expected to provide important evidence with respect to the net positive impact of MPP on software quality and cost.

The approach to evaluating the overall impact of practices on software quality and cost involved (1) establishment of a common set of software characteristics, and (2) development and use of a technique to obtain measures of the nature and extent of the cause–effect relationship between each practice and each characteristic.

In view of particular interest in programming standards, two distinct impact evaluation activities were planned and conducted. The first focused on 18 detailed documentation and coding standards from the current version of the STP Software Standards and Procedures Manual and sought an impact assessment relative to 30 characteristics of software and the software development process. The second impact evaluation activity then concentrated on the 11 more general MPP and sought an impact assessment relative to 12 typical problems that have plagued (and all too often characterize) software development.

It was decided that the basic technique for obtaining impact measures should be a modified Delphi exercise involving several surveys of experienced TRW personnel. Use of this technique not only made the acquisition of comprehensive, detailed impact assessment data a practical task, it also brought into the impact evaluation activities a broad spectrum of project knowledge. To ensure maximum objectivity in the analysis of response data and formulation of a composite impact measure for each practice-characteristic combination, analysis algorithms were established in advance and implemented in the RANK, IMPACT, and MERIT support programs.

In essence, the impact evaluation approach was:

1. Conduct a survey requiring each participant to provide an individual measure (influence rating) of the impact of specific practices on certain characteristics of software development.

2. Analyze the survey response data as necessary to obtain a composite impact measure for each practice-characteristic combination as well as measures of the impact of (a) each practice on all the characteristics, (b) all the practices on each characteristic, and (c) all the practices on all the characteristics.

A.3.3.1 PROGRAMMING STANDARDS IMPACT

The first survey concentrated on detailed programming standards and sought measures of their impact on characteristics of software and the software development process. The survey questionnaire was completed by 54 people representing a cross section of STP personnel as follows:

Tactical Software Design and Development	Operating System Software	Test Support Software Design and Development	Software Integration and Test	Product Assurance and Configuration Management	Other
17	9	11	11	3	3

The Programming Standards Impact Evaluation survey questionnaire contained three parts:

1. A two-dimensional matrix of 18 programming standards versus 30 software characteristics (i.e., 540 "multiple-choice/fill-in-the-blank" questions).

2. A true/false question posed as a restatement of the general MPP hypothesis: "Programming (i.e., documentation and coding) standards, if rigorously defined and systematically enforced with support tools, help make possible the production of software of higher-than-usual *quality* at lower-than-usual *cost*."

3. A request for a free-form statement (in 25 words or less) as to the general effect of programming standards on STP.

Figure A3.3 illustrates the blank survey questionnaire.

Each survey participant was asked to complete as much of the matrix as possible and, from personal experience, to indicate both the nature and

Programming Standards Impact Evaluation Survey

Software Characteristics

Influence rating

+2 Strong positive
+1 Some positive
0 None
−1 Some negative
−2 Strong negative

Software Characteristics (column headers):
Programmer productivity
Logical organization
Core requirements
Execution time
Portability (computer independence)
Coding error frequency
Documentation error frequency
Codability (ease of coding)
Documentability
Completeness
Consistency
Schedule
Cost
Operational reliability
Testability
Code maintainability/usability
Documentation maintainability/usability
Code understandability/readability
Documentation understandability/readability
Testing thoroughness
Customer/contractor relationship
Retesting
Coding rework
Documentation rework
Software integration
Interface consistency
Personnel motivation
Documentation auditability
Code auditability
Requirements traceability

Standards for deliverable documentation:
Text format
Text level of detail
Flowchart format
Flowchart level of detail
Statement label format
Executable statement format
Routine size (modularity)
Calling sequence arguments
Mixed-mode arithmetic

Detailed coding standards:
DO-LOOP usage
Computed GO-TO usage
Labeled common vs. blank common usage
Embedded physical constants usage
Preface common block requirement
In-line commentary requirement
Structured coding requirement
Execution of every program branch requirement.
Naming conventions

A. Programming (i.e., documentation and coding) standards, if rigorously defined and systematically enforced with support tools, help to make possible the production of software:

True False ?
• of higher than usual quality □ □ □
• at lower than usual cost □ □ □

B. (In 25 words or less) STP PROGRAMMING STANDARDS had the following general effect: _____

Name: _____
Mail station: _____

Figure A3.3 Programming Standards Survey Questionnaire

287

amount of influence of each standard on each characteristic by choosing and entering the most appropriate influence rating from the following:

+ 2   Strong Positive Influence
+ 1   Some Positive Influence
  0   No Influence
− 1   Some Negative Influence
− 2   Strong Negative Influence
Blank   Unknown Influence

Upon completion of the survey the mathematical algorithms and support programs were used to analyze and summarize the response data in the form.

"Practice *i* has a positive (negative) influence on characteristic *j*."

The summarized results of the Programming Standards Impact Evaluation survey are presented in Figure A3.4.

The IMPACT program also computed influence ratings for each row (practice), each column (characteristic), and for the total matrix corresponding to (1) the average effect of each practice on the combined set of characteristics, (2) the average effect of the combined practices on each characteristic, and (3) the average effect of the combined practices on the combined set of characteristics. These additional assertion strength/influence ratings can be viewed as a 19th row and 31st column of the matrix, as indicated in Figures A3.5 and A3.6.

The assertion strength/influence rating for the combined practices on the combined characteristics was determined to be Weak/Positive. The weakness of the assertion strength is due to the large number (130) of Indifferent (i.e., no effect) ratings for individual practice-characteristic pairs, while the overall influence rating derives from the ratio of positive to negative influence ratings ($292/17 \simeq 17.2$), which clearly suggests Positive impact.

There are far too many individual elements of the matrix to permit detailed discussion of the assessed impact of each standard programming practice on each of the software characteristics. Four of the impact evaluation results are particularly interesting, however, and are deserving of special mention and, in some cases, further explanation. These are:

1. The Structured Coding Requirement received a relatively positive influence rating. Of the positive ratings, however, only a few were with strong confidence. On the other hand, many of the negative ratings were given with strong confidence. Compared with the other standards, this indicates a relatively dim view of structured coding on the part of STP personnel. There are some good reasons for this to be the case. First, structured coding (unlike most of the other standards) generally requires more core and execution time. Additionally, the standard was not explicitly defined and enforced until

Software Characteristics

Influence rating

Assertion Strength	Strong positive	Positive	Indifferent	Negative	Strong negative	Inconclusive
Strong	SSP	SP	I	SN	SSN	SI
Medium		MP		MN		MI
Weak		WP		WN		WI

Survey Summary

Rating	Frequency
SSP	4
I	130
SSN	0
SP	45
SI	20
SN	10
MP	114
MI	41
MN	3
WP	129
WI	40
WN	4

Software Characteristics (columns 1–30):

1. Requirements traceability
2. Code auditability
3. Documentation auditability
4. Personnel motivation
5. Interface consistency
6. Software integration
7. Documentation rework
8. Coding rework
9. Retesting
10. Customer/contractor relationship
11. Testing thoroughness
12. Documentation understandability/readability
13. Code understandability/readability
14. Documentation maintainability/usability
15. Code maintainability/usability
16. Testability
17. Operational reliability
18. Cost
19. Schedule
20. Consistency
21. Completeness
22. Codability (ease of coding)
23. Documentation error frequency
24. Coding error frequency
25. Portability (computer independence)
26. Execution time
27. Core requirements
28. Logical organization
29. Programmer productivity
30.

Standards for deliverable documentation / Detailed coding standards (rows):

1. Text format
2. Text level of detail
3. Flowchart format
4. Flowchart level of detail
5. Statement label format
6. Executable statement format
7. Routine size (modularity)
8. Calling sequence arguments
9. Mixed mode arithmetic
10. DO-loop usage
11. Computed GO-TO usage
12. Labeled common vs. blank common usage
13. Embedded physical constants usage
14. Preface commentary block requirement
15. In-line commentary requirement
16. Structured coding requirement
17. Execution of every program branch requirement
18. Naming conventions

A. Programming (i.e., documentation and coding) standards, if rigorously defined and systematically enforced with support tools, help to make possible the production of software:

	True	False	?
• of higher than usual quality	85%	4%	11%
• at lower than usual cost	28%	50%	22%

B. (In 25 words or less) STP PROGRAMMING STANDARDS had the following general effect: _____

Name: _____

Mail station: _____

Figure A3.4

Practice Index	Practice Identification	Assertion Strength/ Influence Rating
1	Text format	WP
2	Text level of detail	MP
3	Flowchart format	WP
4	Flowchart level of detail	MP
5	Statement label format	WP
6	Executable statement format	WP
7	Routine size (modularity)	MI
8	Calling sequence arguments	WP
9	Mixed mode arithmetic	WI
10	DO — loop usage	WP
11	Computed GO-TO usage	WI
12	Labeled common vs. blank common usage	WP
13	Embedded physical constants usage	WP
14	Preface commentary block requirement	MP
15	In-line commentary requirement	MP
16	Structured coding requirement	MI
17	Execution of every program branch requirement	WI
18	Naming conventions	WP

"Column 31"

Figure A3.5   Practice Impact on Combined Characteristics

almost 2 years after STP began, and the requirement to restructure working code was felt to be both unnecessary and counterproductive. Moreover, writing structured code in standard Fortran is awkward. Finally, STP has not yet reached the phase during which the major benefits of structured programming (i.e., improved readability and maintainability) are expected to be reaped.

2. Approximately one out of every four of the standard-characteristic pairs received a rating of Indifferent. The Indifferent rating implies a strong assertion of no impact. Although at first the number of Indifferent ratings seems high, careful review of the matrix reveals a very good match with intuition.

3. There are eight software characteristics which received no negative or inconclusive impact assessments. These are: Code Auditability, Documentation Auditability, Customer/Contractor Relationship, Documentation Understandability/Readability, Code Understandability/Readability, Operational Reliability, Consistency, and Completeness. On the other hand, Personnel Motivation received 14 inconclusive ratings. It appears that the overall impact of standards on Personnel Motivation correlates much better with the perceived impact on Cost and Schedule (i.e., only two positive influence

Characteristic Index	Characteristic Identification	Assertion Strength/ Influence Rating
1	Requirements traceability	WP
2	Code auditability	MP
3	Documentation auditability	WP
4	Personnel motivation	WI
5	Interface consistency	WP
6	Software integration	WP
7	Documentation rework	WI
8	Coding rework	MI
9	Retesting	WP
10	Customer/contractor relationship	MP
11	Testing thoroughness	WP
12	Documentation understandability/readability	WP
13	Code understandability/readability	MP
14	Documentation maintainability/usability	WP
15	Code maintainability/usability	MP
16	Testability	WP
17	Operational reliability	WP
18	Cost	MI
19	Schedule	WI
20	Consistency	MP
21	Completeness	WP
22	Documentability	WP
23	Codability (ease of coding)	MI
24	Documentation error frequency	WI
25	Coding-error frequency	MP
26	Portability (computer independence)	WP
27	Execution time	SI
28	Core requirements	SI
29	Logical organization	WP
30	Programmer productivity	MI

"Row 19"

Figure A3.6 Combined Practices Impact on Each Characterstic

ratings for each) than with the above-mentioned eight characteristics. This says something quite positive about the objectivity of the responses: in general, the survey participants did not let their personal distaste for a standard adversely affect their judgment of its effectiveness.

4. The results for the Routine Size (Modularity) programming standard are particularly interesting in that they compare quite well with those of Hoskyns in "Evaluation of Programming and Systems Techniques; Implications of Using Modular Programming." In particular, Hoskyns reports that 89% of those surveyed experienced "easier maintenance" from modular programming. Furthermore, Hoskyns' results on "better program design" and "easier program testing" (85% and 78%, respectively) compare well with ours for Logical Organization and Testability. Notably, fewer of the modular programming users (64%) experienced the benefit of "more reliable programs," again comparing well with our results. On the negative side, Hoskyns reports that 28% of the users claimed "more computer time required during development" and 27% experienced "less efficient final programs," corresponding to our Strong/Negative and Medium/Negative results for Execution Time and Core Requirements. The only obvious inconsistencies between Hoskyns' results and those reported here are for Programmer Productivity and Schedule. Hoskyns' results for "higher programmer productivity" (64%) and "more likely to meet target dates" (63%) are based, however, on a somewhat relaxed interpretation of modularity (i.e., 20 to 2000 statements), while our Strong/Inconclusive ratings relate to a formal standard restricting module size to a maximum of 100 executable Fortran statements.

A.3.3.2 MPP IMPACT

The second impact evaluation survey focused on the 11 previously identified MPP and sought an assessment of the extent to which the practices did (in the case of STP) and could (in a hypothetical software development) contribute to elimination of typical problems that have plagued and adversely affected software development activities. The survey questionnaire was completed by 67 people from a cross section of STP personnel. Of the 67 survey participants, 31 held management positions with varying levels of project responsibility.

The MPP Impact Evaluation survey questionnaire was designed as a booklet containing five parts:

1. A series of individual impact rating matrices, one for each of the 11 MPP. Each page contained a brief definition of the practice and a blank 12 × 5 evaluation matrix. Each row of the matrix corresponded to one of the 12 typical development problems, while the columns offered a choice of five influence ratings. Survey participants were required to enter an "A" in the appropriate column of each row to indicate the nature and extent of the influence of the practice on each problem in the *actual* STP context, and to enter a "T" to indicate the *theoretical,* optimum impact of the practice under ideal conditions. Figure A3.7 illustrates the impact rating matrix used to evaluate each of the MPP.

2. A list of the 11 practices and a request that they be ranked according to relative importance with respect to their positive contribution to elimination of software development problems.

3. A true/false question posed as a restatement of the general MPP hypothesis.

Problem / MPP Rating	High Positive	Low Positive	No Effect	Low Negative	High Negative
Cost overrun					
Development status invisibility					
Unreliability					
Unmaintainability					
Inadequate satisfaction of real requirements					
Inefficient use of resources					
Schedule overrun					
Inadequate planning and control					
Project mismanagement					
Lack of programming discipline					
Lack of conclusive testing					
Poor documentation					

Figure A3.7   MPP Survey Questionnaire Sample Rating Sheet

4. A list of the 12 typical software development problems and a request that they be ranked according to relative significance with respect to their negative effect on quality, schedule, and cost of software production. (The questionnaire format for items 2, 3, and 4 is illustrated in Figure A3.8).

5. A request for a brief free-form statement as to the need for and benefits derived from MPP as applied to STP and in general.

Analysis of the MPP Impact Evaluation survey response data was accomplished with the same mathematical algorithms and support tools used in the programming standards study. Hypothesis testing was applied independently to both the actual (A) and theoretical (T) responses, yielding two

MPP Ranking

MPP	Rank*
Requirements analysis and validation	
Process design	
Incremental development	
Complete preliminary design	
Unit development folders	
Enforced programming standards	
Independent testing	
Software configuration management	
Baselining of requirements specification	
Formal inspection of documentation and code	
Software development tools	

General MPP hypothesis: Rules governing software development, evaluation, and documentation, if rigorously defined and applied, and supported by modern programming practices (techniques and tools), make possible the production:

	True	False	?
• of higher-than-usual-quality software	☐	☐	☐
• at lower-than-usual life-cycle cost	☐	☐	☐

Software development problem ranking

Problem	Rank†
Cost overrun	
Development status invisibility	
Unreliability	
Unmaintainability	
Inadequate satisfaction of real requirements	
Inefficient use of resources	
Schedule overrun	
Inadequate planning and control	
Project mismanagement	
Lack of programming discipline	
Lack of conclusive testing	
Poor documentation	

* Relative importance ranking: Use rank of 1 for "most important," 2 for "next most important," . . ., 11 for "least important."

† Relative significance ranking: Use rank of 1 for "most significant," 2 for "next most significant," . . . , 12 for "least significant."

Figure A3.8   MPP Survey Questionnaire Ranking Sheet

Modern Programming Practices Impact Evaluation Survey

Influence rating

Assertion Strength	Strong positive	Positive	Indifferent	Negative	Strong negative	Inconclusive
Strong	SSP	SP	IND	SN	SSN	SI
Medium		MP		MN		MI
Weak		WP		WM		WI

Survey Summary

A = actual (STP) T = theoretical

Rating	Freq. A	Freq. T
SSP	0	16
IND	4	2
SSN	0	0
SP	24	54
SI	9	1
SN	2	0
MP	45	44
MI	20	4
MN	1	0
WP	23	11
WI	4	0
WN	0	0

Software Problems (columns 1–12)

1. Cost overrun
2. Development status invisibility
3. Unreliability
4. Unmaintainability
5. Inadequate satisfaction of real requirements
6. Inefficient use of resources
7. Schedule overrun
8. Inadequate planning and control
9. Project mismanagement
10. Lack of programming discipline
11. Lack of conclusive testing
12. Poor documentation
- Cumulative effect of a practice on all problems

Programming practices (rows 1–11)

1. Requirements analysis and validation
2. Process design
3. Incremental development
4. Complete preliminary design
5. Unit development folders
6. Enforced programming standards
7. Independent testing
8. Software configuration management
9. Baselining of requirements specification
10. Formal inspection of documentation and code
11. Software development tools
- Cumulative effect of all practices on a problem

(The central matrix cross-tabulates each programming practice against each software problem; each cell is split into an actual (A) and theoretical (T) influence rating.)

General MPP hypothesis rules governing software development, evaluation, and documentation, if rigorously defined and applied, and supported by modern programming practices (techniques and tools), make possible the production:

	TRUE	FALSE	?
• of higher-than-usual-quality software	85%	4%	11%
• at lower-than-usual life-cycle cost	49%	15%	36%

Figure A3.9 MPP Impact Evaluation Survey Results

295

composite assertion strength/influence rating indicators for each practice–problem pair as illustrated in the MPP Impact Evaluation survey summary matrix (Figure A3.9).

The figure illustrates the composite survey response to the general MPP hypothesis true/false question, indicating that 85% of the survey participants agreed that MPP contribute to the production of "higher-than-usual quality software." On the issue of "lower-than-usual life-cycle cost," agreement as to a positive MPP contribution is not nearly as marked; however, the true responses outnumber the false responses by almost 4 to 1.

In the formulation of the average impact of each practice on all problems (i.e., the assertion strength/influence ratings in column 13 of the matrix), equal significance of all problems was assumed. From the cumulative response-frequency distributions for all the practices, it was thus possible to rank the practices in order of their relative impact on the set of uniformly weighted problems. For the purposes of verifying the survey results and further analyzing and estimating the relative value of the practices in differing development activities, several other rankings were obtained.

Analysis of the MPP impact evaluation survey summary results matrix, together with the three practice rankings, prompts the following general observations.

There is strong agreement among STP personnel as to the four MPP of greatest importance and impact and strong agreement on their relative ranking:

1. Requirements Analysis and Validation
2. Baselining of Requirements Specification
3. Complete Preliminary Design
4. Process Design

There is strong agreement on the importance and positive impact of the next three most highly ranked MPP, but the relative ranking among them is less clear:

1. Incremental Development
2. Unit Development Folders
3. Software Development Tools

There is strong agreement on the importance and positive impact of the four lower-ranked MPP, but the relative ranking among them is not at all clear:

1. Independent Testing
2. Enforced Programming Standards
3. Software Configuration Management
4. Formal Inspection of Documentation and Code

Appendix B

Correlation
of MPP Material

The following material correlates the MPP subject matter with MPP companies. In the matrix, for each MPP and company, the paragraph number where that company's use of that MPP is discussed in this book is given.

Company

MPP	BCS	CSC	Martin-Marietta	Sperry Univac	SDC	TRW
Requirements						
Requirements generation			3.1.1.1			
Requirements analysis and validation						3.1.2.1
Baselining and requirements						3.1.3.1
Requirements tracing		3.1.4.2				3.1.4.1
Design						
Design approaches		3.2.1.1 (top-down)	3.2.1.3 (functional)	3.2.1.4		3.2.1.2 (process)
Design reviews	3.2.2.4	3.2.2.1		3.2.2.2		3.2.2.3
Builds		3.2.3.1				
Design control				3.2.4.1		
Implementation						
Structure, modularity, and style		3.3.1.1			3.3.1.2	
Top-down implementation				3.3.2.1		3.3.2.2
Methodologies and tools				3.3.3.1		3.3.3.2

Company

MPP	BCS	CSC	Martin-Marietta	Sperry Univac	SDC	TRW
Management Planning						
Reviews and audits	4.1.2.1		4.1.1.1 4.1.2.2 4.1.2.3	4.1.2.5		4.1.2.4
Technology		4.1.3.1 4.1.3.2	4.1.3.3 4.1.3.4		4.1.3.5 4.1.3.6	
Configuration management	4.1.4.2	4.1.4.1				4.1.4.3
Organization	4.2.1.1 (interdisciplinary)	4.2.2.2 (chief programmer team) 4.2.2.3 (build leader)	4.2.1.2 (advisory board) 4.2.2.4 (cognizant person)		4.2.2.1 (chief programmer team)	
Software quality assurance						
Independent verification and validation		4.2.4.2		4.2.3.1		
Resources	4.3.1 (support libraries)		4.2.4.1 4.3.3 (conversion) 4.3.4 (loading prediction)		4.3.2	4.2.4.3

Appendix C

Glossary

It is important to establish a firm framework of definitions for the material in this book. Communication is always dependent on words having the same meaning, whether it be between speaker and listener, or author and reader. But for the context of this book, a communication framework is especially important. Much of the computing literature uses terms in a fairly consistent and well-defined way. Much of industry does the same. But the vocabulary of terms sometimes differs between the literature and industry, either because one uses terms the other does not, or (occasionally) because one term means one thing in the literature and another in industry.

The material that follows may be both read in context now and used as reference material during further reading of this book.

AN/UYK: One in a series of standard U.S. Navy computers.

Acceptance Test: The formal test process by which the customer and/or user of the software evaluates the capability of the software to meet its requirements. Generally, the acceptance test is conducted by the software developer, and a successful test ends the software development phase and begins the operation/maintenance phase.

Audit: A study of a software process by outsiders to determine if it is proceeding as it should.

Baselining: The process of defining an achieved level of effort, so that further efforts may evolve from a well-defined base. For example, a baseline software configuration is the configuration to which modifications are currently being applied.

Batch: A computer is said to be used in batch mode if the input and output of programs and data is performed in a noninteractive mode.

Build: A portion of a software system whose constituent elements are related to a common set of requirements. Dividing software into builds makes it easier to grasp, plan, and control. Builds are the implementation of one or more "threads" (*which see*).

Change Control: A formal process of evaluating, prioritizing, and tracking software changes by an administrative body.

Chief Programmer Team: A technologist-led software development organization, often characterized by having a chief programmer, several subordinate programmers, and a software-skilled clerk known as a librarian.

CMS-2:   A U.S. Navy standard high-order language.

Cognizant Programmer/Engineer: A cognizant person is both knowledgeable in, and responsible for, all or part of a software system. The cognizant programmer is responsible for its software aspects, and the cognizant engineer for its total system aspects.

Commentary: Information introduced into a computer program whose purpose is solely to assist in its understanding.

Common: An aggregate of globally accessible software data (a Fortran term).

Comparator: A software tool that analyzes two information files and prints out their differences.

Compool: An aggregate of globally accessible software data and program information (a Jovial term).

Configuration Management: The process of controlling a software system to prevent unauthorized changes.

Critical Design Review (CDR):   A final evaluation of software design before the formal coding process begins. (*See also* Preliminary Design Review).

Emulation: The use of computer hardware to imitate some other software or hardware function. One computer can be used, for example, to emulate another.

Firmware: Hardware that is relatively easily changed, usually by microprogramming. The spectrum of changeability moves from hardware (difficult) through firmware (less difficult) to software (by contrast, easy).

Flow chart: A graphical representation of the flow of control (or, sometimes, information) through a software design.

Functional Configuration Audit (FCA):   The formal process of inspecting or testing each software system component to assure that it satisfies the function for which it was developed. (*See also* Physical Configuration Audit).

Guidelines: Recommendations (as opposed to rules) for good software development practices.

High-Order Language: A language for writing software which is closer to human readability than computer readability. Examples include Fortran, Cobol, Jovial, CMS-2.

Indentation: Denoting software levels of logic control by the process of moving the left margin of the listing slightly and consistently to the right for each nested level of control. Indentation is used to improve software readability.

Independent Verification and Validation: The use of a disinterested body, usually a separate company, to verify and validate (*which see*) software.

Integration: The process of putting the components of a software system together. Once software is integrated, it must undergo integration testing to ensure that the system behaves in the proper holistic manner.

Interface: The manner of connection of software components. Software generally interfaces through common data and procedure parameter lists (calling sequences), but sometimes interfaces become more complex than that.

Interpretive Computer Simulation: The use of software to enable one computer to execute programs written in the instruction set of another.

Maintenance: The process of keeping software operational, involving both correction and change.

Modularity: Software is said to be modular if its separate functional elements are found in separate components.

Naming Conventions: Rules for providing names for program elements such as data or procedures. Conventions usually stress mnemonics (the name itself suggests the function of the element) and structure (the name is keyed to the software component to which it belongs).

Performance: The qualities of software having to do with its execution. For example, timing efficiency is an important measure of performance.

Physical Configuration Audit (PCA):   The formal process of ascertaining that all deliverable parts of a software system (e.g., program components, documentation items, etc.) are indeed present. (*See also* Functional Configuration Audit).

Preliminary Design Review (PDR): An early evaluation of software design conducted to ensure that no major misdirection is being undertaken. (*See also* Critical Design Review).

Program Manager: The person responsible for project success in the administrative hierarchic organization approach. (*See also* Chief Programmer Team).

Program Support Library: The information and material needed to assist in software construction. Usually, this is a computerized data base of software components, documentation, and progress reporting information.

Quality Assurance: The activity of analyzing the developing software product to ensure that it will be of high quality. This may range from an auditing role to verify that developers have considered quality process, to hands-on participation in verification, validation, and configuration management.

Real-Time: Software whose functioning must be synchronized with events outside the computing system. For example, software controlling a space vehicle dealing with sensor inputs, or software that interacts with a human being while executing, such as a time-sharing system.

Requirements Tracing: The process of identifying the relationship between all software requirements and all software elements. For example, where is this requirement satisfied in the design? In the code? To what requirement(s) does this code pertain?

Reviews: A study of a software process, usually scheduled in advance, to determine if it is proceeding as it should. *See,* for example, Preliminary Design Review and Critical Design Review.

Scenario: A plan or script, prepared in advance, for the conduct of a software execution. Often used to apply to a real-time test process, where the test environment may be more complicated than the test itself.

Simulation: The process of causing a model to interact with an environment in such a way as to gain information about the properties of the system.

Sizing: The measure of the amount of memory space needed by a software system.

Specification: The formal document defining a task to be performed, or a product to be constructed. For example, a requirements specification or a coding specification.

Standards: Rules (as opposed to recommendations) for good software development practices.

Structured Programming: A set of software standards and guidelines for developing software emphasizing simplified logic structure and early detection and elimination of errors. Specific definitions of the standards and guidelines are subject to some variance and some controversy.

Style: The imprint of a programmer and a suite of methodologies on a program. Style includes such elements as methods of modularizing, naming conventions, kinds of commentary, etc.

Systems Analysis: The study of a problem area to which a computer solution is to be applied. Also called requirements analysis.

Thread: A discrete series of operational activities from stimulus (input) to response (output) which contributes to the satisfaction of a specific system function. A thread therefore links a requirement to the constituent elements of software which satisfy that requirement. Thus, threads are a requirements tracing methodology. The implementation of one or more threads is called a "build" (*which see*).

Timing: The measure of the execution efficiency of a software system.

Tools: An automated methodology—usually, a computer program that assists in the development of other computer programs.

Top-Down Design: The methodology that constructs a software design starting with top-level requirements, and then successively refines the design based on expansion of each level of design to a newer and more detailed level.

Top-Down Implementation: The coding and testing methodology that calls for integration of a total system from the beginning of development, using "stub" (filler) code for components not yet developed. Contrasts with "bottom-up" (unit development, then integration) implementation. Not necessarily related to top-down design.

Unit Development Folder: A respository of software development information with a relatively standardized format and content. Contains relevant documentation, listings, test results, design notes, formal approvals, etc. A UDF is prepared for each software unit.

Validation: The process of ensuring and demonstrating that a total system functions properly.

Verification: The process of ensuring and demonstrating that a software system functions properly.

Walkthrough: The process of reviewing software design or code by stepping through the logic. A relatively informal process, usually relying on a small peer group to identify problems.

Index

Index